Twentieth-Century
BRITAIN

**Modern
Scholarship on
European History**

HENRY A. TURNER, JR.
General Editor

Twentieth-Century
BRITAIN
National Power and Social Welfare

**Edited with an Introduction by
HENRY R. WINKLER**

New Viewpoints

A Division of Franklin Watts

New York London 1976

New Viewpoints
A Division of Franklin Watts
730 Fifth Avenue
New York, New York 10019

Library of Congress Cataloging in Publication Data

Main entry under title:

  Twentieth-century Britain.

  (Modern scholarship on European history)
  Bibliography: p.
  Includes index.
  CONTENTS: Northedge, F. S. 1917–1919: the implications for Britain.
—Marwick, A. After the deluge.—Ehrman, J. Lloyd George and Chur-
chill as War Ministers. [etc.]
  1. Great Britain—Politics and government—20th century—Address-
es, essays, lectures. 2. Great Britain—Foreign relations—20th century—
Addresses, essays, lectures. 3. Labour Party (Gt. Brit.)—Addresses,
essays, lectures. 4. Great Britain—Social policy—Addresses, essays,
lectures. I. Winkler, Henry Ralph, 1916–
DA566.7.T9   320.9'41'082   75–40058
ISBN 0–531–05381–4
ISBN 0–531–05587–6 pbk.

Manufactured in the United States of America

Contents

Twentieth-Century
BRITAIN

Introduction

About fifteen years ago, in a bibliographical essay on twentieth-century Britain, I commented on the obvious scarcity of certain basic sources despite the vast quantity of material available to contemporary scholars. Diplomatic and military archives were particularly difficult of access. Official publication of documents, however carefully they were edited, was not a satisfactory substitute. Constitutional or economic or social historians were better served than their colleagues who studied the history of foreign relations or of defense and warmaking. Their data tended to be public, even though the sheer bulk of evidence posed problems different in scope from those faced by historians of earlier periods.

Since then much has changed. The famous fifty-year rule on the opening of the archives has given place to a thirty-year time limit. Many more scholars concerned with the first half of the century now have the opportunity to be as positive—as they will continue to be equally as tentative—as are their colleagues who specialize in the eighteenth or nineteenth centuries. At the same time, even the years since 1950 have been investigated in a literature that sharply reflects, more often than not, the current concerns and contemporary values of its authors. Many of the most effective interpretations of the very recent past, it should not be surprising, are in the work of sociologists and economists and political scientists rather than in that of practitioners of the historian's craft.

For whatever reasons, much of the new scholarship has appeared in monographs and book-length collections of various sorts rather than in articles published in scholarly journals. Many such articles have, of course, made valuable contributions to our knowledge of the twentieth-century British experience, but they have often tended to be narrow in focus. Their explorations of carefully limited subjects will become the basis for the revised generalizations of the future, but for the present I have often had to seek among books for the overviews that I thought might be valuable in such a collection of essays as this.

What indeed should be the character of a volume that attempts to offer even a few generalizations about three-quarters of a century of history? Some developments are obvious. The two world wars were crucial determinants of Britain's twentieth-century experience. Their civil and military impact was felt in virtually every area of life and in broad terms they accelerated, or at least emphasized, the long-term decline of Britain's position in the world. Economically, too, relative decline appeared to be the rule, although some commentators saw evidence of an industrial or commercial revival of consequence after the lean years between the wars. The pattern of economic life was in fact complicated enough to justify conflicting interpretations, but an overall trend appeared to be evident. The nineteenth-century "workshop of the world" had already begun to slip substantially behind Germany and the United States before 1914. Afterward, although growth continued slowly, the balance of economic power shifted inexorably away from Britain. And whatever the long-run meaning of the change in the nation's economic status, her adjustment to it is a central aspect of her recent history.

Another pivotal theme is the expansion of the social services and the implementation of the concept of universal social security. While one may trace its origins to an earlier period, the "welfare state" really began to emerge in the reforms of the New Liberalism after 1906. From that beginning there is a clear line of development to the legislation passed by the Labour government between 1945 and 1951 and further to the acceptance by all major groups in Britain of the permanence of the welfare revolution. The effects of particular reforms, on the other hand, have been challenged not only by politicians but by prominent sociologists as well. Questions have been raised: to illustrate, about whether or not the welfare state has actually increased equality in British society. Whatever the answer, the evaluation of present programs has understandably helped in the assessment of the whole welfare experience as a central issue in the recent history of Britain.

Changes in the character and procedures of the major political parties have also been of utmost moment. Throughout the period the growth of disciplined party machines is evident, despite occasional revolts among the Conservatives and more frequent differences within the Labour party. Indeed, Robert MacKenzie has argued in his *British Political Parties* (London, 1955) that in their day-to-day operations the Labour and Tory parties are much more alike than they are dissimilar. And while Samuel Beer has made it necessary to modify MacKenzie's conclusions somewhat, his brilliant *Modern British Politics: A Study of Parties and Pressure Groups* (London, 1965) does not completely demolish the latter's contention that the authority structure in both parties is substantially the same. On balance, the major institutional development in political life may well have been the increase in the executive's power over that of Parliament and the courts in the middle years of the twentieth century. While significant changes in the character of local government can be identified, it is the remarkable growth of central government that stands out. The complex evolution of the civil service, the shifting roles of cabinet ministers as policy-makers and as departmental administrators, the heightened concentration upon economic functions are only illustrations of the vital changes that have taken place in the organization of central government.

The collapse of the Liberal party after the First World War was as puzzling as it was consequential. One explanation, illustrated with seductive wit in George Dangerfield's *Strange Death of Liberal England* (London, 1936), is that the Liberal leadership was basically impotent in the face of labor unrest, the suffragette campaign, the Irish troubles even in the halcyon days of the New Liberalism. Other observers have attributed the decline to the clash of personalities—Lloyd George versus Asquith—that tore the party apart after 1916. Some historians have sought a clue to the Liberal malady in the disillusionment of key figures with the foreign policy views of its leaders. A few have seen the problem as evidence of the significant weakening of the British middle classes. And others still have regarded the emergence of a Labour party as a viable alternative to the Conservatives in the exercise of political power as the phenomenon undercutting the position of the Liberals after 1918.

Labour's rise was the most important party development in the seventy-five years of the century to date. Starting unpromisingly as a collection of disparate groups joined together for electoral purposes, the Labour Representation Committee became a party, with substantial though secret Liberal help in its early electoral battles, by the election of 1906. The small new party floundered until World War I when working-class disillusionment with Liberals and Conservatives alike enabled it, aided by a new constitution providing for individual membership and proclaiming its adherence to socialism, to grow in strength. Experience in two minority governments between the wars and participation of

Labour's leaders in Churchill's great World War II coalition led finally to a substantial majority in 1945 and subsequent alternation with the Tories in the political leadership of Britain. The trade unions, too, flourished in the twentieth century, moving from their defensive posture in the nineteen-twenties and thirties to a much more aggressive—some have argued dangerous—stance in the decades after 1945.

Clearly, then, the choice of a few illustrative essays is an almost hopeless task. Volumes of ⁻rticles or of excerpts from books could be gathered together, each devoted to any one of the developments here noted—and to many others. For example, British foreign policy in the interwar years is a fascinating, if depressing, subject. The Munich settlement and its antecedents have been analyzed, praised, condemned by numerous scholars just as, earlier, Britain's role in the outbreak of World War I claimed the attention of some of the most distinguished historians of the period. But I have chosen to finesse dealing with these well-studied subjects. It has seemed to me that three themes are central to Britain's twentieth-century history. The first is the loss of British power and status at home and abroad. To illustrate the issue I have chosen materials that comment first of all upon the impact of the First World War, then turned to authors who address themselves to the more recent indications of domestic stagnation and international weakness. In between, since Lloyd George and Churchill loom so large, I have selected a brief piece that assesses the role of each as a wartime leader. And because so much has been written about British foreign policy as though it were made in a vacuum, I have reproduced an article that examines one single factor that helped shape the making of foreign policy, the relations of Britain with the Commonwealth on matters of defense. It suggests how much more complex were the problems of Britain's position in the world than most of us were prepared to understand for a long time.

The second development of the most profound interest is the growth of the Labour party to a position of pivotal political eminence. That growth, it goes without saying, has been accompanied by a Niagara of analysis, much of it patently bewildered by the conflicting currents that quite evidently run in the stream of Labour party policy. To assess the implications of some of the conflicts I have selected two essays, both in essence summaries of earlier scholarship, which attempt to illuminate both strife and continuity in Labour's history. As a reminder, however, that the Conservative party, not Labour, has won the support of the electorate for the longest span of time in the century, I have turned to a brief essay that speaks to the accommodations of conservatism to the new world after 1945.

Finally, of course, the emergence of the welfare state is the recent historical trend that perhaps overshadows all others. To undertake to encompass its scope in a few brief essays is futile, but I have chosen three pieces of very different character. One is a general survey of the background of the British system of social security. A second deals with what its author claims to be the neglected early role of Labour in its gestation. And the third raises fundamental questions of public policy that put the history of the welfare state into clear contemporary focus.

The result of all this is in some ways an idiosyncratic collection, evidencing my own sense of what has been of primary significance and leaving aside some of the questions that have been most stressed in the standard accounts. These pieces are reproduced as originally published, so that in one or two cases a footnote occurs that refers back to an earlier section of the volume in which a chapter occurs. I should like to thank Ellen Mappen for her help in collecting some of the materials I was seeking. They are far from being a balanced look at Britain in the twentieth century, but I hope they will be useful in illustrating some of the problems of adjustment that were central to her history over the last seventy-five years.

It is commonly accepted that the First World War marked the major turning point in twentieth-century British history. Even before 1914, of course, many observers in Great Britain had begun to sense the erosion of her international position. The war accelerated that erosion, but it was some time, the author of this first selection argues, before most British people apprehended that they were living in a vastly changed world. After more than four years of a bitter struggle, they wanted to be left alone. In such a mood, particularly when internal conflicts over wages, unemployment, and conditions of work dragged on for long years, Britain was uncertain of its response to totalitarian revisionism when it emerged in Europe. F. S. Northedge is Professor and Head of the Department of International Relations at the London School of Economics and Political Science. He is the author, among other works, of British Foreign Policy: The Process of Readjustment 1945 – 1962 *(London, 1962) and* The Troubled Giant: Britain Among the Great Powers 1916 – 1939 *(London, 1966). The article that follows is reprinted from* The Journal of Contemporary History, *III (October, 1968), with the permission of the publishers, SAGE Publications Ltd.*

1

1917—1919: The Implications for Britain

F. S. NORTHEDGE

In 1917 the Allied Powers came within an ace of military defeat; by April the German submarine campaign was eating deep into Britain's merchant shipping resources; in April, too, was launched the catastrophic French offensive on the Aisne, in November came the Italian disaster at Caporetto and the Russian retirement from the war; at the same time Haig's Third Battle of Ypres, designed to relieve the French, was petering out with little of consequence having been achieved; and it would plainly be months before the United States, who entered the war in April, would be making an effective contribution. Yet by the following October the Central Powers were asking President Wilson for peace on the basis of his Fourteen Points speech of 8 January 1918.

The effect of this struggle was to plant in the British mind an abiding fear of war in Europe and of involvement in rival alliance systems which were thought to have dragged the nations into the maelstrom. Hence the dominant aspiration both of British policy-makers and of public opinion in the inter-war period was to prevent at all costs a return to the 1917 situation, and to do so by avoiding the division of Europe into rival blocs; by refusing specific commitments to defend the European status quo in detail, which might touch off again the bloodbaths of 1914 – 18; and by striving for the reduction of land forces which suffered the haemorrhages of those years and the abolition of the submarine which had all but severed Britain's vital supply lines from abroad in 1917. At the same time, the fact that the disasters of 1917 had been surprisingly reversed by the autumn of 1918 meant that the full extent of the French defeat on the Aisne was never properly appreciated. Considering the intact condition of the German army at the end of the war and the unravaged condition of Germany itself compared with France, France, had military justice been done, should have come out on the losing side. The fact that she did not, and that the Peace Conference was held in Paris, persuaded Britain in the 1920s that it was France that had to be feared in future years and Germany, contrary to all the military logic of the last months of the war, which had to be reared up again as a counterpoise.

British ministers after the war remained highly suspicious of the security system which France built up with the successor states of eastern Europe against the day of German *revanche*. Britain's refusal to extend to these states the offer she made to France of a pledge against German aggression caused the failure of the negotiations for an Anglo-French pact in 1920 – 22 and limited the effectiveness of the Locarno Treaties in 1925 for the recognition of the status quo. But the creation of the east European successor states themselves in 1919 had never been an aim of British policy during the war, and this fact again underlay British attitudes towards Germany after 1918, and even towards the Soviet Union after the second World War. Before the Bolshevik Revolution in Russia in November 1917 the British Government had opposed the formation of an independent Poland after the war on the ground that Russia, then thought to be a future ally against Germany, should have a common frontier with Germany in order to be able to invade Germany from the east in any later conflict: precisely what Britain and France could not authorize Russia to do, after their guarantees to Poland, during their negotiations in Moscow for a pact against Germany in the summer of 1939. When Poland was finally being created in 1919, with the patronage and support of President Wilson, Britain fought tooth and nail against any enlargement of its frontiers at Germany's expense, Germany now having become for Britain a potential bulwark against Bolshevism in Europe. The Poles found in Lloyd George, Balfour, and Smuts, their bitterest enemies. As for the other successor states of eastern Europe, Czechoslovakia and Yugoslavia, Britain played no real part in their creation for the simple reason that she had no military forces on the spot to influence events one way or the other. For all practical purposes the Allied Supreme Council could do no more than ratify the actions of local nationalists in those states and try to reconcile the results, in Yugoslavia's case, with the promises in Dalmatia made to Italy in May 1915 when she entered the war on the Allied side. Young men in the Foreign Office, like Harold Nicolson, might say that the only feature of the peace treaties which 'made our hearts sing hymns at heaven's gate' was the formation of the successor states.[1] But high-level official opinion in Britain was well reflected in Lloyd George's statement that the chief task of the Paris peacemakers was 'not to decide what in fairness should be given to the liberated nationalities, but what in common honesty should be forced from their clutches when they had overstepped the bounds of self-determination.'[2]

Small wonder, then, that when the east European settlement was challenged by Germany in the 1930s the British Government showed no great zeal to defend it. On the right wing in Britain the successor states tended to be viewed as idealistic creations of Wilson which took no account of the realities of power, which complicated the main task of reconciliation between the Great European Powers, and which had been imposed on Britain at the peace settlement almost as much as they had been imposed on Germany; the next war, said Lloyd George at the Council of Four in Paris in 1919, will begin in Danzig if it begins anywhere. On the left, while enthusiasm for Czechoslovakia and Poland might have waxed as they came under the Nazi shadow in the thirties, the image of those states was that of highly nationalistic or militaristic regimes, making nonsense of economic facts and dangerously anti-Soviet in their political tendencies. [3]

By 1917 the war had become what Raymond Aron once called 'hyperbolic'; that is, industrialism had produced a *guerre d'usure* which demanded such a mobilization of all the belligerents' minds and emotions that the original war aims were lost to sight; in Britain nothing would satisfy the electorate when it went to the polls in December 1918 but the total destruction of German 'militarism'. The two major demands imposed on the Government in that election, as they prepared for the peace conference, were German money to pay for the war and the German Kaiser's head on a platter. But these Armistice Night feelings soon gave way to worries about unemployment, demobilization, industrial unrest, and about a possible German refusal to sign a harsh treaty and hence a return to the horrors of war. In this sudden switch of feeling the realities of power in Europe were lost to sight. When war came again in 1939 British writers began to explain 'how we won the war and lost the peace'. But the truth was that the war was never won—certainly not by the Entente Powers—and hence the peace, based on a false victory, was easily lost. It would have been lost almost whatever Government had been in office in Britain in the thirties.

By November 1917 Germany had utterly defeated Russia and so mauled the French army that its recovery seemed for a time doubtful. Italy was to all intents knocked out of the war and Britain was struggling in the mud of Flanders with no other hope than that, in the end, Germany would fall faint to the ground a few moments before Britain herself did. In effect only the prospect of the seemingly inexhaustible resources of the United States being tipped into the scales on the Allied side ended the conflict. Yet in the 1930s Russia was alienated from Britain and, despite the Franco-Soviet pact, from the bulk of French opinion too; Italy and Japan were belligerently on the other side; the United States was completely out of the picture. British ministers knew that, if Hitler's challenge were taken up, the balance of military force was against Britain and France, as the first World War had shown. We now know that Hitler's war machine was never as fully mobilized as Britain and France believed at the time. But, considering the strength that Germany had put forth in the first World War, it did not need to be; the psychological effect was enough. Hitler counted on that, and it worked.

Despite all the calumny heaped since 1939 on the pre-war British National Government, there was a certain logic in the conclusions they seemed to have drawn from 1917 – 19: first, that no war on that earlier scale should be embarked upon unless it was clear beyond all doubt that Germany was seeking the mastery of Europe, not merely the redress of grievances arising from the peace treaties; second, that any war between Britain and France on one side, and Germany on the other, could not be begun with hope of victory for the former unless other Powers, notably Russia, were brought in, and there was no knowing how a war started in those circumstances would end; and third, that the European balance of forces could not be redressed, as 1917 – 18 had shown, without American assistance, and the prevailing isolationism in the United States necessitated the postponement of a European conflict until American intervention was in sight and the taking up of the dictators' challenges only on the kind of issues on which American public opinion was likely ultimately to throw its weight on their side. The balance of forces in Europe in 1917 – 19 was thus misunderstood in Britain in the 1920s and realized, only too late, in the 1930s.

The Russian Revolution and Allied Intervention

The most important fact about the two Russian Revolutions of 1917 from the British viewpoint was that they occurred in the course of a life-and-death struggle against a powerful enemy and overtook an ally whose contribution up to that time in relieving the pressure on the Western Front was immense, if destructive to itself. British ministers were ignorant about and on the whole uninterested in the political and social issues of the revolution; on the very eve of the fall of the Tsar in March, Lord Milner returned from a mission to Russia with hardly an inkling of coming events. The sole questions for the British Cabinet when the monarchy, and later the Kerensky Government, fell, was how this would affect Russia's and Germany's war effort; how far it might change the image of the Allied Powers prevailing abroad, especially in the United States; whether it would rivet the ordinary people in the Allied countries more closely to the war effort or, if Russia left the war, increase their own war weariness and suspicions of Allied war aims. How to keep Russia in the war despite the revolution; how to use the revolution to improve the attractiveness of the Allied cause; and, if Russia left the war, how to organize in that country enough anti-German forces through Allied intervention so as to reduce the benefits to Germany from the revolution: these were the major considerations.

Hence the March Revolution was conceived at first in Britain as a revolt, not against the war, but against Tsarist inefficiency in conducting it. Attempts were made to seize the opportunity, first to increase supplies to Russia from the West, and second, to extract from the new regime some modification of Russian war aims, in the Near East for example, in order to modify the annexationist complexion of the Allied case. When the Bolsheviks seized power in November, a primary consideration was to avoid driving them into the arms of Germany by too hostile an attitude; but, with the increasing signs of the new regime's determination to make a separate peace, this gave way to a more ambivalent position: a search, on the one hand, for some kind of accommodation with Trotsky, the first Bolshevik Foreign Minister, to prevent him signing the Brest peace and quitting the war, and, on the other, a policy of encouraging anyone throughout Russia who was prepared to carry on the fight and pin down German forces. When the first of these endeavors failed, with the signing of the Brest peace on 3 March 1918, the way was open for Allied intervention on a full scale, with Japanese assistance in Russia's Far Eastern provinces. But however much Winston Churchill, as Minister for War, strove to turn Allied intervention into an anti-Bolshevik crusade, campaigning with the French for this at the Paris Peace Conference in 1919, there was really no heart for it in Britain. There was little dissent in the House of Commons on 16 April 1919 when Lloyd George defined the Government's policy as helping to stop the flow of Bolshevik lava into Europe but leaving the volcano in Russia itself to burn itself out. No-one worked harder in the Council of Four than the Prime Minister, not even Wilson himself, to bring Lenin's regime somehow into the negotiations, if only on an island refuge for lost dogs in the Sea of Marmara.

The Russian Revolution thus made its first impact on Britain in a context of Russian military defeat, and no doubt this explains the consistent under-estimation of Soviet military power by Britain in the 1930s, and also the National Government's belief that Russia might defect in a war against Hitler as readily as she had in the war against the Kaiser in 1917. The impact of the social implications of the Russian Revolution came later, when signs appeared immediately the Armistice was signed of industrial unrest in Britain and the risks of a spread of Bolshevism in Europe. Suspicion of Russia as a stimulus to working-class militancy in Britain reached a climax in the 1926 General Strike and resulted in the breach of diplomatic relations with Moscow in 1927. But it is interesting, too, to see how a Conservative like Viscount Cecil of Chelwood felt that the existing international system must somehow be made to work better, as by the creation of an effective League of Nations, or otherwise the working man would follow the Russian example.[4] It was all too evident, also, how fear of communism spreading into Europe from Russia committed the British Government to a moderate peace with Germany and later to a struggle with Russia to win the support, first of Germany, then of Kemalist Turkey, for the West, culminating, in Germany's case, in the Locarno Treaty in 1925 and Germany's entrance into the League of Nations a year later, and in the Lausanne Treaty of 1924 in Turkey's. At the same time, Lloyd George's policy of attempting to reintegrate Russia into the European economy in the interests of reviving international trade after the war was played as a counter-motif, setting the tone for the curious ambivalences towards Soviet Russia which have characterized British policy ever since.

The Anglo-American Alliance

It is a remarkable fact that, despite the effect of American arms in hastening the end of the war, and despite President Wilson's extraordinary hold over radical opinion in Britain in 1917–19, the British Government entertained mixed feelings about a United States entry into the war before that entry was actually effected in April 1917. To Britain, America had been more valued in 1915 and 1916 as a source of supply than as a potential belligerent; the equipment of her own forces for battle, it was thought, might have the effect of diverting war supplies away from the European allies. Above all, Wilson's idealistic approach to the political and territorial issues of the war was revealed in his detached offer to the belligerents on 18 December 1916.[5] It was clear that if he entered the war he would expect to put all the inter-Allied secret treaties for the division of the spoils into the melting pot. Fear that the President would allow all the hard-earned gains of the war to slip through the Allies' fingers was especially rife as the Supreme War Council in Versailles reviewed the correspondence between the German Government and Wilson in October 1918.

And yet, as generally tends to happen with idealists, Wilson proved even more exacting towards the Germans after America entered the war than the British; Lloyd George disagreed with him, for instance, in his demand that no peace could be made with Germany until it had acquired a representative form of government.

In the event, President Wilson proved on the whole a distinctly pro-British arbitrator between Britain and France at the Council of Four. He opposed Britain over the new Polish – German frontiers and the recovery of the whole costs of the war from Germany, which the British delegation at first tried to extract, but on the occupation of the Rhineland, the Saar, the Russian question, and the military clauses of the peace treaties, Wilson and the British worked together, as symbolized in the abortive Anglo-American guarantee to France in return for Clemenceau's agreement to withdraw his demand for a separate Rhineland state. When the United States retired from the implementation of the peace treaties, it was felt in Britain as the loss of a moderating force on France. (Lloyd George continued to hope against hope for an American mandate over European Turkey as a counter-weight to France in the Near East.) The effect of the American withdrawal from the peace settlement was in fact quite contradictory for Britain and France respectively. For Britain it strengthened the case for moderation towards the late enemies—during the negotiations on the Dawes Plan in 1924, for instance—on the assumption that the United States was more likely to return to the enforcement of a moderate peace than to that of a harsh one. The French, more realistic about the prospects of an American return to Europe, drew the opposite conclusion: namely that now America had left the scene the door must be bolted even more securely against German *revanche*.

It was rather in the extra-European world that America's entry into world politics in 1917 was most acutely felt in Britain. At the Peace Conference President Wilson worked himself into a fury against the colonial appetite of the British Dominions, especially Australia, and determined that America's new naval power would never be used to defend such ill-gotten gains. Later, at the Lausanne negotiations with Kemalist Turkey in 1923 – 24, the American observer, Joseph Grew, watched with similar distaste the rival machinations of Britain and France in the Near East and encouraged American companies to take their share of Middle East oil concessions without staining America's official hands with imperialism.[6] Above all, the seeds of the later, and rather absurd, Anglo-American naval rivalry (later equilibrated by the Washington Naval Treaty of 1922 and the London Naval Treaty of 1930), were planted in the sharp disagreement between the United States and Britain over the Japanese proposal, which Britain backed with certain reservations, for intervention by Japan in Russia in the early months of 1918.

The extraordinary tergiversations of President Wilson in the face of the strongest British pressure over this expedition bore witness to his dilemmas: his deep-seated suspicion of Japanese designs in Asia and Japanese demands for unrestricted immigration into the United States, and, on the other hand, his unreadiness to see the Anglo-Japanese alliance further consolidated by their joint expedition into Russia's Far Eastern provinces if America held aloof.[7] This incident bequeathed to the United States the determination to destroy that alliance if it were humanly possible, an ambition achieved at the Washington Conference in 1921 – 22. What Britain had to face, with the rise of Japanese imperialism in the 1930s, was the problem of co-operating with an America which remained too suspicious of Japan's ambitions against America's protégé in the Far East, China, to work with Britain in attempting to satisfy some of Japan's aspirations and hence limiting her advance in Asia, and yet which was too emotionally committed against British imperialism to work with Britain in opposing Japan.

After 1919 British politicians recognized that in the United States was a force always thereafter to be counted with: as an ally in moderation and pacification in Europe, and as a suspicious, censorious opponent elsewhere. But, after the non-ratification of the peace treaties by the Senate in March 1920, there was no acceptance of the fact that American assistance was essential to balance the rival forces in Europe, or that it would be forthcoming if it were. Sir Austen Chamberlain, as Conservative Foreign Secretary, was able to say in the House of Commons on 24 March 1925 that it rested with the British Empire to determine whether there should be war or peace; and as late as 1937 Neville Chamberlain was saying, with some appearance of reason, that 'it is always best and safest to count on nothing from the Americans but words'.[8] The Anglo-American alliance of 1917 – 19 was a wartime phenomenon; when it ended the British Government felt that the European equation of forces remained much the same as it always had been.

The Fall of Empires

The war saw the collapse of four empires: Austria – Hungary, and the German, Ottoman, and Russian empires. The Austro – Hungarian and Russian empires were, of course, multinational agglomerations in Europe, while the Ottoman empire extended over the Arab lands of the Fertile Crescent and was titular sovereign in Egypt, although Britain had declared a protectorate over that country on the outbreak of war in 1914. Only the German empire, with its possessions in Shantung, its island territories in the Pacific and its colonies in Africa, was an overseas dominion in the traditional sense.

While the British Government, as in Lloyd George's statement of war aims to a meeting of trade union leaders in London on 5 January 1918, welcomed the prospect of 'genuine self-government on true democratic principles' for the national peoples of Austria – Hungary, the dismemberment of the Habsburg Empire was never an element in official British war aims.[9] The hope rather was that after the war a viable Austria would remain in being as a counterweight to Germany, much as it had served in that role in relation to Prussia in the German Bund of 1815; as we have seen, the 'balkanization' of East and Central Europe which might result from an Austro – Hungarian dissolution tended to be feared, at least in government circles in London, as a factor of weakness. It was no doubt on this account that the government in 1937 and 1938 felt no strong obligation to resist the *Anschluss* of Germany and Austria, if this could be achieved by peaceful means.

Almost the same could be said of the process of self-determination which attended the flaking of Russia's western periphery as a consequence of the Soviet announcement of freedom for the non-Russian peoples of the Tsarist empire and their military inability in any case to hold on to these possessions of the Romanovs if they wanted to secede. It is true that in June 1918 the Supreme War Council was at odds with Admiral Kolchak, whom it was backing against the Bolsheviks, because of his unwillingness to commit his regime to self-determination for Russia's western border peoples, the Finns, the Baltic states, and the Poles.[10] But this was largely due, on the British side at least, to the Council's wish to rally world support, especially in the United States, for intervention in the Russian civil war; as we have seen earlier, no commitment to an independent Poland existed in Britain before the Bolshevik seizure of power. The situation had however changed by July 1920, when Lloyd George gave his celebrated personal guarantee to the Poles in the Russo – Polish conflict.[11] But here again it was not so much the principle of self-determination in itself which motivated the Prime Minister, as the desire, stated in his Commons speech of 16 April 1919, to hold up the flow of Bolshevik 'volcanic lava' and prevent it rolling into Europe. Thus the collapse of the Austro – Hungarian and Russian empires in Europe, though they could be conveniently presented to the world as consistent with the more abstract Allied war aims, was by no means an unmixed blessing for Britain; in so far as it created areas of weakness on Germany's eastern borders it was regarded as inconvenient if not positively dangerous.

The loss by Germany of its overseas possessions was quite a different matter, giving no cause for regret in Britain. Germany's stake in Shantung and her island dependencies in the Pacific north of the equator, always a thorn in the flesh of the British navy before 1914, could be handed to Japan, then one of Britain's closest allies, while German islands south of the equator were available for distribution as mandates within the British Empire. With the winding up of the Anglo – Japanese alliance at the Washington conference in 1921 – 22, Britain was able to join with the United States in securing from Japan the retrocession to China of Germany's former Shantung properties. This total disappearance of Germany as a Far Eastern Power, coupled with the scuttling of the German High Seas Fleet at Scapa Flow in the summer of 1919, gave rise to no misgivings in Britain, especially since, unlike the situation in the Middle East, it was not accompanied by struggles with France to fill the void. The United States at once replaced Germany as Britain's chief naval competitor in the Far East, and the acceptance by the Admiralty of naval parity with that country in March 1921 ensured a certain equilibrium in that respect in the Pacific. [12] The United States, however, had little of the commercial and investment stake in mainland China which the European Powers enjoyed; hence, when Britain was engaged in the 1920s in struggles with the Chinese nationalists in defence of her rights and concessions in the Yangtse valley, she found little support among her European partners, and practically none from the United States. It was partly for this reason that the British Foreign Secretary, Sir John Simon, could look with a certain sympathy on Japan's campaign in Manchuria in 1931 and 1932. There was no common European front to face the onslaught of the Chinese nationalist revolution against foreign rights in China, and Japan, though no longer supported by her former alliance with Britain, was regarded as fighting much the same kind of defensive action as Britain had in the mid-1920s.

As for Germany's former possessions in Africa, the lion's share of this fell, of course, to the British Empire, Tanganyika becoming a British and South West Africa a South African mandate, while in West Africa the Cameroons and Togoland were divided between Britain and France as mandates, with Ruanda – Urundi in Central Africa going to Belgium. The effect of this was, on the one hand, to achieve a dominant British Imperial war aim, the acquisition of the major portion of Germany's dependencies, and, on the other, to open the way to the unification of the whole of East Africa, from Cairo to the Cape, under the British aegis. The mandates system, however, though at first regarded by experienced colonial administrators as little more than a thinly disguised form of annexation, did serve to inhibit British colonial policy in East Africa, and to that extent the mandated territories' former master, Germany, could derive a certain wry satisfaction from observing the consequences of the loss of her colonies on the beneficiaries. In the first place, the principle of accountability for colonial administration, reflected in the mandates article of the League Covenant, undoubtedly helped to promote the nationalist protest against colonialism among dependent peoples and hence, thirty years later, made its own contribution to the decolonization process after the second World War. Second, the mere fact that Britain was answerable to the League for Tanganyika meant that the government's hopes in the 1920s of federating the East African territories, Kenya, Tanganyika, and Uganda, and hence of entrenching the political supremacy of the white minority there, could not be realized. [13] Tanganyika came to serve, not so much as annexation-in-disguise, but as an obstacle to irresponsible annexation almost everywhere else in Africa. Where, as in South West Africa, the principle of international accountability was never taken seriously, the seeds of an emotional alienation between South Africa and strands of British opinion which did take this principle seriously were well and truly planted.

Compared with the collapse of the three empires already mentioned, the process by which Turkey came to be restricted to its Anatolian core was protracted in the extreme, the final act being played out only with the signing of the Treaty of Lausanne on 24 July 1924. The reasons for this were the Kemalist revolution in Turkey itself, which nullified the Carthaginian Treaty of Sèvres imposed by the Allies on the Sultan's ministers in August 1920, the Greco – Turkish war culminating in the massacre in Smyrna in September 1919, differences between the British Foreign Office on one side, and the India Office on the other, about the expulsion of Turkey from Europe, and the quarrels between Britain and France over their influence in the new Turkey and the Arab states which emerged from the settlement. For Britain, however, this protracted settlement proved not only to be lasting (more so than any other of the post-war settlements), but consistent with most of Britain's aims and interests in the area.

In the first place, the Sultanate was replaced by a reformist national state which renounced its pan-Turkish ambitions, previously regarded as so disturbing in India and other territories with Moslem populations governed by Britain. Contrary to first impressions, Kemalist Turkey showed no tendency to become a satellite of Soviet Russia, and in the new Straits Convention negotiated at Lausanne, Britain secured the right to send warships into the Black Sea, as against the Bolshevik demand that defence of that sea should be exclusively a right of the riparian powers. In the second place, while the Anglo – French

Sykes – Picot Agreement of May 1916 for the partition of the Arab portions of
the Ottoman Empire was frustrated by Arab nationalism and the mandatory regime of the League, Britain had little difficulty in 1919 in winning the sympathy
of the Arabs as against the French. While France forcibly ejected Prince Fai-
sal from Syria in July 1920 after he had been somewhat unwillingly lifted to the
throne by the Syrian nobles in Damascus, Britain unostentatiously agreed to
his installation as the ruler of Iraq. Moreover, Britain's mandate over that
country became the guarantee of her access to the oil of its territory and the
later construction of some of her chief Middle East air bases there. Thirdly, the
implementation of the Balfour Declaration of 2 November 1917 in regard to
Palestine ensured, in theory at least, that it would serve under British mandate
as a friendly neighbour to the sea route to the Suez Canal and the Far East.
And, finally, the formation of the Arab states as League mandates and the
withdrawal of Turkey to its Anatolian core meant that Egypt was now securely
under British control, an arrangement given formal shape in the Anglo-Egyptian Treaty of 1922, while to the south lay the Anglo-Egyptian Sudan, in fact a
British colony and playing the part of a link with British East and Southern Africa. These were substantial by-products of the war effort.

The trouble which lay in store for Britain after the peace settlement in the
Near and Middle East did not arise, like those in Europe, from revisionism in
the defeated Power, but from the unwillingness of the liberated peoples to accept the settlement of their affairs which the Entente Powers had arranged on
their behalf. In eastern Europe the successor states appealed to Britain and
France to help them defend the status quo resulting from the peace treaties; in
the Middle East the Arab states increasingly revolted against the status quo
which the Allies had created, especially in Palestine, and in doing so they
found an ally in the resurgent Germany of the 1930s, with its own brand of dissatisfaction with the status quo. Had Britain never committed herself to the
idea of a national home for the Jews in Palestine in 1917 her subsequent relations with the Arab states would no doubt have been smoother; on the other
hand, the Balfour Declaration had been a wartime expedient designed to secure world-wide Jewish support for the Allied war effort. Had it never been issued, the Allied victory, which was the condition of Arab emancipation, would
have been that much harder to achieve.

The League of Nations and the British Empire
In the last year of the war British ministers deprecated over-much talk of a
League of Nations after the war lest it distract attention from the business of
winning the military conflict. It is also doubtful whether more than a very small

proportion of Conservative leaders (Viscount Cecil always being the exception), ever considered that the traditional rules could be superseded by the kind of 'talking shop' President Wilson seemed to have in mind. [14] It was quite evident, nevertheless, that a commitment to some more rational means of conducting diplomatic relations was essential in order to make sense of the bloodletting in Europe, and by the time Lloyd George recognized the 'need to establish by some international organization an alternative to war as a means of settling international disputes' in his war aims speech of 5 January 1918, he was voicing what had become a common aspiration of almost the entire Liberal and Labour parties and the trade unions.[15] Indeed, in some ways the Cecil plan for a League which the British Government accepted in principle in November 1918 was more detailed even than that of Wilson and House; it envisaged, for example, the use of sanctions against states which rejected machinery for pacific settlement of disputes, while Wilson was primarily interested in the exchange of obligations to defend territorial frontiers.

With the development of Anglo-French differences on the treatment of Germany at the Council of Four, however, a new function of the League began to shape itself in the British mind, one which loomed especially large after the American Senate refused to ratify the peace treaties. This was its potential role, to which British governments clung throughout the inter-war period, as a means of moderating the allegedly vindictive features of the peace treaties, which in the British view stood in the way of the reconciliation of Germany to the European comity of nations. This was the spirit in which Lloyd George recommended the peace treaties, with the League Covenant forming the first 26 articles of each of them, to the House of Commons on 3 July 1919; it was the reason why the British delegation at Paris had striven for the famous 'peaceful change' clause, article 19, in the Covenant; and it explains the emphasis laid by British governments in the 1920s on filling the 'menacing vacant chairs' in the League Assembly, first those of Germany and the United States, then Russia's. The whole basis of the British conception of the League, in sharp contrast to that of France, was of an organ for the reconciliation of nations, not for the organization of restraints by one group of nations against another.

And yet, of course, this attitude had its dangers and drawbacks. Britain in the 1920s might have thrown her weight on the side of France and the successor states in defence of the regime of the peace treaties; the League, being in the British mind an instrument for reconciling the nations, not for ranging them in armed coalitions against each other, tended to rule that out. So deeply did the mystique of Geneva sink into the mind of the prevailingly pacifist British public that any suggestion of Britain joining a military alliance against another nation or group of nations became abhorrent, as did the rearmament of the country to meet its foreign dangers. The paradoxical thing is, however, that when League supporters in Britain were roused to demand sanctions, for instance against Italy in 1935, the British government still felt that it could not act, since to do so would be to alienate Mussolini at a time when his help was needed, as a Locarno guarantor, to help preserve the balance in Europe.

The League may thus be said to have complicated the tasks of British diplomacy, while not greatly advancing the basic British aspiration for international reconciliation. The League threatened, as a consequence of French influence, to draw Britain into the defence of every detail of a peace settlement, much of which British ministers had strenuously disapproved in 1919. It bred the illusion that a company of nations existed, ready to stand foursquare against armed aggression anywhere in the world, whereas in reality Britain and France were the sole effective guarantors of the status quo, and they were inhibited from developing their military strength by the prevailing League psychology, especially in Britain. But the League also tended to stereotype for many well-meaning British people the form in which they expected furture breaches of the peace to occur. Following the precedent of 1914, the League Covenant assumed that aggression meant the crossing of the frontiers of an innocent state by the armed troops of a guilty one. Hence League supporters rose to the cry of 'sanctions against Italy' in 1935. But, as Sir Austen Chamberlain used to say, any definition of aggression is in danger of becoming a signpost to the guilty. The really dangerous aggressor of the 1930s, Germany, realized that it was much safer, in a League world, not to cross Czechoslovakia's frontiers by armed force, but to feed the resentment of Germans inside Czechoslovakia to such a pitch that that country had to be dismembered by the Great Powers to prevent Germany entering it to rescue her countrymen. The League Covenant was not designed for that kind of situation; the situation was framed in the light of the League Covenant.

There was a further implication of the foundation of the League for Britain, namely that it consolidated and symbolized the independence in home and foreign policy which the Dominions—Australia, Canada, New Zealand, and South Africa—had to all intents achieved by the end of the war. The Dominions and India (though Indian foreign policies were still made in London), were separate members of the League and were separately answerable to the Geneva organization for such mandates as they administered. Attempts were made at the Peace Conference to co-ordinate British and Dominion foreign policies through the device of the British Empire Delegation. For all practical purposes this meant the modification of British policy so as to eliminate features or nuances unacceptable to the Dominions, though they, and especially Australia, made their own voices felt in no uncertain manner on colonial questions. Moreover, the close alignment in outlook between Britain and the Dominions on all the major issues of the European peace settlement and on the proposals for reforming the League Covenant after the peace settlement, meant that British governments were rather more conscious of their freedom to use the Dominions as excuses for avoiding European commitments like those proposed by France, than they were of obstructions placed in their path by Dominion statesmen. It remains true, however, that after 1919 the British Empire was not to enjoy again that unity of foreign policy, based on control from London, which it could take for granted before. It did not need the Balfour resolutions of 1926, or the Statute of Westminster of 1931, to establish the point that Britain could never again automatically count on the support of the Dominions in critical foreign policy issues unless it was clear that the course of action proposed was in their interest as well as her own.

The Mood of Britain

The overwhelming desire of the British people when the war ended was to retire into a quiet civilian life as soon as possible. It was assumed that internationally things would continue in much the same way as they always had. Germany would not be able to get up to her tricks again; on the other hand, France had to be watched lest she provoke the Germans to distraction. The League of Nations would no doubt help to make international affairs rather more rational and orderly, but in any case the world had surely had such a surfeit of war that the risk of its recurrence for ten years at least was considered remote. The United States had emerged from isolation, but even if it returned, Europe was slowly rising to its feet and could probably get on without America. There had been altogether too much war; now was the time for tranquility, for cultivating one's garden. Besides, the rumblings of industrial unrest and troubles in Ireland and India demanded that Europe be left alone for the present.

This mentality is understandable, but it took little account of the vast changes in the world scene which were enacted in the last months of the war and during the peace settlement: the permanent imbalance in Europe resulting from Germany's industrial and military power, however latent for the time being the latter must be; the weakness of the east European settlement; the dangerous estrangement of Russia from the West; the rise of nationalist feeling outside Europe, especially in the Arab world; the ascent of Japan to front-rank military status and the slow emergence of China from civil war. These events sounded only a distant echo in a Britain settling down to long and bitter internal conflict over wages, unemployment and conditions of work. When revisionism later sprang to life in Europe in the totalitarian states, it encountered a Britain unwilling to defend a peace settlement much of which it never endorsed, and preferring a quiet life to the stridencies of world politics. Because Britain fought in 1914 to avoid certain things—especially being excluded from the peace settlement—rather than to gain something, the idea spread in Britain that 'war settles nothing'. Had the war then been a gross mistake? The British were not entirely sure. But if it had been a mistake they would need much convincing before they would make the same mistake twice.

NOTES

1. *Peacemaking, 1919* (London, 1934), p. 113.

2. David Lloyd George, *The Truth about the Peace Treaties* (London, 1938), I, 91.

3. R. B. McCallum, *Public Opinion and the Last Peace* (London, 1944), 101 – 3.

4. Viscount Cecil, *All the Way* (London, 1949), 159.

5. HMSO, Misc. No. 39 (1916), Cmnd. 8431.

6. Joseph C. Grew, *Turbulent Era, 1904 – 45* (London, 1953), I, Chapters XVIII – XXI.

7. George F. Kennan, *Soviet-American Relations, I, Russia Leaves the War* (London, 1953), Chapter XV.

8. Sir Keith Feiling. *The Life of Neville Chamberlain* (London, 1946), 325.

9. *British War Aims* (HMSO, London, 1918), 9.

10. *Documents on British Foreign Policy,* 1919 – 1939, ed. E. L. Woodward and Rohan Butler, First Series, III (HMSO, London, 1949), 362 – 69.

11. Cabinet Minutes and Conclusions, CAB 23/22 (20) Appendix II, Public Record Office.

12. See speech by Lord Lee of Fareham on 16 March 1921, quoted in *The Times,* 17 March.

13. See B. T. G. Chidzero, *Tanganyika and International Trusteeship* (London, 1961), Chapter II.

14. See H. R. Winkler, 'The development of the League of Nations idea in Great Britain, 1914 – 19', *Journal of Modern History,* June 1948.

15. *British War Aims,* 12.

There are many assessments of the domestic consequences of World War I. Most scholarly articles, however, have focused attention upon some relatively narrow aspect of policy or behavior and the broader assessments have appeared generally in the wide range of books dealing with the war's impact. Arthur Marwick, Professor of History in the Open University, has written extensively on the British labour movement, on historiography, and especially on social history. Among his works in the latter field are: The Explosion of British Society, 1914 – 62 *(London, 1963);* The Deluge, British Society and the First World War *(London, 1965); and* Britain in the Century of Total War. War, Peace and Social Change, 1900 – 1967 *(New York, 1968). In* The Deluge *he assesses the shattering effects of the war on British society, but gives attention to what may be called its constructive results as well as to the disastrous. The following excerpt is Chapter 9 of that illuminating book and is reprinted by permission of A. D. Peters and Company.*

2 | After the Deluge

ARTHUR MARWICK

[I] Daddy, What Did the Great War Do to You?

Where history differs as a scholarly pursuit from a science is in the inability of the historian to conduct anything in the nature of a controlled experiment. In summarizing analytically the material presented chronologically in the course of this book, we find that there are not many topics in which we can say this or that was caused by the war, *and nothing but the war.* If we attempt to list the bed-rock direct consequences of the war, we shall find that we are dealing as much with the *method* by which the war affected society as with the actual effects in society.

The direct consequences, which we can limit to seven, reacted with a multiplicity of other forces creating a tremendous range of side effects and indirect consequences. First and second are the obvious tangibles, the loss of life and limb, and the destruction of what contemporary writers liked to call 'treasure'. Third is the wholesale disruption caused by the war in the old mechanism of international trade and finance. Fourth is the huge physical demand of the war for manpower and machines, which, given, of course, the deeper pressure of the will to survival, created an irresistible pressure for the reorganization and reorientation of society; what forms the reorganization took, what lessons were learned from it, depended on other circumstances, but the immediate and eventual ramifications were immense. Fifth is the way in which the war, in one sense the ultimate expression of the German challenge to British supremacy, brought to Britain a sharp sense of her deficiencies and a sharp determination to remedy them. Sixth is the mass of domestic problems piled up by the war's interruption of normal social development. Seventh is the scale, horror, and excitement of the war, calling forth all sorts of different responses from all sorts of different people, and necessitating the mobilization, not just of men and machines, but of minds, which in turn created all kinds of reactions and by-products.

The loss of 745,000 of the country's younger men (leaving aside the unknown proportion of the 1.6 million wounded who were gravely mutilated) amounting to about 9 per cent of all men under 45, meant a definite alteration in the population balance, which can be presented with reasonable statistical precision, but whose full emotional effects cannot be precisely assessed. In 1911 there were 155 males aged between 20 and 40 per thousand of the population in England and Wales; in 1921, for every thousand of the population, there were only 141. The balance of females over the age of 14, therefore (discounting any other minor factors involved), rose from 595 per thousand in 1911 to 638 per thousand in 1921, and the proportion of widows per thousand of the population rose from 38 to 43.[1] There is no exact measure of the quantity of personal agony concealed behind these figures, but society, in later years, exhibited all the signs of having suffered a deep mental wound, of having undergone a traumatic experience, to which the agony and the slaughter, as well as the more generalized horror over the destruction of an older civilization and its ways, which we shall consider in a moment, contributed. In the inter-war years the birth rate declined even further than it had in Edwardian times, but although the loss in the war of potential fathers was a contributory factor a later Royal Commission concluded that it was not in itself a significant one.[2] Other by-products of the war—the wider diffusion of contraceptives or the pruning of large family establishments for example—reacted within the broader trend. Already by 1921 the average number of children under 14 per family had declined from 1.29 to 1.12, bringing the important incidental consequence of a raising of living standards.[3]

Much was written in the years after 1918 on 'the lost generation'. We have seen the statistical basis—one in ten of the generation aged between 20 and 45 during the war, missing. What the figures do not make so clear, but what has often been pointed out, is that the missing were the cream of the generation, the first volunteers, the junior officers; out of Oxford University's total roll of service of 14,561, 2,680 were killed.[4] A faint touch of myth, perhaps, was mixed with the grim reality, which was mainly stressed by those articulate men who had themselves been Oxford men, junior officers, early volunteers. Society, very hesitantly, was turning towards the idea of choosing the occasional leader elsewhere than from the university officer class, but there is no doubt that much of the political weakness of Britain in the inter-war years can be attributed to the paucity of young talent of quality. To avoid getting one's generations hopelessly mixed, it is worth recalling that the survivors of the lost generation were men like Clement Attlee and Harold Macmillan, who reached political eminence in the forties and fifties when they were not noticeably deficient in colleagues of high calibre. Where the loss of the tithe of a generation did also seem to make itself felt—this is problematical ground—was in the weakening of any possible mediatory agency between the old generation, entrenched in power by virtue of the Coupon Election, and the young generation which grew up in the maelstrom years of the war.

While the wartime damage to Britain's capital assets (with the notable exception of shipping) was not of great significance, the immense financial cost of the war, through the high taxation which it necessitated and the inflationary trend which it created, did have powerful social effects. First of all the trend towards the compression of disposable incomes intensified, drawing classes closer together, making it difficult for the upper classes, and very nearly impossible for the middle classes, to maintain the lavish standards of pre-war days. Secondly the landed classes received the final series of blows, which, in combination with other political developments, finally knocked them out of their political and social primacy. Thirdly, as the 'tax line' dropped to incomes of £130 at the same time as working-class earnings began to rise above this figure, it virtually ceased to exist as the sort of social demarcation that it had been in Edwardian times. The sale of War Savings Certificates was another financial expedient which contributed to this spreading of the pale of respectable citizenship.

The dislocations of the old international economic system were extremely serious for a trading nation such as Britain and created problems which helped to give rise to mass unemployment in the inter-war years. But the immediate effect was to demonstrate the falsity of many of the economic dogmas associated with that system. Despite the effective departure from gold, the economy not only survived, but was able to produce enormous sums of money for the prosecution of the war. It almost began to look as though economics could be the servant of man, rather than man the servant of economics. The same conclusion could be drawn from the vast experiment in state control developed step by step to meet the needs of war. The lesson was not immediately learned: what was wrong with Britain in the twenties was that she suffered from what the war had done, and failed to profit from what the war had taught—her governments were composed of sadder but not wiser men. But the story does not end there. In the first place the precedents had been set, establishing in fact a new measure of tolerance for large-scale State intervention. Thus the collectivist measures which were enacted at the end of the war, the big ones like the Housing Act and the Unemployment Insurance Act, and, later, the setting up of the B.B.C., and the little ones like the establishment of the Forestry Commission in 1919, created little stir. In the second place ideas which could in pre-war years be laughed off as Utopian fantasies, denounced as contrary to economic law, or displayed as evidence of the sinister intentions of socialism, had been put to work and had been seen to work. In the years after the war, as the country entered upon economic depression and mass unemployment, more and more political thinkers began to argue that escape could only come through the revival of some of the policies of the war years. In 1927 four young Conservatives, Robert Boothby, Harold Macmillan, John de V. Loder and the Hon. Oliver Stanley pointed out that:

> The war period shattered preconceived economic notions, proved possible theoretic impossibilities, removed irremovable barriers, created new and undreamt-of situations. Yet by far the greater part of the legislation which today governs trade and industry dates from before that period. We are surely entitled to ask whether it is now adequate to meet the vastly changed conditions of the modern economic era. [5]

Under the impact of the great crash of 1931 collectivist economic policy was greatly extended in the thirties; it became dominant in the nineteen-forties, and although there have been slight relaxations since then, no serious politician today, save perhaps Mr. Enoch Powell, would contemplate a return to the orthodoxy of Edwardian Britain.

The shortage of manpower contributed along with the other shortages to the wartime extension of State control, but its main effects were more subtle. The working class as a social class, though suffering many hardships and grievances, derived a number of permanent advantages from their favourable market position—wage rates were doubled, the average working week was reduced from 55 hours to 48—and, more important still, they got a taste of the better material comforts of modern civilization. That the working class made as much as it did of its favourable situation was in large measure due to the efforts of the organized labour movement, which was already developing in strength and cohesion before 1914; but the need of the Government for the cooperation of the leaders of the labour movement in maximizing the war effort meant that they also gained immensely in prestige and status, even to the extent of taking Cabinet office. The political side of the movement, the Labour

Party, was strengthened sufficiently for it to be able to wring advantage from the divisions and weaknesses in the Liberal Party. The working man, in factory or mine, or conscripted into the army, not only was, but was seen to be, fully implicated in the country's survival. A handful at least of politicians and opinion-makers began to stress his claim upon a fuller citizenship, making this claim a major motivation behind the extension of the franchise in 1918, and one among several behind the social legislation of the same period.

The gaps in the home front left by men summoned to the fighting front had to be filled, and they could only be filled by women, and, to a lesser extent, by children. The manner in which the situation was exploited owed much to the experience the women's leaders had derived from the pre-war suffrage movements; it is also true that before the war the doors to a number of professions were already slowly opening. Yet it is difficult to see how women could have achieved so much in anything like a similar time-span without the unique circumstances arising from the war. Almost certainly when the time came for a further Reform Act in the great series extending back to 1832 they would, or some of them would, have been included in the new franchise, and the vote would no doubt have assisted the fight for further economic, social, and civic freedoms. But the war brought opportunity in concentrated and varied form, and from the stock of patriotic bombast paid the women a valuable bonus: men and women joined together to praise women's contribution to the war effort, bringing a confidence in their new role to women, and an acceptance of it among men, which might otherwise not have been easy to create.

The straight demand for mighty weapons of offence and defence inevitably gave a great prestige to science and a stimulus to technological, if not scientific, research. At least as important an influence on public and private research, however, was the sense of insecurity and desperate challenge brought home to British society by the war. In the really major advances of twentieth-century science the war was totally irrelevant, and Sir Charles Parsons rightly pointed out that

> the work of the scientists during the war has perforce been directed more to the application of known principles, trade knowledge, and the properties of matter to the waging of war than to the making of new and laborious discoveries. [6]

Yet even from such work there came developments—aviation and broadcasting being two of the most striking—of the utmost importance for society in time of peace. The two major features of the process were the desire of commercial companies to exploit the new technological potential they had developed for purposes of war, and the creation, through the drama of war, of a popular interest in, and appetite for, such developments. It must, however, always be borne well in mind that science is international, and that the influence of war was often very secondary to the influence of, in particular, the United States of America.

The interruption by the war of normal domestic, social and economic development undoubtedly contributed to the economic ailments of the inter-war years. At the same time by inflating such problems as housing and education to enormous size it brought them within the vision of the most myopic politician. The will to action was enhanced by the contemporary collectivist experience, by the need to appease the working class and the desire to accord its members some of the privileges of citizenship, and above all by the present supreme struggle which brought out Britain's defects in the physical well-being of her people, as it had exposed her weaknesses in scientific equipment. Here is part, the major part, of the explanation for the burst of social reform at the end of the war. We must qualify it by recollecting what the Wickwars [7] stress in discussing the Addison Housing Act, that the collectivist 'tendency was already at work before the war of 1914'. They then add that 'the end of the war gave an illusion of dramatic suddenness to what might otherwise have been a gradual and almost imperceptible process'. But in this book, following Miss Marion Bowley, [8] I have described the Housing Act in its scope and provisions as revolutionary. In reality, there is no conflict: the problem is the same as that involved in the new freedoms gained by women—no doubt they would have come eventually as an 'almost imperceptible process', but in fact, because of the war, they came in a sudden burst. Similarly, by an only slightly less direct train of causation, the Housing Act, and the other social legislation, in the form in which it actually came, was a consequence of the war.

But what were the consequences of these pieces of social legislation? Here we run up against the complicated chemistry of social improvement in modern society, which involves 'a rare and fascinating phenomenon, the rise of a new standard of living, the pursuit of which has made a profound difference to the poverty-stricken of all classes'. [9] Once it has started, this phenomenon is to some extent self-perpetuating, but at its centre are the material products of scientific advance and the extension of collectivist social welfare. The importance of the reconstruction legislation of the war period is that it forms the basis of this subsequent extension, and thus makes a large contribution to the overall process. Although the Addison Housing Act was stifled, half a million houses were built under its important successor, the Wheatley Act of 1924, which greatly extended the subsidy policy. Similarly, some of the ideals of the Fisher Education Act, destroyed in 1921, were restored after 1924. Many of the other wartime developments—the growth of women's spending power, for example—fit into the chain-reaction; by accelerating pre-war trends, they create still greater acceleration.

Our final direct consequence of the war is a multiple one. The war was exciting as well as horrible. Where the world was not really, as Blumenfeld put it, 'topsy-turvy', people tended to want to believe that it was; the wish became the father to the thought, and the thought became acceptable. Early twentieth-century Britain had been a disturbed society, but those who openly railed against its conventions were a small minority: the emotional excitement of this greatest of all wars gave a certain universality to the concept of change, gave a moral sanction to the disruptions and transformations demanded by the physical needs of war. When enthusiasm flagged, propaganda stepped in. For the ordinary citizen, despite dark liberal talk of truth being the first casualty of war, the poison did no more than prolong the emotional debauch a little longer than it might otherwise have lasted, leaving behind little but a bad taste and perhaps—among ex-soldiers at least—a certain healthy scepticism of the printed word: 'whatever your pastors and masters tell you had best be assumed to be just a bellyful of east wind'. [10] Pastors indeed did their own cause great harm by their pulpit propaganda.

The havoc of the war, in the apt word of E. L. Woodward, had a 'scorching' effect on the minds of British intellectuals:

> The novels and poems of D. H. Lawrence, the early novels of Aldous Huxley, Lytton Strachey's *Eminent Victorians*, Mr. Keynes's *Economic Consequences of the Peace* bear evidence of minds 'scorched' by war, and reacting against a nervous strain which was almost unbearable. The strain was caused not by any doubt about the issue of the war, but by the very fact of a European war and the breakdown of accepted standards. [11]

Woodward obviously regretted the disappearance of old virtues; he obviously disliked the tone of, say, Lytton Strachey's closing description of the service of remembrance held for the martyred Victorian hero General Gordon:

> The service was conducted by four chaplains—of the Catholic, Anglican, Presbyterian, and Methodist persuasions—and concluded with a performance of 'Abide with me'—the General's favourite hymm—by a select company of Sudanese buglers. Every one agreed that General Gordon had been avenged at last. Who could doubt it? General Gordon himself, possibly, fluttering, in some remote Nirvana, the pages of a phantasmal Bible, might have ventured on a satirical remark. But General Gordon had always been a contradictious person—even a little off his head perhaps, though a hero; and besides he was no longer there to contradict . . . At any rate, it had all ended very happily—in a glorious slaughter of twenty thousand Arabs, a vast addition to the British Empire, and a step in the Peerage for Sir Evelyn Baring. [12]

To attribute the cynicism of Lytton Strachey or the mystical hatred for industrial civilization of D. H. Lawrence solely, or in any sizeable degree, to the experiences of the war would be ludicrous. The serious attack on Victorianism began in the 1890's and developed under the leadership of Shaw, Wells, Davidson, Fry and many others in the Edwardian period but it was in the nature of the war, murderous beyond all proportion to moral or material gains made, to foster scepticism, irony, irreverence.

Of religion not a great deal has been said so far, since no clear trend really emerges till the end of the war. It was in keeping with the exaltation of the times that the churches should be well patronized during the war, and they seemed a natural focal point of Armistice celebration and thanksgiving. Ministers of religion had embarked with enthusiasm upon the 'Holy War'. 'The Church', as the Minister of St Giles Cathedral, Edinburgh, recalled,

> to an unfortunate degree, had become an instrument of the State and in too many pulpits the preacher had assumed the role of a recruiting sergeant. Almost every place of worship throughout the length and breadth of the land displayed the Union Jack, generally placed above the Holy Table, while some had great shields carrying the flags of all the allied nations. The first thing I did myself when I went to St Paul's, [Greenock] was to have a huge Union Jack and the national flag of Scotland displayed upon the east wall of the chancel. Being young, and owing to the inflamed feelings of the times, I said many things from my pulpit during the first six months of my ministry that I deeply regret. It is no excuse to say that many preachers were doing the same thing. I still feel ashamed when I recall declaiming on one occasion—about the time of Haig's 'Our Backs are to the Wall' message—that anyone who talked of initiating peace negotiations with the rulers of Germany was a moral and spiritual leper who ought to be shunned and cut by every decent-minded and honest man! This monstrous and stupid utterance, of which the Press got wind and duly lauded, so moved one of my patriotic hearers, the Manager of the Greenock Docks, that he startled the congregation by involuntarily shouting 'Hear, hear!' [13]

But sensitive believers were already secretly in revolt. C. F. G. Masterman, formerly a staunch Anglican, complained to his wife that a service at Westminster Abbey seemed like an activity at Wellington House, and remarked that the only religious leader who emerged with credit was the Pope, because of his appeal to the warring nations, and that the body which came through best was the Quakers. [14] After the war there was an immense reaction against the fervour and bigotry which had displayed itself in its most nauseating forms during the war. The brutal horror of the military war had a direct effect on religious belief: in February 1918 Masterman, in his diary, was musing upon the possibility that

> God is a devil who rejoices in human suffering. He may be. There's no evidence to show He isn't. [15]

Many other long-term forces are involved in the decline of organized religion, not the least of them being the failure of the churches, from the time of the industrial revolution, to capture the interest of the proletariat. If anything, there did seem during the war to be a positive attempt to meet this situation, as Churchmen asked 'why should it be the exception rather than the rule for the workers to feel that the Church is their home?' [16] In the social reorganizations of the war, the Churches, though they may have been assisted towards interdenominational unity through the sharing of ministers, were, on the whole, adversely affected, especially from the breaking-up by war-service of the old close-knit dissenting communities. [17] The extent to which, in the perspective of three decades of change, the Churches suffered, can be seen from Rowntree's 1935 survey of York:

> the number of adults attending church has fallen from 17,060 in 1901 to 12,770 in 1935, notwithstanding the fact that during that period the adult population of the city has increased from 48,000 to 72,248. . . . In 1901 adult attendances amounted to 35.5 per cent of the adult population; in 1935 it amounted to only 17.7 per cent. [18]

The direct 'scorching' of the war reacted with the indirect consequences of the social transformations wrought by the war and with the broader trend of intellectual scepticism to create one great denominator, 'a widespread impatience of authority as such,' [19] which was both a part of, and an influence on, the social climate of the inter-war years. It could be seen in the 'new morality', [20] it could be seen in the decline of 'deference', it could be seen in religion. But, alas, it had only a negative influence on politics: that was the supreme equivocation bequeathed by the war, and the key to the tragic aspects of Britain's inter-war history.

[II] The New Society

Geography, naturally, did not change much between 1914 and the 1920's (Southern Ireland gained independence at the end of 1921). In the twenties, however, a new population drift from the areas which in 1914 held the main concentrations of industrial power towards the Home Counties and the South East becomes apparent. While the population of London and the Home Counties increased by 18 per cent between 1921 and 1937, that of the Midland Counties increased by only 11 per cent, that of the West Riding, Notts and Derbyshire by only 6 per cent, the Lowlands of Scotland by only 4 per cent (although the Scottish birth rate was higher than the English) and that of Lancashire by less than 1 per cent. The population of South Wales declined by 9 per cent, and that of Northumberland and Durham by 1 per cent. [21] This trend was the geographical expression of the depression in coal mining and the old heavy industries, which accounted for the high and steady figure of 1½ million unemployed throughout the decade, and of the growth (though insufficient growth) of the new light, science-based industries. London and its motorized traffic problem had already caused concern before the war, and it already had its extensive environs inhabited by 'suburbans'; but it was in the twenties that the great development of commuterland—Hendon, Morden, Wembley, etc.— began, so that the total population of Greater London rose to over eight millions. Before the war it was London with its sweated trades which housed the most notorious swamps of poverty while the miners and the skilled workers in the heavy industries had been the most prosperous members of the working classes.

Clearly the movement towards the new technologies was inevitable, and signs of it were apparent enough well before 1914. It can be argued that, apart from the wider interruption of international trade, the war had an adverse influence in that it brought a final intensive development and exploitation of the old industries, when there should instead have been a steady conversion to new industries. [22] There is some, but not a lot of, force in this, since the war did also bring a stimulus to the new industries. What was ironic about the wartime industrial experience was the great, and justified, sense of power and importance it gave to the miners and heavy engineering workers, who were then, after the war, to find themselves working in conditions of falling demand. And although that same experience demonstrated not just the value of science-based industry but also the uses of Government direction and control, no attempt in the twenties was made towards sending new industry where it was required to absorb unemployment. So the pattern established itself: a prosperous, bustling south producing a tremendous range of new consumer goods; a decaying north.

The war had a dissolving effect on the class structure of Britain, the elements working the change being both economic—taxation especially—and emotional: the sense of 'topsy-turvydom', the sense of common citizenship. But Britain was still, as it is today, very much a class-conscious society. At the top the landed class, which had been the dominant component of the political élite of Edwardian times, moved into political, though not so obviously into economic and social, eclipse. Much attention, in the first years of peace, was focused on the extensive land sales which took place: 'England is changing hands', became a stock remark. By March 1919 about half a million acres were on the market, and by the end of the year over a million acres had been sold. In 1920 sales were still greater, with the Duke of Rutland making the pace by selling off about half of his Belvoir estate, 28,000 acres in all, for

£ 1½ million. [23] One firm of estate agents claimed that within a single year land equal in area to an English county had passed through their hands. [24] There were three main reasons for these sales. They could first of all be simply the continuation of a policy initiated at the beginning of the century whereby the landowner sought to consolidate his income by selling off outlying holdings; that is to say, financial impoverishment was not necessarily involved. Second, however, there was the question of high taxation, initiated as far as the landowner was concerned in the years before 1914, but greatly extended during and at the end of the war, when the 1919 budget raised death duties to 40 per cent on estates of £2 million and over. The frequent deaths in battle of young aristocrats made the burden of death duties even greater than it might otherwise have been. Third was the fact that, because of wartime exploitation of agriculture, land values had greatly risen, while rents had not; by selling, the landowner could put the increased value straight into his pocket. Economically, then, the position of the landowners was not too serious: they

emerged into the inter-war period still in residence in their country seats, with their territorial empires considerably reduced, but with their incomes—once debts had been cleared and reinvestments made—probably much healthier than they had been for very many years. [25]

But their feudal dominance of the countryside was almost at an end, as their own tenants took the opportunity presented by the land-sales to set themselves up as owner-farmers. The sale of urban land, opening the door to the small domestic landlord, and to a new type of property developer, took place at the same time as the sale of landed estates. Town houses, now that the upkeep of large establishments was so difficult, were sold too, symbolizing the movement of aristocratic high society away from the centre of the London political stage. [26]

The new flow of political power within the topmost class was given its first big boost by the events of December 1916, and was ratified in the 1918 general election. It was expressed in the notorious energy with which Lloyd George created new peerages—98 between 1917 and 1921, his fall from office unfortunately preventing him from completing his century—in the passing over of Lord Curzon in favour of the 'countrified businessman' Stanley Baldwin for the Prime Ministership of 1922, and in the formation of the influential 1922 Committee of Conservative backbenchers—most of them businessmen. It was, naturally, a matter of deep regret to aristocrats like Lord Henry Bentinck who believed that the Conservative Party was being 'thoroughly commercialized and vulgarized', and Plutocracy 'ennobled, decorated, knighted and enriched'.[27] The upper class, then, is still, as in Edwardian times, a composite class, but the balance has moved definitely from the landed to the business interest. It was this class, or the younger members of it, which, drawing upon the hectic hedonism of the war, created the gay high-life associated with the nineteen-twenties. It was this class which occupied the literary attentions of Aldous Huxley, and of John Galsworthy, the chronicler of the fortunes of a Victorian business family. Galsworthy, making a not very funny joke at the expense of social investigators who talked of the ten per cent below the poverty line, said that he was concerned only with the ten per cent above the property line. [28] Inequality in the division of income and wealth was still very marked, but not quite as marked as before the war: in 1910 1.1 per cent of the population took 30 per cent of the income; in 1929 1.5 per cent took 23 per cent of the income, and two thirds of the wealth was owned by 2½ per cent of the population. Bowley and Stamp, in their analysis of the national income as it was in 1924, pointed out that, while in 1911 individuals with incomes above £5,000 drew 8 per cent of the aggregate national income, in 1924, those earning £9,500 (the equivalent, given the rise in prices between 1914 and 1924) drew only 5½ per cent. They then proceeded to the very cautious summing up:

> When the full effects of taxation are taken into account the real income available for saving or expenditure in the hands of the rich is definitely less than before the war. The sum devoted to luxurious expenditure is (allowing for the rise of prices) definitely less than in 1911, but it is still sufficient to bulk large in the eyes of the public, since it is concentrated in small areas, enlarged by the spending of visitors from overseas and advertised by the newspapers. [29]

When we move into the middle classes, the outstanding and incontrovertible statistical fact is the increase over the war period in the salaried class from under 1.7 millions in 1911 to over 2.7 millions in 1921, a rise from 12 per cent to 22 per cent of the occupied population. [30] The figures themselves are inflated because of the inclusion in this category of low-paid shop assistants, clerks, etc., and the expansion is exaggerated because the classification in 1921 was rather more rigorous. None the less the growth is striking. Itself a social phenomenon of outstanding importance, it reflects the expansion of four important groupings in the community: the professions, for whom rising material and welfare standards brought a new demand; the Civil Servants and clerical administrators, needed by the growing bureaucracy; the managerial class required for the running of large-scale modern industry; and those women who held on to the opportunities opened to them during the war (in 1931 there were 5½ million women in employment, 37 per cent of the female population between 14 and 65). [31] The other important feature of note is the decline in ser-

vant-keeping among middle-class households. The total decrease in the number of servants in the country over the war period, about a third, is less than is
sometimes suggested; despite what observers during the war thought, many
women were forced back at the end of the war into this degrading occupation.
Still, the decrease that did take place came largely out of the households of
the middle classes. In the commuter areas of London the number of resident
servants per 100 families declined from 24.1 to 12.4, whereas in the West End
it only edged down from 57.3 to 41.3. [32] In the whole of Liverpool the decline
was from 13.5 to 8.3; in suburban Wallasey from 22.4 to 14.5. [33]

The decline in servant-keeping helped to weaken the barriers between the
middle and lower classes, though a comparison between John Galsworthy's
Tony Bicket in *A Modern Comedy* and E. M. Forster's Leonard Bast do not suggest any great change in upper-middle-class attitudes. The 'tax line' had all but
disappeared in 1919 – 20 when there were 7¾ million tax-paying citizens, [34]
six times the number in 1914, though this total fell again when the exemption
limit was shortly raised to £150 per annum. When Bowley conducted a second social survey in 1924 with the express purpose of finding out whether
working-class poverty had diminished since 1913, the problems of deciding
which were working-class households and which were not had subtly
changed:

> In general, our principle has been 'when in doubt, rule out.' In the previous inquiry the
> inclination seems rather to have been the other way. [35]

The lines of distinction between middle and working class, that is to say, have
become much more blurred than before; the feeling is that the clearly defin-
able working class has got a little smaller. This feeling is borne out by the figures in the 1921 census: the total number in the 'wage-earner' category, the
main core of the working class, has fallen to under 15 millions, [36] other vari-
ables being at least cancelled out by the increase meantime in the population.
Carr-Saunders and Caradog-Jones, in their inter-war studies of the social
structure of England and Wales, it may be noted here, refused to use the language of social class, belligerently in the first study when they asserted that
'the belief in the existence of social classes . . . is the result of studying social
theory of doubtful value and of neglecting social facts', [37] less belligerently in
the second, when they merely inquired, "is it not a misreading of the social
structure of this country to dwell on class divisions when, in respect of dress,
speech, and use of leisure, all members of the community are obviously coming to resemble one another?' [38]

The working class in 1914 was large and it was poor. In the early twenties it
was not quite so large, and it was not quite so poor. Bowley referred to his ear-

lier pronouncement that 'to raise the wages of the worst-paid workers is the most pressing social task with which the country is confronted today', and continued:

> It has needed a war to do it, but that task has been accomplished, so far as rates of wages are concerned, though employment has not been permanently possible for all at those rates. [39]

There was the achievement, and there the qualification upon it. Real wages for full-time employment were up by 20 per cent, the average working week down from 55 hours to 48 hours. But there was also, in certain areas, continuous unemployment on an unprecedented scale. Where 11 per cent of the families in Bowley's previous survey had been in primary poverty, the new wage rates should have reduced this figure to 3.6 per cent; because of unemployment the actual figure was 6.5 per cent. In the mining village of Stanley, which has basked in the coal boom of 1913, conditions were actually slightly worse now that coal-mining was a depressed industry: 7.5 per cent in primary poverty in 1924 as opposed to 6 per cent in 1940. [40] In the long view the achievement was much more important than the qualification; but in the meantime the qualification brought much misery.

The great flux in material conditions, mental attitudes, and leisure activities contributed to the blurring of social distinctions. The decline in drunkenness, in itself a most important social fact, also helped to bring working-class behaviour into the area of the middle-class norm. While mentioning 'the immense present-day volume of drinking which takes place', the *New Survey of London Life and Labour* stressed that 'the outstanding points are,

> the decrease in the amount of drinking per head, as distinct from the amount spent on drink, and the decreased extent to which actual excess, and the economic and physical effects of excess, are found. The social status of drunkenness has steadily fallen in the eyes of the working-class population. Where once frequent drunkenness was half admired as a sign of virility, it is now regarded as, on the whole, rather squalid and ridiculous.' [41]

A levelling out in the opposite direction was suggested by Mary Agnes Hamilton, writing in 1935 of 'the new morality':

> in this respect the practice of the middle-class now tends, with variations of its own, to resemble that previously common enough among what were then called the 'lower orders.' [42]

A similar sort of social communion was to be found in widespread religious non-observance.

The most potent force of all was the growth of the mass media of communication. This was at first treated by the politicians with something of the same fuddy-duddy obscurantism as brought the return of much of the old economic orthodoxy in 1920 and 1921, but was shortly made the occasion for the enlightened application of the wartime collectivist lesson. In March 1919 a wireless telephony (i.e. the broadcasting of speech and sound as distinct from code signals—wireless telegraphy) transmitter was set up at Ballybunion in Ireland by the Marconi Company, and, under the direction of H. J. Round, successful transmissions were made to America. This led to the installation of a more powerful 6-kilowatt transmitter at Chelmsford, where, in addition to the testing of speech and long-distance transmission, short transmissions of musical items were also made. The product of the experimental work at Chelmsford was a standard Marconi transmitter for commercial purposes. In February 1920 a new 15-kilowatt station at Chelmsford began broadcasting two half-hour daily programmes of news items and live and canned music, which were enthusiastically picked up by the owners of receiving sets. The *Daily Mail* gave a lead to popular interest and arranged the celebrated Melba broadcast from Chelmsford of 15 June 1920, which has been widely recognized as 'a turning-point in the public response to radio'. But many vested interests, particularly among the military, regarded these developments as entirely frivolous, and issued grave warnings on the plight of airmen seeking guidance in bad weather who received only musical entertainment. Accordingly the Chelmsford broadcasts were banned, though transmitting and receiving licences continued to be issued to those who could provide testimonials to the seriousness of their scientific interest. Serious or not, there was nothing to stop the owners of receivers listening to broadcasts from Paris and the Hague; from January 1922 the Marconi Company was again allowed to broadcast speech and music, and this it did at Writtle, and at 2 L O—Marconi House in the Strand—where broadcasts of one hour a day began on 11 May 1922. But the Post Office insisted that broadcasts must be broken off every seven minutes to allow a pause for the reception of official messages, a restriction which Professor Briggs has likened to the old prescription that motor cars must be preceded by a man with a red flag. The chief influence on 2 L O broadcasting was Arthur Burrows, who argued that although there should be a large number of items of 'a really popular character' the attempt should also be made to 'lift' the public above its 'present standard of musical appreciation'. [43]

The Marconi Company was not alone in its interest in broadcasting; other companies wished to exploit the new potential which they had developed for war purposes. At a meeting of the Wireless Society of London in 1920 the British Thomson-Houston Company displayed a radio receiver which could be in-

stalled in the home for about £ 30. By the summer of 1922 both the Metropoli-
tan-Vickers Electrical Company (now Associated Electrical Industries) and
the Western Electric Company were preparing to make transmissions. Each
had American associations, and it was indeed the tremendous radio boom
which took place in the United States at the end of the war (demonstrating the
international quality of technological advance), combined with the pressure of
the British companies, which helped to bring about the next development, a
'treaty' between the Post Office and the 'Big Six' (the four companies already
mentioned, plus the Radio Communications Company and the General Electric
Company). The outcome was the British Broadcasting Company, which began
operations at the end of 1922, and moved in April 1923 to the home always associated with it, at Savoy Hill. [44] With the Calvinistic Scot, John Reith, as General Manager, and, inside a year, Managing Director, and Arthur Burrows as
Director of Programmes, standards were high, but the Company was in essence a commercial company working for private profit through expanding
sales of radio sets. The State at first had shown a narrow suspiciousness of
broadcasting; but from August 1923, when a Departmental Committee on
Broadcasting presented a glowing appreciation of its potential as a medium of
mass communication, [45] governmental attitudes began to change. A second
Broadcasting Committee, reporting in 1925, declared:

> Broadcasting has become so widespread, concerns so many people, and is fraught
> with so many far-reaching possibilities, that the organization laid down for the British
> Broadcasting Company no longer corresponds to national requirements or responsi-
> bility. Notwithstanding the progress which we readily acknowledge, and to the credit
> of which the Company is largely entitled, we are impelled to the conclusion that no
> company or body constituted on trade lines for the profit, direct or indirect, of those
> composing it can be regarded as adequate in view of the broader considerations now
> beginning to emerge. [46]

Acting on the Committee's recommendations, the Conservative Government
of the day established a public corporation in place of the private company.
The founding of the British Broadcasting Corporation, embodying the application of the collectivist method to one of the most potent of the social relations of science, symbolizes very neatly the union of two of the major forces
discussed in this book.

  A similar comment could be passed on the enactment of the British Cinema-
tographic Films Bill in 1927, which, by instituting a system of quotas and
subsidies, was designed to break the American monopoly and encourage the
making of British films. The war had taught the value of propaganda and the

afterglow of war flames up strongly in report of the Moyne Committee (1936), which described the cinema as

> undoubtedly a most important factor in the education of all classes of the community, in the spread of national culture and in presenting national ideas and customs to the world. Its potentialities moreover in shaping the ideas of the very large numbers to whom it appeals are almost unlimited. The propaganda value of the film cannot be over-emphasized. [47]

If it was the propaganda value of films which helped to bring about the necessary legislation for the protection and development of the native industry, it was their entertainment value which most affected British society in the early twenties. More than this, as the *New Survey of London Life and Labour* noted,

> The influence of the films can be traced in the clothes and appearance of the women and in the furnishing of their houses. Girls copy the fashions of their favourite film star. At the time of writing [1934], girls in all classes of society wear 'Garbo' coats and wave their hair *à la* Norma Shearer or Lilian Harvey. It is impossible to measure the effect the films must have on the outlook and habits of the people. Undoubtedly they have great educational possibilities which have so far been very imperfectly attained. But the prime object aimed at is not to instruct or 'uplift', but to amuse, and in this object the cinema has proved very successful. It is estimated by the Cinematograph Exhibitors' Association that the aggregate weekly attendances at London cinemas now amount to a third of the population. Certainly today the cinema is *par excellence* the people's amusement. [48]

State intervention also took place in a third technological development greatly stimulated by the war, aviation, whose importance for society, however, was for the time being trivial compared with that of the cinema, or even radio. Holt Thomas's new Aircraft Transport and Travel Company began the first daily air service for passengers and goods between London and Paris in August 1919. Only two or three passengers were carried at a time:

> One would walk into the little office where the clerk . . . was seated and ask: 'How many have you got for today?' 'Two,' he would answer, with an air of satisfaction. 'And how many for tomorrow?' . . . 'Three,' he would reply, with an even greater pride. [49]

The passengers, 'resigned but still apprehensive', would be packed into the 'small aeroplanes like sardines in a tin.' [50] By January 1920 three British companies were operating regular cross-channel services. But despite the Atlantic and Australian flights undertaken in the Vickers 'Vimy' (an adaptation of the wartime bomber) in 1919, which helped to preserve the romantic image which aviation alone brought untarnished from the war, [51] civil aviation simply did not pay. Temporary government subsidies to the three British companies were followed by the establishment in 1924 of Imperial Airways, with a government subsidy and certain government-appointed directors.[52] The major government assistance to the motor-car industry had come in the form of its wartime tariff policy. In 1920 there were 550,000 motor vehicles (including motor-bicycles) on British roads; in 1922, 952,000 and in 1930, 2,218,000. [53]

British society in 1914 was strongly jingoistic and showed marked enthusiasm at the outbreak of war. The strongest single popular sentiment on international politics after 1918 was 'It must never happen again'. There was doubtless nothing very heroic about this and indeed the envenomed European atmosphere of the early twenties suggested that, like it or not, it might very well happen again. Yet the 'war to end war' talk, the early Liberal idealism, the successful economic co-operation which had taken place between the Allies, and the realistic revolt against the possibility of another bloodbath, had produced the ideal represented by the League of Nations. The ideal was bedevilled by the bitter divisions and the cynicism also thrown up by the war, but there can be no doubt that, as represented by the League of Nations Union, it got stronger and stronger in Britain in the inter-war years. Misguided and confused though it was, British society seemed to be seeking something at once finer and more rational than the emotional clap-trap which had led it into war in 1914: thus in October 1933 the electors in the safe Conservative constituency of East Fulham rejected the fire-eating blimp, Alderman W. J. Waldron, in favour of the young Labour candidate, J. C. Wilmot, fighting on a programme of, among other things, disarmament and international co-operation through the League of Nations; and in 1935 eleven million people expressed through the 'Peace Ballot' (or 'Blood Ballot' as the *Daily Express* wittily called it) their belief in the League of Nations.[54] Yet in 1939 this island paradox of Britain once again entered into a world war against Germany. It is to the political basis of the paradox that we must now turn.

[III] The Same Old State

The political scientist draws a distinction between 'Society' and its political and administrative organization, 'the State'. A rough and ready way of explaining the paradoxical aftermath of the First World War would be to say that while society had changed, the State had not. Or one could say that the war had thrown the forces of social change and the forces of political change out of joint. A society of new ways and new attitudes had been created. New organs of government, sources of endless self-congratulation on the part of the War Cabinet, were elaborated, yet the Ministry of Reconstruction was denied any really effective executive authority, the Ministry of Health was a mere shadow of what it might have been, and the much-vaunted Haldane Committee on the

Machinery of Government, presenting its Report a few days after the election, produced only a rigid and unrealistic blueprint which no one, in any case, made any attempt to put into force. [55] In economics important new lessons were learned, but in the end most of the old structure was restored. In politics old-style Liberalism was destroyed, but, despite the advances of Labour, the supremacy of Conservatism was established for two decades. Other countries had revolutions; Britain had a Coupon Election.

Not that a revolution in Britain was either likely (political and economic tensions were never sharp enough, there were no shattering blows of occupation or defeat) or desirable (Germany with its Weimar and then Nazi 'revolutions' fared far worse than did Britain). But the Coupon Election, in the size and calibre of the Conservative majority which it riveted on the country, was a misfortune. Equally unfortunate was Lloyd George's apparent acceptance that he was the captive rather than the leader of that majority. Thus votes given for Lloyd George and reconstruction, where they were given as such, became votes for Conservatism and reaction. But most votes were given as the last gesture in the long patriotic debauch (the defeat of Asquith is the most vivid piece of evidence of this): the Conservatives, after Lloyd George, 'the man who won the war', could, with justice, claim to be the best patriots; and many of them had the coalition coupon to prove it.

Over the war period there were changes in the composition of the Conservative Party. Ironically, these, if anything, were changes for the worse: Baldwin and Neville Chamberlain, businessmen both, had many admirable qualities, but neither had great gifts of political leadership. Why was there no successful challenge to the low-grade leadership of the inter-war years, even within the Conservative Party? Some of the men who might have raised it were dead. Many survivors, swept by the post-war tide of bitterness and disenchantment, conceived a healthy contempt for politics and all its ways. Men younger still, the generation too young to fight in the war, seemed completely remote from the ageing world of politics. The first inter-war decade was marked by a sceptical and bitter-sweet detachment from politics, the second by a firm and bitter, but utterly futile, commitment to violence and extra-parliamentary action.

These, however, are minor considerations compared with the key political fact at the end of the war, the absence of a strong party of the Left. Consider the Liberal and Labour Parties as two cars on a funicular railway: it was during the war that the Liberal Party, going down, met the Labour Party coming up. The image is not really very apt, since it implies that the Liberal Party was inevitably foredoomed, which was not so. What happened, as we saw, was that the

Liberal Party was prevented by the war from gaining the necessary time in which it might have resolved its own internal contradictions. Prior to 1914 one or two Liberals like Arthur Ponsonby and C. P. Trevelyan who disagreed with the imperialistic trends in the Party, apparent after Lloyd George's Mansion House speech of 1911, were beginning to look with favour on the internationalist aspirations and keener devotion to social reform of the Labour Party; but their idea clearly was that Labour should be a subordinate partner to a radically-minded Liberal Party.[56] At the end of the war these same men flocked into the Labour Party, largely, they said, on the grounds that it, and especially its important component part, the I.L.P., was the only party with anything like a true internationalist spirit, but also because they now saw no hope of further social reform from any other party.[57] They were joined by others, enthusiastic upholders of the war effort, like Leo Chiozza Money, E. F. Wise, the live-wire Civil Servant from the Ministry of Food, and Christopher Addison, the Minister of Health whose attempt to build homes fit for heroes was frustrated by a Government whose concern turned to maintaining a land safe for investments. These men argued that socialistic theory had vindicated itself during the war, and regretted its abandonment.[58]

The Labour Party, then, strengthened and consolidated within itself by developments during the war, also benefited from an influx of new recruits; and this was just at the time that the Liberals were bitterly split between the majority trapped in the Lloyd George coalition, and the 'Wee Frees' who continued to follow Asquith. The long-term results were immense, but for the time being neither the twenty-six Asquithite Liberals returned in 1918 (actually, by an irony implicit in the 1916 crisis, the more reactionary section of the party) nor the 59 Labour M.P.s, ineffectually led in the absence of their pre-war leaders, could present an effective opposition to a Coalition Government with a parliamentary strength of 474. In 1922 the Conservatives dropped Lloyd George; the election which followed gave Labour 142 seats, the Asquith Liberals 60 and the Lloyd George Liberals 57. By January 1924 Labour with 191 seats had taken office; arrayed against it were 259 Conservatives and a reunited (more or less) Liberal Party of 159.

As a new party regarded with the utmost suspicion in many quarters, Labour, once again under the able but not very adventurous leadership of Ramsay MacDonald, set itself two tasks: to demonstrate its fitness to govern, and to establish its independent status as one of the two major parties of State. It was primarily for the latter reason that no attempt was made to strengthen the Government's parliamentary position by seeking an understanding with the Liberals (who were anyway, in many respects, more out-moded in their politi-

cal ideas than the Conservatives, especially since their more radical members
had joined the Labour Party). The upshot was that, apart from the Wheatley
Housing Act, the first Labour Government hardly scratched the surface of the
major problems of the day. The Conservatives under Baldwin then aggravated
the economic situation by restoring the Gold Standard in 1925; at the same
time their attempts to carry out the policies of 'Tory Socialism' roused the opposition of their own right-wing extremists. The ultimate expression of political
confusion and economic failure came in the great crisis of 1931 which once
again entrenched a solid Conservative majority in power. If there ever was an
effective two-party system in Britain, it was not very apparent in the inter-war
years; if ever a two-party system was needed, it was needed in the inter-war
years. All attempts to form new groupings, planning groups, popular fronts,
proved unsuccessful. Finally the Government and the country, determined to
avoid the mistakes which had led to the First World War, blundered into the
Second World War.

[IV] 1914—18 And All That

The First World War was, to borrow from *1066 And All That,* 'a bad thing', and
no one but a callous rogue would wish to deny the validity of the bitterness
which followed it; would wish, say, when talking of the emancipation of women
to forget that a vote won might coincide with a husband or son lost. But no one
but a romantic reactionary would wish to regret the world which disappeared
in the deluge of 1914 – 18. In her *Testament of Youth,* one of the most moving
of all descriptions of a private life shattered by the war, Vera Brittain incidentally brings out how the narrow conventions of provincial middle-class life
by which girls were confined in pre-war days were also shattered. It is right to
stress the hysteria, the phoney religion, and the nauseating propaganda; but it
is worth remembering that British Governments did at least have the conscience to make provision for conscientious objection, that Walter Long, the
Tory squire at the Local Government Board, worked hard to see that conscientious objectors got their legal rights, and that a few crusty individualists
did stand up for them.

Doubtless a new age in Britain would have been ushered in more slowly and
more agreeably if there had been no war, if social and political forces, spared
its distorting effects, had been left to march more closely in unison. But the
war is a historical fact, whose consequences, in the end, can only be
presented, not argued over. Its greatest significance is as a revelation, not so
much of the folly of statesmen, but of the irrationality and love of violence bed-
ded in human society.

NOTES

1. The figures, drawn from the Census reports of 1911 and 1921, are presented in convenient form by A. L. Bowley and M. Hogg, *Has Poverty Diminished?*, 1925, p. 3.

2. *Report of Royal Commission on Population;* P. P., 1948 – 49, XIX, Cmd. 7695, p. 46.

3. Bowley and Hogg, p. 4.

4. Woodward, *Short Journey*, p. 115.

5. R. Boothby, *et al.*, *Industry and the State*, 1927, p. 35. See generally A. Marwick, 'Middle Opinion in the Thirties: Planning, Progress and Political Agreement', in *English Historical Review*, April 1964.

6. *Report of British Association 1919*, p. 10.

7. H. and M. Wickwar, *The Social Services*, 1949 edn., p. 137.

8. M. Bowley, *Housing and the State*, pp. 9-35.

9. H. and M. Wickwar, p. 289.

10. C. E. Montague, *Disenchantment*, p. 94.

11. Woodward, p. 122.

12. L. Strachey, *Eminent Victorians*, 1918, p. 309.

13. C. L. Warr, *The Glimmering Landscape*, 1960, pp. 118 – 19.

14. L. Masterman, *C. F. G. Masterman*, p. 290.

15. (14 February 1918) quoted in ibid., p. 305.

16. Society for Propagation of Christian Knowledge, *The Church and the People*, 1915.

17. G. Spinks (ed.), *Religion in Britain since 1900*, 1952, pp. 68, 75.

18. B. S. Rowntree, *Poverty and Progress*, 1940, p. 420.

19. National Council on Public Morals, *The Ethics of Birth Control*, 1925, pp. 2-3.

20. ibid.

21. P.P., 1939 – 40, IV, Cmd. 6153 (Barlow Report), pp. 36-7.

22. M. Abrams, *The Condition of the British People, 1911 – 45*, 1945, p. 21. Cp. Scott and Cunnison, *Industries of the Clyde Valley*, p. 185.

23. A. F. Thompson, *The English Landed Aristocracy in the Nineteenth Century*, pp. 330 – 31.

24. C. F. G. Masterman, *England After the War*, 1922, pp. 45 – 6.

25. Thompson, p. 337.

26. ibid., pp. 335 ff.

27. H. Bentinck, *Tory Democracy*, 1918, pp. 2 – 3.

28. *A Modern Comedy*, p. x.

29. A. L. Bowley and J. Stamp, *The National Income 1924*, pp. 57 – 9.

30. ibid., pp. 11 – 12.

31. R. Strachey (ed.), *Our Freedom and its Results*, pp. 137 – 8.

32. *New Survey of London Life and Labour*, Vol. II, 1931, p. 465.

33. D. Caradog Jones (ed.), *Social Survey of Merseyside*, 1934, Vol. II, pp. 301, 306 ff.

34. D. C. Marsh, *Changing Social Structure of England and Wales*, 1955, pp. 216 – 17. Dr. Marsh expresses this as one quarter of the population over twenty. It is, of course, a much higher proportion of heads of familes.

35. Bowley and Hogg, *Has Poverty Diminished?*, p. 28.

36. Bowley and Stamp, p. 11.

37. A. M. Carr-Saunders and D. Caradog Jones, *Social Structure of England and Wales*, 1927, pp. 71 – 72.

38. ibid., 1937, p. 66.

39. Bowley and Hogg, p. 20.

40. ibid., p. 36.

41. *New Survey of London Life and Labour*, Vol. IX, 1935, p. 245.

42. *Our Freedom and Its Results*, p. 268.

43. A. Briggs, *The Birth of Broadcasting*, pp. 45, 47 – 53, 70 – 9.

44. ibid., pp. 53, 59 – 68, 82 – 3, 88, 93 – 142.

45. P.P., 1923, X, Cmd. 1951, pp. 5 – 7.

46. P.P., 1926, XX, Cmd. 2599, p. 240.

47. P.P., 1936 – 37, IX, Cmd. 5320.

48. *New Survey of London Life and Labour*, Vol. IX, p. 47.

49. R. Harper, *The Romance of a Modern Airway*, 1931, pp. 9 – 10.

50. ibid.

51. J. D. Scott, *Vickers*, 1962, pp. 174 – 6.

52. See esp. A. Plummer, *New British Industries in the Twentieth Century*, 1937, pp. 156 ff.

53. ibid., p. 103.

54. See Marwick, *Clifford Allen*, pp. 159, 200 – 1.

55. *Report of the Committee on the Machinery of Government*; P.P., 1918, XII, Cmd. 9230. P. Abrams in *Past and Present*, 1963, pp. 51 – 52.

56. See esp. A. Ponsonby, *Social Reform versus War*, 1912, and C. P. Trevelyan, *From Liberalism to Labour*, 1922.

57. Trevelyan, *op cit.*

58. C. Addison, *The Betrayal of the Slums*, 1922, *Practical Socialism*, 1926. L. C. Money, *The Triumph of Nationalisation*, 1921.

David Lloyd George and Winston Churchill have been the two towering political figures in twentieth-century Britain. Lloyd George had by far the greater influence upon the domestic scene, although Bentley B. Gilbert has shown—in "Winston Churchill versus the Webbs: The Origins of British Unemployment Insurance," American Historical Review, *LXXI (April, 1966), 846–62, and especially in* The Evolution of National Insurance in Great Britain: The Origins of the Welfare State *(London, 1966)—that Churchill's contribution to the "New Liberalism" before 1914 was a substantial one. But in a century in which two fateful wars dominated British history, both men will be remembered above all for their leadership of the nation embattled. Here John Ehrman, one of Britain's outstanding military historians, summarizes his assessment of the two wartime prime ministers, their styles, and their skills. His article, originally a speech, appeared in the* Transactions of the Royal Historical Society, *fifth series, II (1961), 101–15.*

3 | Lloyd George and Churchill as War Ministers [1]

JOHN EHRMAN

In March 1915, when the Dardanelles campaign was at its crisis, F. S. Oliver, the author of *The Endless Adventure,* who had long known many of the leading political figures and the background to politics of his day, wrote to his brother in Canada: 'The only two men who really seem to understand that we are at war are Winston and Lloyd George. Both have faults which disgust one peculiarly at the present time, but there is a reality about them and they are in earnest, which the others aren't.'[2] This affinity was recognized by the two men themselves. Churchill's admiration and affection for Lloyd George are well known. 'There could be no doubt . . . ,' he has written, referring of all years to 1940, 'that he was our foremost citizen'; [3] and his final verdict on Lloyd George's death was 'The greatest Welshman . . . since the age of the Tudors'. [4] Lloyd George returned the affection to the full, and the admiration to a great, though not to the full, extent. 'Men with such gifts', he once remarked of Churchill, 'are rare—very rare. In an emergency they ought to be utilized to the full, and if you keep a vigilant eye on their activities, they are a greater asset than a legion of the conventional sort.'[5] And while he failed to recognize the great development of Churchill's character and judgment in the Second World War, he continued to the end, though critically, to appreciate that he and his younger contemporary together formed a unique phenomenon in public life, a species somehow different from the more prosaic figures by whom they were surrounded and so often obstructed. It is perhaps not without significance that Churchill was the only one of Lloyd George's political associates to address him regularly by his Christian name.

This similarity between the two men is particularly noticeable if we confine outselves to their careers as Prime Ministers in the two World Wars. Then, indeed, a personal comparison becomes obvious and compelling. Both, to begin with, were politically non-conformist. Lloyd George found a convenient resting-place for a long time in the Radical wing of the Liberal Party (though it is worth remembering, as one of the oddities of politics, that if he had not, in his youth, mistaken the date, he would have appeared on a platform in Birmingham as an avowed supporter of Joseph Chamberlain and the Unionist party against Gladstone's Home Rule, and would thus presumably have found himself, at least for a spell, a Conservative). But he ended by splitting and then breaking the party of which he had been a member all his life. Churchill has plagued, adorned and resigned from both of the great parties of his youth, has twice tried to rally new political groupings around himself, and, like several of the great Conservative Prime Ministers, ended by presiding over a party with which he was often out of sympathy. Both men, again, were fertile in imagination and fluent in argument, and both were led into conflict—though in greatly differing degrees—with their professional advisers from the armed forces. Each, in his different way, could dominate his Cabinet. Both were good Parliamentarians, and came to be adept at handling the House of Commons on big occasions. Both could be spellbinders—Lloyd George of almost any audience he chose, Churchill more particularly of a small audience already sympathetic to him, though he could on occasions deeply impress a larger meeting. Both, in the crisis of war, were found to possess exceptional qualities of moral courage and resilience, and the capacity to bear the gravest responsibilities. Both—and this was by no means a foregone conclusion—then showed themselves entirely single-minded in their devotion to achieving victory. Both had that rare and indefinable quality, of catching the imagination of their times. And both, as I have remarked, recognized in each other, despite their many differences, a rare and kindred spirit.

Those differences, however, were also considerable, and indeed at times such as to conceal the points of similarity. Thus, whereas Lloyd George approached strategy rather as H. G. Wells approached history—as an essentially simple subject which had been unnecessarily complicated by the professionals—Churchill approached it as a professional manqué, and differed from his advisers rather in claiming—and often rightly—that his professional arguments were better than theirs. One might say, as a generalization, that Lloyd George preferred to ignore military detail, Churchill to plunge enthusiastically into it. There was moreover a great difference between them in their handling of military men. For when the inevitable disputes arose, Lloyd George was prepared in the last resort to 'go it alone', while Churchill—influenced, it has been suggested, by his experiences in the Dardanelles controversy of the First World War—emphatically was not, and would not move, if it came to the point, without the concurrence of his Service advisers. In their oratory and powers of persuasion, too, the two men were very different. Take the famous account of Lloyd George by Maynard Keynes—a superb picture of a highly sophisticated intelligence surrendering consciously, surprisedly, but only half-reluctantly to an unfamiliar, incalculable and largely distasteful brand of political genius:[6]

> 'How can I convey to the reader, who does not know him, any just impression of this extraordinary figure of our time, this syren, this goat-footed bard, this half-human visitor to our age from the hag-ridden magic and enchanted woods of Celtic antiquity? One catches in his company that flavour of final purposelessness, inner irresponsibility, existence outside or away from our Saxon good and evil, mixed with cunning, remorselessness, love of power, that lend fascination, enthralment, and terror to the fair-seeming magicians of North European folklore . . . .
>
> Lloyd George is rooted in nothing; he is void and without content; he lives and feeds on his immediate surroundings; he is an instrument and a player at the same time which plays on the company and is played on by them too; he is a prism, as I have heard him described, which collects light and distorts it and is most brilliant if the light comes from many quarters at once; a vampire and a medium in one.'

All this is a far cry from the robust, obstinate, weighty, sentimental, healthily self-centred and unprismatic genius of Churchill at the summit of power.

It is symptomatic of this difference that Churchill, while compelling and often overwhelming in argument, seldom proved able in the event to convince an initially unsympathetic audience; and in some *milieux* he was definitely unsuccessful. He was not in fact a good negotiator, if only because he was excessively sensitive to an atmosphere of hostility, and too eager to secure a form of agreement in cases where agreement did not really exist. Lloyd George, on the other hand, was a superb negotiator, if one is looking simply at the process of negotiation. His failures in diplomacy usually came from too great a success at the conference table—and it is all the more remarkable that so alert and tactful a man should have lost his peculiar flair whenever he came to deal with the leaders of the armed forces.

Again, though each pre-eminent in his way, the two Prime Ministers treated their Cabinets very differently. Lloyd George was a good listener, and liked to surround himself with men of independent stature, capable of argument. Churchill, though he too disliked the taciturn and tongue-tied (such as Lord Wavell), was more at the mercy of a sensitive nature, and preferred—though he was not always able to secure it—to have around him able subordinates rather than figures of genuinely independent importance.

Again their characters as well as their personalities—if I may use such terms—were very different; and Churchill's was undoubtedly the bigger of the two. He was far more generous in big issues, more loyal to his associates, possessed of much greater humanity, than one who was, as Keynes divined, ultimately remorseless and rootless. I think it is impossible to imagine Churchill at the height of his power in his later career ruining a great political party, and causing the eclipse of an Administration (as Lloyd George did in 1922), by the mistrust with which he was generally regarded. And it is impossible to imagine him, at the same stage, allowing exclusion from office to drive him into some of the inconsistent follies and worse of Lloyd George in the same state. It is easier, in fact, to accuse Churchill of obstinate adherence to a cause than of an undue willingness to abandon it for its opposite. The central sanity of his character—supported and strengthened, I think, by his historical sense, a quality entirely lacking in Lloyd George—became increasingly apparent as time went by. So did the central irresponsibility of Lloyd George.

But it is scarcely profitable to pursue this personal comparison beyond a certain point. For such an exercise, after all, becomes relevant only if it takes place within a context of comparable situations. It is because the two Prime Ministers were placed in much the same kind of position, and faced much the same kind of problems; because both came to power in similar circumstances, as the result of dissatisfaction with the conduct of a war, because both thereafter dominated the scene until the war ended, and because the wars themselves were at once alike in many respects and unlike anything that had gone before, that it becomes interesting and necessary to examine the qualities of the two men. To study Lloyd George and Churchill, in fact, is to study the work of a Prime Minister in war as it has been known in this century; and to assess their achievements, we must therefore look briefly at what such work involves.

In doing so, I should perhaps say in advance, I do not propose to discuss the familiar—the wearisomely familiar—subject of the personal strategies favoured by Lloyd George and by Churchill: not only because it is in fact pointless to debate such questions except in full detail, but also because to attempt to do so in a short talk would, I think, obscure the proper perspective. For while it is obvious that the formulation of strategy is one of the most important tasks for which a wartime Prime Minister must be responsible, and is indeed the one by which he will finally stand or fall, it is not by any means the only task, and in fact cannot itself be tackled successfully unless the other tasks are under control. For it is often forgotten, or not appreciated, that while the demands of war are very different from those of peace, the work of the Prime Minister, as the head of Government, does not completely change, but on the contrary consists largely of seeing that the inherited methods of peace— through which alone the war can be fought—are adapted as effectively as possible to needs and pressures which are unfamiliar to them.

A Prime Minister in war has, I would suggest, three main functions to perform. First, he should if possible inspire, and at least sustain, the morale of the nation. Secondly, he should evolve, or cause to be evolved, the most reasonable strategy possible, within the framework of an Alliance if one exists, and—as part of that function—should get the strategy accepted by his allies. And thirdly, he must harness, or cause to be harnessed, the national economy and administrative system to such a strategy, again as part of the Allied effort if there is an Alliance.

For the first of these tasks, which we may call that of inspiration, both Lloyd George and Churchill were exceptionally well equipped. It is indeed their glory that at times of uncertainty and crisis they identified the country so fully with themselves. Nor is this quality one that should be underrated. For there is perhaps a certain danger of those, such as administrators and historians, who are interested in the conduct of government and war, dismissing it or taking it for granted. Such a neglect, where it occurs, is obviously foolish. In the intensely hierarchical atmosphere produced by modern war, an immense amount must depend on the degree of inspiration generated by the head of Government; and whatever other qualities a wartime Prime Minister may possess, it is fairly certain that without this quality he will not survive for long in hard times. Asquith in 1916, Neville Chamberlain in 1940, fell at least partly because they lacked it. Lloyd George and Churchill—particularly Churchill—will live as much by its possession as by anything else.

But, equally clearly, inspiration by itself is not enough; and indeed it is one of the difficulties of those who try to explain Lloyd George and Churchill on that ground alone that they cannot in fact do so. I suppose that Carson and Kitchener in the First World War, and Lord Beaverbrook in the Second, may be described, in their different ways, as inspiring personalities. But one has only to compare them with Lloyd George or Churchill respectively to see that something more is required. For, of course, inspiration itself will fail after quite a short time if it is not based on competence; and while a Prime Minister in war must not only be, but must seem to be, the man for the job, the first half of that truism is as important as the second. A wartime Prime Minister, in fact, must be capable of handling, of 'gripping', to use a favourite word of Churchill's, a complex and hard-strained system of government. And for this he needs knowledge and experience, as well as the imaginative flair to exploit them in unusual circumstances. Both Lloyd George and Churchill, it is well known, possessed the imaginative flair. It is not so often appreciated to what extent they also possessed the knowledge and experience to which such a flair must be geared. Both in fact were very good administrators for war, to whose personal efforts it is very largely due that this country, alone of the major powers that endured the full course of both World Wars, survived without destroying or devitalizing its familiar institutions. Both men certainly kicked against the administrative pricks, as one can read in the memoirs of those who had to deal with them. But it does not seem to me particularly surprising that this should have been so, or that the imagination which could see what was required should, in the course of securing it, strain and sometimes distort the system which it was doing so much to create.

In forging this war system, Churchill was undoubtedly more fortunate in his conditions than Lloyd George, if only because he had his predecessor's experience and achievements behind him. Lloyd George indeed entered upon a thoroughly discouraging inheritance, at a time, as we can see in retrospect, of peculiar importance and difficulty. It is now widely accepted that the years 1915 – 17 mark the watershed between the worlds of the nineteenth and twentieth centuries, and that many of our political and social assumptions derive from the experiences of that period. It was then that we were first afflicted by war on the scale, and with many of the implications, which we now take for granted. The failure of the Dardanelles campaign in 1915, removing the last real possiblity of turning the enemy's flank, left no alternative—unless a new war-winning weapon was to be introduced—to a costly war of attrition, with results which were soon to be shown for the manpower, production and social patterns of the belligerent States. The year 1916 saw the first manifestations, partial, hesitant but unmistakable, of total war. For the first time it became necessary for Government to intervene in, and begin to control, the distribution of the national economy, where previously it had been necessary for it only to stimulate and supervise production. In such revolutionary circumstances, the traditional methods of government, inherited from the nineteenth century, were bound to prove inadequate. It is one of Lloyd George's achievements that he grasped this very early in the process. On assuming power at the end of 1916 he at once—within a month—drastically revised the structure of administration, creating several new Ministries and Departments and overhauling others. His division of functions and responsibilities, indeed, has remained the basis for subsequent developments, and proved an admirable model for a similar expansion in the Second World War. At the same time, he recognized that the central direction was proving inadequate to the military conduct of the war. A Cabinet of peacetime dimensions was still combined uneasily with a succession of War Councils or War Committees, designed to supervise the day to day conduct of the war but with a membership and procedure which, deriving as they did from pre-war military committees, were more suited to providing study and advice than responsible decisions. As a result, it was impossible to say on any one occasion where responsibility rested, and to take the firm and rapid decisions necessary in war. It was equally difficult, given such circumstances, to organize satisfactorily the subordinate system for providing professional advice, when the two distinct functions were muddled in this way. The Dardanelles campaign finally showed the urgent need for a change, but the second Asquith Government seemed incapable of providing it. Lloyd George at once found an answer, and again in a form which, with modifications, has endured. In December 1916 he abolished both Cabinet and War Committee, and replaced them with a small War Cabinet, the final repository of power, most of whose members were freed from departmental duties. The new body was in fact a Committee of Public Safety, relying on a political coalition between Lloyd George Liberals and Conservatives to relieve it of the burden of Parliamentary preoccupations, and on the revised departmental system to preserve it from the detail of administration.

This pattern was repeated at the outset of the Second World War. The Chamberlain Government then set up the group of fresh Departments which had been prepared in peace, and a small War Cabinet, though one whose members were not divorced so sharply as before from departmental duties. This was all right as far as it went; but it did not go far enough. For while the new arrangements repeated the virtues of Lloyd George's system, they failed to avoid some of its shortcomings, for which further development was required.

Those shortcomings existed particularly in the liaison between the War Cabinet and the many agents of government which it had directly to control. In the First World War, various means had been tried to make this vital link more effective: to render the whole vast range of departmental administration more manageable by the small body at the top, particularly when most of its members were no longer themselves heads of Departments; to establish satisfactory relations between the War Cabinet and the Service chiefs and staffs; and to co-ordinate the complicated demands of the military and civil sectors of government. The answer had been provided, in the last year or so of the war, in the shape of standing Cabinet committees, on which the Ministers of the War Cabinet presided over Ministers, officials and officers from the various executive agencies. But this system did not have time to settle down or to develop very far by the end of the war; and although thereafter, in the years between the wars, the military committees expanded greatly, they did so—as their predecessors had done before 1914—for purposes of study and advice rather than of decision; while the central civil committees scarcely developed at all. It was on this sector of government, accordingly, that Churchill concentrated in the Second World War. On coming into office, he at once remodelled the military committee system, to concentrate power more effectively in himself and his professional advisers, the Chiefs of Staff; and a year later, partly of his own volition and partly this time on advice, he greatly extended and altered the system of civil committees, in a form which, basically, has endured since the war for the central planning and supervision of economic and administrative affairs. These changes, in fact, carried a stage farther the work begun by Lloyd George, in adapting the traditional system of Cabinet government to the needs of total war.

The modified system worked a great deal better under Churchill than its predecessor had done under Lloyd George. On the military side, in particular, the Prime Minister and the Chiefs of Staff worked together much more harmoniously in the Second World War than in the First. They did so for several reasons. In the first place, everyone in Whitehall in the Second World War was determined not to repeat, if possible, the costly frontal assaults which had characterized the campaigns of 1915 – 18; and the expulsion of British forces from the Continent in 1940 at once made this ideal a practical possibility. There were no 'Easterners' and 'Westerners' in the formative years of the Second World War. The problems, in so far as they were not defensive, were for long of a different kind. How far should the productive effort be put into bombing? Where best to strike at the circumference of the Axis position? What resources, in such circumstances, could be spared for the Far East? And when at last the Western Allies could pass to the offensive, the determination to avoid the experience of the past ensured that, whatever their differences, all authorities in London agreed basically on the strategy to be adopted in Europe. Their most serious disputes were in fact reserved for the Far East, where strategic alternatives were fundamental and, thanks largely to the paucity of resources, extremely hard to resolve. Even so, the choice here depended ineluctably on a factor beyond British control—the rate of American progress through the Pacific. And angry as the Chiefs of Staff and the Prime Minister became with each other, all appreciated in the end that events in the Far East might overtake the debate, and that, in the last resort, their decisions for that theatre were, in the largest sense, marginal.

In arguing these matters, moreover, both sides had reflected, and been taught, a good deal about the experiences of politicians and soldiers in the First World War, and again were determined if possible that those should not be replaced. We have heard a lot recently about Churchill's behaviour to his military advisers; and it is of course entirely true that he was often exceedingly difficult to work with. Probably only those who have experienced his exceptional powers of interference and obstinacy can appreciate exactly how difficult he could be. But that must not blind us to the fact that he always kept those powers within limits—even if of his own choosing—and that he never allowed himself to go to the lengths, or to adopt the sort of methods with his Service advisers, to which Lloyd George was driven, or sank, in the First World War. However exasperating he might be—and it must not be overlooked that very often he had good cause—the Chiefs of Staff knew that he would not intrigue, that he would not abandon them in secret, and that in the last resort he would listen to their opinion. And the Chiefs of Staff, for their part, were men of a higher calibre than the Service chiefs in the First World War. It was indeed fortunate that such men as Portal and Alanbrooke came to sit on the supreme working military committee, and by their intelligence and character ensured both that it functioned on the whole efficiently and—equally important—as a unity, whose members were known not to intrigue. This was perhaps a matter of chance. It is possible to think of several eminent officers, both slightly senior and slightly junior to the Chiefs of Staff themselves, whose appointments might easily have been unfortunate in both respects. But it was not entirely chance; for whatever the shortcomings of individuals, the development of the central military committee system between the two wars had taught senior officers a good deal about co-operation between the Services and between them and the whole range of civil government. Churchill thus found himself working with more experienced men, in a far more sophisticated system, than Lloyd George had encountered a quarter of a century before. And finally, he himself was in a much stronger position than his predecessor. The political and personal conditions in which he came to office—the fact that there was no obvious rival from the start—saved him from the uncertainties and embarrassments which dogged Lloyd George's every move for over a year, and favoured the system he exploited and the means by which he did so. On the one hand he was able, as only a politically secure Prime Minister could have done, to work closely with his Service advisers without having to worry too much about political reactions: on the other, his unique record and experience—the fact that he had been a Service Minister when the Chiefs of Staff of the Second World War were young subalterns and lieutenants, and a household name when they were at school—gave him a prestige which the socially undistinguished Radical Lloyd George, whose very name was anathema to the average Admiral and general of his day, entirely lacked at the start, and fought savagely to gain. It may seem odd to say that the conditions for Churchill in 1940 were easier than those for Lloyd George in 1916. But it is true, if by that we mean not the conditions of the war itself, but for his conduct of it.

The result, in Churchill's hands, was a triumph. Government in a hard-fought war inevitably breeds bitter disputes and personal antipathies. But allowing fully for all this, it can hardly be doubted that the last war was conducted more smoothly and efficiently from London than any war in British history. It therefore remains surprising at first sight that the Prime Minister, more secure and powerful than any of his wartime predecessors since Chatham, should have failed in its later years to have his way on any major strategic decision. Indeed, he was perhaps less successful in this from 1943 to 1945 than Lloyd George, with all his setbacks and difficulties, had been in 1917 – 18. Again there are various reasons. But the most important lies in the nature of the Alliance. For if Churchill's domestic conditions were easier than those of Lloyd George, the conditions which he worked with his allies were in many ways less promising.

Again, this may perhaps seem a strange statement to make. The Alliance of the First World War embraced an ill-assorted group of nations, which was subjected, by defeat in some cases, by disaffection or revolution in others, to a series of appalling strains, and emerged victorious only after a final convulsion, in the spring of 1918, that almost proved disastrous. The Alliance of the Second World War, by contrast, weathered its most dangerous moments early in its course, was clearly gaining strength thereafter, and in the West achieved a remarkable cohesion between the two major powers of Britain and the United States. The combination of Churchill and Roosevelt had no parallel in the First World War; nor, despite the serious differences that arose from time to time between their Governments, did the working alliance of the British and American forces. But this pattern, for which Churchill in person may take a lion's share of the credit, was set in the first phase of the Alliance; and as the war progressed it became increasingly endangered. It was only by the exercise of great tact, skill and magnanimity that the Prime Minister managed in the later years to retain as much influence for his country as he did. After 1943 Britain gradually and inevitably sank in the balance between the two larger powers of the United States and Russia and in the last year of the war that fact could no longer be obscured. In the First World War, on the other hand, the latent strength which she possessed at the outset was felt increasingly as time went by, so that by 1918 Lloyd George was representing the strongest power in the Alliance. Despite, therefore, the many difficulties he encountered—and again it was he in person who may claim a lion's share of the credit—he was well placed to make the British influence felt, and to secure the adoption of his partners of the improved British methods for waging the war. In this, he may have been assisted by the very fact that defeat remained a real possibility almost to the end, thereby helping to preserve those ties of common funk which the obvious but gradual approach of victory weakened from 1943 to 1945. In the First World War, in fact, the Alliance grew stronger and more coherent in the final stages, and Britain emerged as its most powerful member. In the Second World War, the Alliance began to disintegrate as Russia and the West came more closely into contact, and Britain had to fight increasingly hard to maintain her position in the Western partnership itself.

In handling their very different Allied problems, both Lloyd George and Churchill displayed great skill. Indeed, I am not sure that Lloyd George at least was not at his best as an Allied leader. Certainly, his exceptional sensitivity to atmosphere, his intuitive understanding of natures very different from his own, were seen to enormous advantage on the international stage. Churchill achieved his very great standing within the Alliance of his day by an almost contrary process: by subordinating, rather than exploiting, his instinctive attitudes, and keeping within strictly defined bounds his natural propensity to dominate and argue. One might indeed see in his domestic disputes over the Far East in 1944 a compensation for his recognition—which was quite conscious—of the limits within which he must act abroad. Both Prime Ministers of course made their mistakes in handling their allies. Lloyd George's quarrels with his Service advisers at home led him to adopt some strange expedients in promoting his contacts abroad—expedients, it may be noted, which he was content to let drop when his domestic opponents had been quelled. Churchill, for his part, did not always handle the American Chiefs of Staff well, and in particular might have gained more strategic concessions in 1943–44 by a greater reliance on Field Marshal Dill in Washington, at the expense, by then, of Harry Hopkins. But such shortcomings, in the last resort, are matters of detail. Broadly speaking, both men understood very well how to make an Alliance work. Despite the very real limits to what they achieved, both acted as catalysts for their Alliances. It was they who, more than any one else, brought those combinations into effective being and sustained them in hard times. 'Nations', it was remarked almost a century ago, 'touch at their summits.' [7] If they did so in the two World Wars, it was on each occasion very largely due to the British Prime Minister.

As Allied war leaders in the strict sense of achieving military victory, one can hardly indeed cavil at the achievement in either case. Whether Lloyd George or Churchill exploited that achievement as best they could in pursuing the objects of victory is a wider question, and one less easy to answer. In a sense, Lloyd George's task here was perhaps more difficult than that of Churchill, in that the very nature of the settlement to be imposed on the losers, and the very shape of Europe after so rude an end to a century of stability, were problems of a new kind. British influence, morever, although strong by 1918, was exercised within a traditional structure of European powers still sovereign in the nineteenth-century sense of the term, and conscious of a somewhat uneasy relationship with the potent but puzzling addition of the United States. These difficulties must be judged in assessing Lloyd George's failure to realize his aims at Versailles—for, at least at first, he did not favour the kind of settlement ultimately adopted. In 1945, the victors had their predecessors' experience in peacemaking to guide or to warn them, and a greater disposition both on the part of the Western European powers and of the United States to work closely together, and to surrender sovereignty in some respects to a wider association. The great obstacle in this case was the fact that a powerful potential enemy had come into sight before the war ended, and in the complicating guise of an ally. The critical period for peacemaking, therefore, came on this occasion while the war was still in progress, and the diplomatic future was affected by strategic decisions. How far Churchill's prescient fear of Russia might have been transmitted into effective action with American support, must remain a matter of opinion. For what it is worth, I would be inclined to say, hardly at all. Certainly, I think, this applies to the last stage of the war in Europe as it developed in 1945. And if we go back a stage further, and ask—as so many Americans have recently been asking—if a Western invasion of south-east Europe might not have proved a better basis for diplomatic action than the strategy that was adopted, I think we must remember that Churchill himself was not committed to the idea of such a campaign at the expense of one in north-west Europe, and that if it had taken place the Russians might have switched their efforts, with the forces thus released, to achieve a position of greater strength elsewhere—say to the west and north of Poland as well as to a more limited extent to the south and south-east.

These are might-have-beens. Two other questions may perhaps be put as a conclusion to these remarks. First, it may be asked if one is justified in attaching so much weight, in scenes of such complexity, to the personal efforts of the two men. I would suggest that one is. In the last hundred years or so, the Prime Minister has become increasingly, to quote a phrase of Lord Morley's before the First World War, 'the keystone of the Cabinet arch'. His powers are great in peace, greater in war, and, with a Prime Minister such as Lloyd George or Churchill whom war is apt to produce, very great indeed. Provided the conditions themselves allow, he is then much more free than usual to exploit them, and to mould the form at least of short-range events—and short-range events, after all, are then extremely important. It is no doubt an exaggeration to say what Churchill himself has said of Lloyd George, that 'when the English history of the first quarter of the century is written, it will be seen that the greater part of our fortunes in peace and in war were shaped by this one man'.[8] But it is not such an exaggeration, I suggest, to say that the fortunes of war could not have been the same without him.

And secondly, it may be asked—it has often been asked—which of these two wartime Prime Ministers was the greater. It is not a question I should like to answer: so many different elements, so many differences even between the points of similarity, must be taken into account. Nor is it, I suspect, the sort of question that historians think should be asked, at least of them; for a confident answer would run counter to the way in which historians are trained to approach their problems. Perhaps we may conclude, therefore, with the safe remark that together the two men formed an extraordinary combination, and that it is fortunate, for the survival of the country itself and of its traditional institutions in this century, that the normal political world should have thrown up such a figure on each occasion, to work within its framework and to preserve by his unusual methods a tried and familiar form of government. Of the two men themselves, we can only say of each what Gibbon, in less complimentary vein, said of Andronicus Comnenus: that placed 'in every deed of mischief, he had a heart to resolve, a head to contrive, and a hand to execute'.[9]

NOTES

1. I have not attempted to disguise in print the colloquial character of this paper as it was read, or the personal nature of its judgments.

2. *The Anvil of War,* ed. Stephen Gwynn (London, 1936), p. 92.

3. *The Second World War,* ii (1949), p. 503.

4. *Parliamentary Debates, Fifth Series,* vol. 409, col. 1380.

5. David Lloyd George, *War Memoirs,* iii (London, 1934), p. 1072.

6. *Essays in Biography* (1951 edn.), pp. 35 – 36.

7. Walter Bagehot, *The English Constitution* (London, 1867), p. 152.

8. Quoted in Thomas Jones, *Lloyd George* (London, 1951), p. 290.

9. *The History of the Decline and Fall of the Roman Empire,* ed. J.B. Bury, v (1911), p. 248.

The breakup of the modern British empire after World War II, the emergence of the multi-national Commonwealth and its dubious viability have all tended to obscure the importance of Commonwealth relations before that war and the problems of defence posed by those relations. Rather than deal in general terms with British foreign policy in the twenties and thirties, a subject that has properly been widely controverted in the literature devoted to the international politics of the period, the essay that follows illustrates one of the problems behind the issue of Britain's relations with continental Europe. D. C. Watt is Professor of History at the London School of Economics and Political Science. He has served as editor of the annual Survey of International Affairs *published by The Royal Institute of International Affairs and is the author of* Britain Looks Towards Germany *(London, 1965),* Personalities and Policies *(Notre Dame, Ind., 1965), and editor (with K. Bourne) of* Studies in International History; Essays Presented to W. Norton Medlicott *(London, 1967). This essay first appeared in the* Journal of Commonwealth Studies, *I (May 1963), 226–81 and is reprinted by permission of the Leicester University Press.*

4

Imperial Defence Policy and Imperial Foreign Policy, 1911—1939: A Neglected Paradox?

D. C. WATT

Any student of British foreign policy between the wars must begin by being struck by the fact that the vast bulk of comment on that policy has been couched in terms that either deny the importance of the development of consultation with the Commonwealth, or more commonly ignore this consultation altogether.[1] The student who attempts to fill this gap begins of course by running his head on what seems at first sight a total absence of documentation. But perseverance in study reveals two factors of importance: first, the psychological vulnerability of members of all governments to representations from the Dominions; and secondly, that one and the same organ advised both British and Dominions governments on the strategical factors underlying their position in the world, namely the Committee of Imperial Defence, with, since 1924, the Chiefs of Staff Sub-Committee. And what seems to be a curious paradox emerges. The political membership of the C.I.D. also dominated Cabinet discussion and formulation of British foreign policy. Yet in matters of foreign policy, they spoke for Britain alone (unless otherwise authorised by Dominion governments); in matters of defence, in matters of that ultimate sanction of force which is, in domestic and foreign affairs alike, the *ultima ratio regum,* they acted for, and were responsible for the defence of the Commonwealth as a whole.

Attention had been called to this paradox indirectly by Sir Edward Grey before the First World War, although he approached the matter from the opposite angle, that of the existence of separate Dominions, armies, and naval forces.[2] Speaking to the 113th meeting of the Committee of Imperial Defence at which the Dominions delegates to the Imperial Conference of 1911 were present he said:

> It is possible to have separate fleets in a united Empire but it is not possible to have separate fleets in a united Empire without having a common foreign policy—the creation of separate fleets has made it essential that the foreign policy of the Empire should be a common policy. [3]

At the time his words fitted accurately enough into the anxieties of his listeners. The main aim of the Conference in the eyes of its conveners, or at least of one of them, was achieved: Dominion aid, moral, material and financial for the mother country staggering under the weight of the increased armament expenditure made necessary by the menace of Germany, was secured; [4] the Pacific Dominions increased their naval expenditure still further, and the very next year, impressed by the evidence put before him during his attendance at meetings of the Committee of Imperial Defence, the Canadian Premier, Sir Robert Borden, introduced into the Canadian Parliament a bill providing for the construction on Canada's account of three dreadnoughts to be presented to the Royal Navy. [5] In the event his bill was defeated in the Canadian Senate; but the actual onset of war in 1914 found the Dominions more or less at one with Britain on the policy which had involved Britain in the war and the defence policy with which she entered it.

The machinery by which this comparative unanimity had been achieved was two-fold. Colonial and Imperial Conferences had in fact met at biennial intervals in 1907, 1909, and 1911; on each occasion problems of defence and foreign policy had been reviewed in detail. The Admiralty and the Imperial General Staff had provided advice on military and naval problems, and the whole field of defence policy had been thrashed out at Cabinet level in Britain through the machinery of the Committee of Imperial Defence. The 1907 Colonial Conference had provided for meetings of imperial conferences every four years, and had established an Imperial Conference Secretariat, while at the 1911 Conference the delegates had agreed that representatives of the Dominions governments could be invited to attend meetings of the Committee of Imperial Defence when questions of defence which affected the overseas dominions were under consideration. They had agreed also that Committees of Defence, patterned on the C.I.D. should be established in each Dominion; and between 1911 and 1914 Canadian, New Zealand, Newfoundland and South African representatives attended meetings of the Committee of Imperial Defence, which had come to assume the role of the key co-ordinating force in imperial affairs "a forum first for shared information and later an undefined but united share of defence policy making." [6]

Three themes which stand out in these years were to dominate post-war developments, each a different aspect of the same central problem. First, there was the conflict between the home defence anxieties of the individual Dominions and the equally clear truth that a defeat of Britain meant, as Grey pointed out in 1911, that each Dominion would be left on its own; that the major threat to the Dominions came from Europe. Secondly, there was the problem of the organisation of imperial defence, in which Dominion nationalism and the isolationism of the non-English speaking peoples in Canada and South Africa pulled one way, and the Admiralty, the Committee of Imperial Defence and neo-imperialist ambition pulled the other. Thirdly, there was the brute fact that every major move towards the Dominions made in Britain was made because of the disparities between Britain's defence commitments and obligations and Britain's own resources. The Empire before 1914, the Commonwealth after 1931 were equally dominated by Dominion dependence on Britain and independence of one another, a cluster of bilateral alliances, rather than an interlocking multilateral alliance. Without Britain there was neither rhyme nor reason in the Commonwealth. The principal threats to the Commonwealth came from European challenges to Britain. And Britain herself was decreasingly able to handle them or to measure up to them on her own.

In the meantime, behind the operation of the machinery developed by 1914, there lay a fairly determined body of opinion in Britain, voicing itself at one stage through the theorists of the *Round Table,* and at others in the quiet extension of the pattern of consultation by the secretariat of the C.I.D., especially as developed by Lord Hankey, which was set on developing the Commonwealth into a quasi-federal organisation with common economic, common defence and common foreign policies. A great deal of study and sophisticated thinking, a great deal of quiet, persistent lobbying and a gradual permeation of the higher civil service [7] all very much heightened by the events and pressures of the war, led in 1917 to the next stage, the summoning of the Imperial War Conference and the establishment of the Imperial War Cabinet. Again the motives impelling the British Cabinet to take these steps were as much dictated by British needs as by neo-imperialism. The original prompting came from Lord Milner. [8] But Lloyd George's letter to the Colonial Secretary, Walter Long, of December 12, 1916, puts the matter in terms of naked want:

> I am convinced that we should take the Dominions into our counsels in much larger measure. . . As we must receive even more substantial support from them before we can pull through, it is important that they should be made to feel that they have a share in our Councils as well as in our burdens. [9]

But the Premiers of three of the Dominions came to London determined to attack the Admiralty and the Foreign Office for ignoring their position in the Pacific in 1914 and to make certain that machinery should be devised to prevent a recurrence of this situation. The two New Zealand representatives devoted the fourth and fifth days to a detailed criticism of the Admiralty for ignoring the pre-war agreements with Australia and New Zealand and leaving the South Pacific almost undefended before the German Pacific squadron in 1914. They ended by presenting a resolution calling upon the Admiralty to work out a scheme of naval defence for the Empire as soon as the war was over. A resolution of equal force was presented by Sir Robert Borden, the Canadian Premier, which spoke of the "Dominions' right to an adequate voice in foreign policy and in foreign relations" in calling for "effective arrangements for continuous consultation in all important matters of common Imperial concern."[10] It was agreed that the Imperial War Cabinet should meet annually or more often if possible. Borden's approach was essentially governed by his conviction first voiced in 1910 that co-operation in imperial defence should carry with it the right to an effective voice in determining the foreign policy of the Empire. And alone of Dominion premiers before 1914 he had agreed to the Canadian High Commissioner being a regular member of the C.I.D., and had appointed Perley simultaneously as Minister without Portfolio and High Commissioner in London.[11]

The position attained in 1917 – 1918 was to last formally until the Imperial Conference of 1923. It marks the high-tide of the pan-Imperial movement in the Dominions. Beneath the surface signs of its weakness were evident in two directions. First, an Imperial foreign policy could only be carried out on a basis of continuous consultation. This Borden, William Hughes of Australia, Massey of New Zealand, and Smuts of South Africa readily realised was in itself technically difficult except where a British Empire delegation attended an international conference. It raised great difficulties in spheres where a basic difference of approach between the Dominions became apparent. And it depended on there being one recognisable source of advice and action at the head of the conduct of British foreign policy, and one moreover prepared to consult and take notice of consultations with the Dominions. Secondly, the conduct of a single Imperial defence policy was comparatively simple where there was the unity of purpose between the Dominions and the home country, with priority for expenditure on imperial defence, and unity of command. None of these survived the end of the war. To achieve agreement on an imperial defence policy came to necessitate as careful a set of compromises as did agreement on an Imperial foreign policy.

To take the theme of foreign policy first. At Versailles a good deal of care was taken to maintain a unified policy as between the Dominions and Britain. The demands of the Australian Prime Minister, Hughes, were backed by Britain, even where they conflicted directly with American ideals as set forth by President Wilson. [12] Smuts and Borden played a considerable part in hammering out much of the Peace Treaty and the Covenant of the League of Nations, incidentally providing Wilson's Republican critics with a good deal of ammunition by their insistence on separate votes in the League for the Dominions ("Six votes for the British Empire"). [13] These developments have been admirably summed up in a recent study: [14]

> The strategic circumstances of the First World War had produced a major revolution in the diplomatic relations of the English-speaking world. The self-governing Dominions with Great Britain had taken on a joint responsibility for foreign policy. Joint responsibility of governments required unanimous agreement. The British Government knew that the experiment with the Imperial War Cabinet and the continued Dominions aid in the war could founder on the abyss of disunity. Consequently it became peculiarly sensitive to Dominions' demands. Hidden behind each Dominion's demands lay a threat fraught with dire consequences for the Empire's survival. Where earlier in the history of the Empire Great Britain could sacrifice Dominion interests to the needs of British foreign policy, now Britain was compelled to heed Dominions' advice and take up their causes, even if these were not what the British government itself would have desired.

But once the Conference was over, the Treaty signed, and the British Empire delegation dispersed, differences rapidly began to develop between the various Dominions and Britain, Canada and South Africa particularly moving back into an isolationism almost as extreme as that of the United States. Reactions against the final form the peace treaties had taken was fairly uniform both in Britain and among Dominion representatives. Indeed it was with backing from the British Empire delegation that Lloyd George succeeded in getting the terms on Upper Silesia altered but failed to secure a revision of those governing the occupation of the Rhineland. But despite their intense dislike of the Treaties necessity forced the British into attempting to operate them, particularly in the Near East. The Dominions felt no such urgency and began very swiftly to lapse back into that curious attitude, half resentment, half automatic assumption of British leadership, which had been so marked a feature of their earlier reaction to Britain's European preoccupations. In Pacific matters meantime the growth of American-Japanese hostility and the question of a renewal of the Anglo-Japanese alliance brought to the fore an issue where the Dominions themselves were divided.

To these divisive forces was added one which it lay within British power to remedy, the absence of a clear and single recognisable source of advice and action to the controls of Britain's own foreign policy. The coalition Cabinet of 1918 – 1922 was one of the ablest, most brilliant and, be it said, least responsible, governments Britain has suffered under. But its foreign policy was bitterly divided both on personal and on ideological issues, the only common bonds between Lloyd George, Curzon, and Churchill being the detestation of France shared by the first two and of Bolshevism shared by the second two. British constitutional practice has always admitted, moreover, of two interpretations of the powers of the Foreign Secretary. He can be the agent of a Cabinet policy acting as the delegate of a united Cabinet, or he can be the initiator of foreign policy acting in the Cabinet's name but as their representative. Most of the great Foreign Secretaries have held to the second interpretation. But this interpretation is one which it is impossible to reconcile with the conduct of an Imperial foreign policy resting on consultation with the Dominions. Thus Lloyd George consulted no-one, not even Curzon. And Curzon could not conceive of prior consultation with the Dominions other than as an exercise of prerogative to be acted on only if time permitted or Dominion statesmen were unduly importunate.

The issue of the renewal of the Anglo-Japanese alliance and its effect on Imperial-American relations brought the differences between the Dominions into the open. Basically the division lay between Canada and South Africa for whom good Anglo-American relations and the avoidance of "entangling alliances" were paramount and Australia (with New Zealand in support) for whom security against Japan in the Pacific was most important. The subsequent clash between Arthur Meighen (who had succeeded Sir Robert Borden as leader of Canada's imperialists) and Hughes paralleled the similar division within the British Cabinet between those who regarded America with distaste and resentment as a factor to be included and reconciled with their calculations, and those for whom American policy was one of the basic principles from which those calculations should start. This latter division had been reconciled in the plan which Curzon and Lloyd George presented to the conference (and which Hughes himself favoured), of coupling the renewal of the alliance with Japan with the summoning of a Pacific conference in which a tripartite relationship with America and Japan should be so far as possible substituted for the alliance as a guarantee of the peace and *status quo*. But Meighen revealed himself as being thoroughly against the renewal of the alliance in any form, and went on to demand that in questions where the interests of one Dominion were "peculiarly concerned" Imperial policy should be shaped by that Dominion. The proposal arose logically out of the attempt to

conduct a foreign policy by consultation between separate cabinets responsible to separate electorates. But it was rebuffed in this instance by Lloyd
George and Hughes who denied its applicability to Imperial-American relations; and the question Meighen raised of continuous consultation went by
default when the American government won by a hair's breadth the race to call
a Pacific Conference. [15]

This was, however, a clash within the Empire in which the British government could to a certain extent play a mediatory role. It fitted, albeit with difficulty, into the general framework of consultation with the Dominions representatives on an agreed line of policy in which the British Foreign Office could act
as executive agent for the Empire as a whole. Not that there were not further
inconsistencies underlying this theory. For British ministries to act as advisory
agents to the Empire as well as to Britain was difficult enough to reconcile with
the theory of equality within the Empire between Dominions and mother country. That they should act as executive agents as well (despite the attempts to
make the Foreign Service more imperial in its sources of recruitment), was
clearly anomalous. But given goodwill, this could be represented as a transitional stage. What was to bring to an end the attempt to evolve machinery for
the formulation of an Imperial foreign policy based on consultation was the behaviour of the Coalition Cabinet during the Chanak crisis, first in bringing the
Empire to the verge of war without a shadow of prior consultation, and secondly in publicly appealing to opinion in the Dominions simultaneously with an
approach to their Governments.

The Imperial Conference of 1923 thus saw the abandonment of any attempt
to formulate a common foreign policy to be executed by the British Foreign
Secretary and his agents. The new Canadian Liberal Government under Mackenzie King rebuffed *ab initio* Lord Curzon's claims to have acted on behalf of
the Empire as a whole at Lausanne, the more so as they found themselves during the Conference confronted with important telegrams dispatched in their
name by Curzon without prior consultation. The agenda again included the
item of measures to secure a common foreign policy which had found a place
in that of the 1921 Imperial Conference. But the line taken by Mackenzie King,
and backed by Smuts, made any further progress towards such an objective
impossible. Instead, the Conference was compelled to accept the passage of
a series of individual resolutions on individual points of policy, and to devise a
formula for the signature of treaties which reserved ratification to the parliaments of the individual members. [16]

Mackenzie King's veto put an end to the efforts to evolve closer machinery
for policy formation though not to the drive of the neo-imperialists for consulta-

tion. Their efforts seem thereafter to have been forced into new directions. The first of these was the development of the Dominions Office and the High Commissioners as a means of avoiding a repetition of the disastrous Chanak manifesto, in which they rightly saw the cause of the miscarriage of their earlier plans. The second was to face them with the necessity of putting a stop to activities of the Curzonian kind, which they realised were irritating the Dominions into the suspicion that their change in status from colonies who obeyed the central government to equality as governments of the Crown was regarded by the British government as one of form only. [17] The effect of this was to impose on those who formulated British foreign policy the need continuously to consult Dominion representatives, and, where such consultation was impossible, to operate within the limits of what they felt the Dominions would accept. This latter difficulty became larger as Imperial Conferences became less frequent. Three years elapsed between the 1923 and 1926 conferences; four before the 1930 Conference met and seven before the next (the 1932 Conference was purely economic in its interests). [18] An illustration of these differences can be seen in the attempt to summon a Conference to deal with the Geneva Protocol. [19] And in 1929 Austen Chamberlain commented to Sir Esmé Howard: [20]

> The conduct of foreign affairs in present conditions presents an entirely novel problem. In matters of this importance Great Britain can no longer act as the spokesman of the Empire unless with the individual consent of the other governments.

Two factors aided them in their efforts. The annual meetings of the League of Nations Assembly and of the Preparatory Commission to the Disarmament Conference provided a regular meeting ground for British and Dominion representatives at a ministerial level. And support of the League of Nations itself provided them with an external frame of reference on which their policies could converge; thus they evolved a regular system of appropriating initiative on matters before the League among the representatives of the various Dominions.

This necessitated avoiding any measures designed to turn the League into more than a permanent international conference. Perhaps the most remarkable agreement on this was achieved in the rejection of the Draft Treaty of Mutual Guarantee and the Geneva Protocol, essentially on the same grounds, that in Smuts's words, they would tend to turn the League into an "armed alliance to maintain the status quo" in Europe. The members of the Commonwealth came therefore to have a vested interest in the maintenance of the League of Nations as an external point of reference around which their differing interests could coalesce; Canada and South Africa could continue the isolationist policies necessitated by their white non-Anglo-Saxon elements; Australia and New Zealand could mark their pre-occupation with Pacific problems; Britain on the other hand could indulge under Austen Chamberlain her proclivities for leadership in Europe. And the Empire could divide on the obligation assumed at Locarno towards France and Belgium since these were linked with the League and in any case were designed, it is not too strong to say, to create a state of circumstances in which they would never need in fact to be fulfilled.

This position could only last while the League itself functioned as an instrument to maintain the peace without any major effort being actually called for from its signatories. But before considering the dilemmas which the end of this happy state created for the Commonwealth it would be as well to examine the question of Imperial Defence. Here the burden lay most heavily on Britain, and the weapon of defence most centrally concerned was the Royal Navy. In 1917 as related above, the Admiralty representative at the Imperial War Conference had been most royally roasted for the Navy's failure to live up to its promises to maintain a reasonable force in the Pacific. And the Conference had passed a resolution calling upon the Admiralty to draw up a plan for Imperial Defence as a whole once the war was over. The Admiralty in fact anticipated this date, largely, one supposes, because, in late 1917, it had at last acquired a genuine Naval War Staff. The scheme itself was submitted to the Imperial War Cabinet in an Admiralty memorandum of May 1918. [21] It called for a single Imperial Navy, responsible to an Imperial Navy Authority, whose precise constitutional status was left unclear until the form "in which it may be ultimately decided to give expression to the desire for closer union" was apparent, but which was to be headed by the First Lord of the Admiralty with a Board on which the Naval ministers of the Dominions were to sit at least once a year, and would, it was hoped, be more continuously represented. These proposals were rejected immediately by the Dominion Premiers, Borden taking the lead. [22] Instead the Admiralty were forced to accept the standardisation of Dominion navies, and an absence of control over their naval estimates (one of the most important items concealed but implied in the Admiralty scheme). In December 1918 Admiral Jellicoe was dispatched, on the invitation of Dominion premiers, to advise them on naval organisation, so as to ensure homogeneity between the practice of the various Dominion navies and the Royal Navy. Jellicoe so far exceeded his instructions as to draw up a major scheme for a British Far Eastern fleet of sixteen capital ships, to be paid for on a contributory basis, either in cash or kind in proportion to their population and the value of their overseas trade. [23]

In the meantime the British government set up in May 1919 an inter-Service

Committee on Imperial Defence Organisation, on which the Dominions were by invitation represented, to prepare proposals to be submitted to the Imperial War Cabinet before the Dominions Prime Ministers returned home. [24] The Committee does not seem to have been able to report in time to meet this dead-line, but what was presumably the Admiralty's contribution was sent to Jellicoe in November 1919. This called reluctantly for the building up of separate Dominion navies, with separate budgets, etc., but still asked for the creation of an Imperial Naval Council to consider matters of policy and for the representation of the Dominions on the Admiralty Naval Staff. [25] Jellicoe's proposals were equally praised and ignored in the Dominions he visited (he did not visit South Africa). Some of his ideas were later incorporated into long-range Admiralty planning, but the bulk of his recommendations as to expenditure and size of fleets, etc. were wildly unreal in the financial circumstances of 1919 – 1920. The Admiralty returned to the charge, however, in 1921. Again they expressed their view that the ideal was a unified navy under a single command with a quota of men and ships supplied by the Dominions and talked of an "Empire Fleet" even if Dominion sentiment made it necessary to concentrate on the development and coordination of separate Dominions Navies. Their main recommendations lay in the need for the Empire of a chain of oil-fuelling stations and the development of Singapore as a naval base. [26] Both of these recommendations were accepted by the Dominions representatives. [27]

The provisions agreed at the Washington Naval Conference and embodied in the Naval Treaty only added force to these recommendations, since British capital ship strength was now rudely limited to a mere fifteen ships in 1936, where the Admiralty could normally have expected an increase in the fleet to something approaching its pre-war dominance once the initial period of financial stringency which followed the war had passed. At the 1923 Imperial Conference, Amery, the new First Lord of the Admiralty, outlined a new Imperial strategy to take care of the possibility of a war in the Far East by the development of the Singapore base as a *place d' armes* to which part at least of the battlefleet could be speedily transferred on the imminence of hostilities. [28] He failed, however, to secure Canadian approval, until Smuts's intervention; and the differing support in the Dominions for the Singapore base policy was revealed in 1924 when Ramsay Macdonald asked for Dominions' views on the proposal to stop work on the base; [29] the Canadian and South African governments both approved, while the Pacific Dominions protested violently. The old policy was resumed when the Conservative government returned to office in November 1924, and the Pacific Dominions and Colonies in fact contributed very considerably in cash to the development of the base.

For the 1926 Imperial Conference the Admiralty at last came to terms with reality so far as the Dominion navies were concerned. In their view the single collective Empire fleet which would have to exist in war consisted of three categories, the Main Fleet, detached forces to control lines of communication distinct from the main theatre of operations, and the local defence forces necessary to stave off local enemy pressure. Dominion navies would, they hoped, pass through four phases of development. In the first they would provide local defence forces. In the second they would provide seagoing forces in addition to the local defence forces. In the third, they would take over responsibility for their home station, on which a squadron of the detached forces would be based. In the fourth they would, it was hoped, provide additional units for attachment to the main fleet. [30] From the published resolutions of the 1926 Imperial Conference and Dominion support of Britain's stand on the cruiser question at the ill-fated Three-Power Naval Conference at Geneva the following year, it must be assumed that the Dominion representatives accepted the Admiralty's analysis and proposals. A powerful and unavoidable inducement to them to do this was the refusal by foreign governments (especially the U.S.A.), made clear to them at the Imperial Conference, [31] to treat the Dominion navies as separate from the Royal Navy when considering the allocation of quotas for naval construction in the categories of smaller warship in which the Dominion navies were interested. This was peculiarly irksome to the Canadian government, especially since it would be taken as providing a precedent for the limitation of Dominion military and air forces. [32] The Americans, however, remained adamant and the Dominions were forced to accept their inclusion in the British quotas established in the London Naval Treaty of 1930. The matter appears to have been raised in private conversations at the 1930 Imperial Conference and reluctantly accepted; at any rate Commodore Hose R.C.N., was able to make effective use of this fact to defeat in 1933 a cut in the Canadian Naval estimates which would have entailed an abrupt disbandment of the Canadian Navy and the sale of its four destroyers to Britain. [33]

In the meantime the arrangements proposed by the Admiralty in 1923 and 1926 for the exchange of ships and officers, the attachment of Dominion officers to the Naval Staff College had developed easily and freely, being duly chronicled every year in the statements accompanying the British Naval Estimates. A further unifying force had come with the establishment of the Imperial Defence College. The Committee of Imperial Defence now reinforced by the establishment of the Chiefs of Staffs Sub-Committee in 1924 and a rapidly increasing network of civilian subcommittees continued its role as adviser not merely to the British Cabinet but also to the Dominions governments. At the 1926 Imperial Conference the Prime Minister of Britain, Baldwin, called the attention of the Dominions again to its work, and to the need for Dominions equivalents agreed on in 1911; and a number of Dominions senior officers of all Services attended the Imperial Defence College thereafter.

Thus by 1932 despite the defeat of the Admiralty's schemes for a single Imperial Navy, the Commonwealth amounted for defence purposes virtually to a permanent alliance with armed forces which were at least as integrated as those now comprising N.A.T.O.'s striking forces, with a common centre of advice on defence matters both between the individual armed Services and in the C.I.D. as a whole. There was of course no compulsion upon the individual governments to take such advice as was given. Yet on all matters of standardisation of equipment, training, etc., financial considerations and the virtual lack of domestic armaments industries operated with those of imperial sentiment to hold them on this common course even where the two bilingual Dominions were concerned. All this coupled with the existence of a world-wide network of bases available to the armed forces of the mother country, operated, as has been pointed out, to make the Commonwealth "in the matter of sea-power, to some extent an alliance with a certain contractual basis".[34] Yet this was an alliance without a common policy and a common enemy, as was to become apparent after 1933, when its varying members began to find themselves faced with different enemies. In February 1934 the Defence Requirements Sub-Committee set up the previous year on the joint promptings of the Treasury and the Chiefs of Staff Sub-Committee as an organ of the C.I.D. reported in strong and pungent terms on the threat from Germany and Japan. The reaction in the Dominions again showed very marked differences. The Canadian Government felt obliged to adopt a policy in public even more cunctatory than that pursued by its American neighbour. The South African government plunged boldly into a series of ill-considered attempts to mediate between Germany and Britain, meanwhile pressing Britain not to take any action against Germany. The New Zealand Government held out bravely for collective security. The Australian Government on the other hand was deeply disturbed by the development of a European threat which might prevent the dispatch of the Fleet to the Far East in the face of the increasing bellicosity of Japan. It was presumably in part to allay these anxieties and to advise them in the face of this threat that Lord Hankey visited Australia in the summer of 1934;[35] possibly in part to allay any anxieties on the part of the Home government as to Dominion action in the event of war.

Divided counsels continued to bedevil British ability to evolve an agreed policy to deal with the complete breakdown of European security. Neither South Africa nor Australia were at all happy about the accident which made Italy the first enemy, situated as Italy was across the line along which the transfer of the British fleet to Far Eastern waters should take place. But the obvious inability of the League to prevent the Italian conquest of Abyssinia deprived the whole Commonwealth of the factor which had enabled them to paper over their divisions and avoid the questions that had threatened to disrupt their society between competing nationalisms.

In these circumstances, the last Imperial Conference to meet before the war met under distinctly unhappy auspices. The main motif of the British Government's proposals marked a return to the circumstances of 1911 and 1917, the need for a considerable increase in Dominion contributions to the armaments burden of the Commonwealth as a whole. Particularly were they interested in investigating the possibility of developing native armaments industries in Canada and Australia. To justify the increased expenditure in armaments they embarked upon in 1936, the Commonwealth ministers were given an unvarnished account of Britain's inability to cope with Germany, Japan and Italy together, and of the efforts being made to reach a *modus vivendi* with each of them. They were told of the decision reluctantly made by the Chiefs of Staff that year that Italy had to be counted as a potential enemy. The Chiefs of Staff themselves pointed out that even with France as an ally the naval position would be extremely precarious. But they did their best to assure the Pacific Dominions that even if the Eastern Mediterranean had to be divided the utmost would be done to maintain Britain's position at Singapore. An appeal was made for an increased naval effort from the Dominions. But behind the scenes there was little unity. The Canadian representative, though sufficiently impressed to undertake, in the course of a forthcoming visit to Germany, to warn Hitler seriously against the idea that the Dominions would not support Britain, continued to maintain that the function of an Imperial Conference was limited to discussion and review. The South African representative delivered a warning as gratuitous as it was unhelpful that South African aid could not be relied on in the event of British involvement in a war originating in a dispute between Germany and Czechoslovakia. The New Zealand delegate appealed for the stationing of a capital ship squadron in the Far East in peacetime, and lectured the Conference on the virtues of simple morality in deciding the course to be followed in international politics. The Australian representative, acting it is believed on promptings from Britain, appealed for the preparation of Commonwealth defence plans by mutual arrangement between those members of the Commonwealth who might be interested. In the event only bilateral talks with Britain were held, and the Australian delegate delivered himself of an appeal for a Pacific Security Pact, which the Permanent Under-Secretary to the British Foreign Office told the American Ambassador in London surprised him very much though "nothing very much would come of it". [36] As the Australian official historian has commented, the Conference

> never ventured beyond the edge of those vital questions which were facing the British Commonwealth and each of its members. [37]

Even the proposal to encourage the development of a native armaments industry in Canada proved on examination to rest on nothing but rather vague cerebration and to be unbacked by any serous intention to place orders on the scale necessary to call such an industry into being. On the general problems facing the Conference, the British Premier was certainly correct in his view that

> in no part of the Commonwealth was opinion then ready for a firm commitment against Hitler by force. [38]

It is surely then of significance that the two initial moves in Chamberlain's new policy of appeasement, the invitation to Baron von Neurath, the German Foreign Minister, to visit London, and his first private letter to Mussolini should follow so immediately on the close of the Conference, the more so as all hope of an accommodation with Japan, talks for which had been in progress since October 1936, collapsed with the outbreak of the "China incident" at the end of July 1937. This is not the place to set out the policies followed towards Germany and Italy thereafter or the parts played by the Dominions in support of them. [39] It is enough to quote again from Mr. Duncan Hall, himself no friend of appeasement: [40]

> The policy of appeasement was not merely the policy of the Government of Neville Chamberlain. It was a policy shared in varying degrees by all the Dominion Cabinets and persisted in until the fall of Prague in March 1939. It was as near to being a common foreign policy of the whole British Commonwealth as any policy since 1919.

In March 1939, Dominion opinion reacted as positively to Hitler's entry into Prague as did that of Britain itself, and was, we are told, [41] a factor which determined Chamberlain in his open abandonment of appeasement in his speech of March 19 at Birmingham. Even then according to the same source, anxiety about French Canadian opinion was a factor in the hesitancy of his approach to Russia. [42] In the event, however, with the exception of Eire, the Commonwealth entered the war as a whole, though with nearly as bitter divisions in South Africa as in 1914.

Conclusion

Looking back we can see that it was not as Sir Edward Grey thought the establishment of separate Dominion armies and navies, but the establishment of separate Dominions whose governments were primarily responsible to their own electorates which threatened the Empire with the alternatives of disruption or the evolution of a common policy in the field of defence or foreign policy alike. Until 1923 the existence of a common European enemy and the dominance of varying degrees of imperialist sentiment in the Dominions achieved this unity, and a habit of consultation developed which made "imperial" the consultative machinery evolved to solve the problems of civil-military relations in the home country. After the Canadian refusal in 1923 further to countenance the practice by which the executive organs of the mother country acted in foreign policy in the name of the Empire as a whole, part of that unity was disrupted. The common defence policy continued, however, in part because it suited the pockets of the Dominions and the pride of the mother country, in part because foreign countries refused to accept the Commonwealth as anything but a unity in their defence and disarmament calculations. To avoid publicly acknowledging the effects of the Canadian action and facing its implications in the field of defence, the home government continued to consult on its own initiative where it could and to act within the scope of what it imagined consultation would approve where it could not. Imperial foreign policy became a matter of the Emperor's clothes; or would have become that had not an exterior frame of reference, equally unreal in many respects, been provided by the existence of the League of Nations. When the League's failure to cope successfully with the Abyssinian and Rhineland crises revealed the unreality of the League, the British government tried to return to the atmosphere of 1911; but the lack of a common imperial sentiment and the existence of a threat *more real to the Pacific Dominions than to Britain herself* made this attempt a failure. Britain continued to act as she imagined the Commonwealth would approve until March 1939 awoke the Dominions to the reality of the threat from Europe and recreated the atmosphere of 1911. In the meantime British statesmen had got into the habit themselves of consulting their own individual ouijaboards as to what Dominions sentiment would or would not approve, and the Dominions seemed mainly to prefer this to direct consultation of the kind which might face them with a choice on which their domestic public opinion was itself too unrealistic to prove of effective guidance.[43] Is the position so very much changed today?

NOTES

1. See Arthur J. Marder, *From the Dreadnought to Scapa Flow* (London, 1961) Vol. 1; Donald C. Gordon, "The Admirality and Dominions Navies, 1902 – 1914", 33, *Journal*

of Modern History, (1961); Brian Tunstall, "Imperial Defence, 1900 – 1914", *Cambridge History of the British Empire,* (1959), Vol. III.

2. These strictures are not intended to cover works specifically intended to deal with problems of Commonwealth as opposed to British foreign policy, such as P. N. S. Mansergh, *Commonwealth Affairs, Problems of External Policy 1931 – 1939,* (London, 1952); Gwendolen Carter, *The British Commonwealth and World Security,* (Toronto, 1947); W. Y. Elliott and H. Duncan Hall (Ed.), *The British Commonwealth at War,* (New York, 1943); J. D. B. Miller, *The Commonwealth in the World,* (London, 1958); though there are differences of emphasis between these works and the approach adopted in this paper.

3. *British Documents on the Origins of the War, 1898 – 1914,* G. P. Gooch and Harold Temperley, Vol. VI, Appendix V.

4. Already in 1902, during the Colonial Conference of that year, Joseph Chamberlain had spoken in somewhat highly coloured language of the "Weary Titan" struggling under the "too vast orb of its fate". On the impressions left on the minds of Dominion Premiers see Lord Hankey, *The Supreme Command, 1914 – 1918,* (London, 1961), Vol. I, 129.

5. Gordon, *op. cit.;* Gilbert M. Tucker, "The Naval Policy of Sir Robert Borden", 28, *Canadian Historical Review,* Vol. I, 1948.

6. Franklyn Arthur Johnson, *Defence by Committee, the British Committee of Imperial Defence 1880 – 1959,* (London, 1960), 121. See also Lord Hankey, *The Supreme Command,* Vol. 1, 124-136.

7. See Hans E. Bärtschi, *Die Entwicklung vom imperialistischen Reichsgedanken zur modernen Idee des Commonwealth im Lebenswerk Lord Balfours,* (Berne, 1957) 125-131, 136-138.

8. Hankey, *The Supreme Command,* Vol. II, 657. That the motives underlying this move included the desire to take advantage of the moment of crisis to advance further towards the Imperial super-state is suggested by a memorandum in Austen Chamberlain's papers which analyses the characters and attitudes of the Dominion representatives scheduled to attend the Conference, from the point of view of their views and openness to Imperial considerations.

9. David Lloyd George, *War Memoirs,* (London, 1933 – 36), Vol. IV, 1733.

10. *Public Archives of Canada, Sir George Foster Papers,* File 75; *Imperial War Conference 1917, Minutes of Proceedings,* etc. Cmd 8566 (1917); See also Sir Robert Borden, *Memoirs,* Vol. II, 693 – 96; M. Ollivier (Ed.), *The Colonial and Imperial Conferences from 1887 – 1937,* (Ottawa, 1954), Vols. II, III.

11. Hankey, *op. cit.,* Vol. I, 134; Tucker, *op. cit.*

12. Hughes had considerable support inside the British Cabinet from those who disliked the Fourteen Points, and resented the way the Allies had been compelled to allow the conclusion of an armistice with Germany on this basis without prior consultation. See *Public Archives of Canada, Sir Robert Borden Papers,* minutes of Imperial War Cabinet meetings of December 30, 31, 1918. (The minutes of the first meeting are also to be found in Colonel House's papers, Sterling Library, Yale.) On the Peace Conference, see Seth W. Tillmann, *Anglo-American Relations at the Paris Peace Conference,* (Princeton, 1961).

13. This was one of the few items on which Lord Grey was not allowed to offer any compromise in his mission to the United States in the last few months of 1919. *Docu-*

ments on British Foreign Policy, 1919 – 1939, edited by Sir Llewellyn Woodward and Rohan Butler, Series I, Vol. V, Chapter II, *passim.*

14. Neville Kingsley Meaney, "American Attitudes towards the British Empire, 1919 – 1922", (unpublished Ph.D. Thesis, Duke University, 1959), Library of Congress Microfilm 59-2387, 150.

15. This account is based on the following sources: J. Bartlet Brebner, "Canada and the Anglo-Japanese Alliance", *50 Political Science Quarterly* (1935); John K. Galbraith, "The Imperial Conference of 1921 and the Washington Conference", *29 Canadian Historical Review* (1948); William Farmer Whyte, *William Morris Hughes, his Life and Times,* (Sydney, 1957); memoranda in *Public Archives of Canada, Arthur Meighen and Sir George Foster Papers.*

16. This summary is based on Ramsay Cooke, "J. W. Dafoe at the Imperial Conference of 1923", *41 Canadian Hist. R.* (1961); R. Macgregor Dawson, *William Lyon Mackenzie King* (Ottawa, 1960), Vol. I; M. Ollivier, *op. cit.,* Vol. III.

17. Leo Amery's activities here are of the first importance in view of his personal friendship with Mackenzie King and Smuts.

18. There appears to have been some kind of an unofficial conference on defence matters during the Jubilee Celebrations in May 1935.

19. See Cmd. 2458 (1925). *Protocol for the Pacific Settlement of International Disputes. Correspondence relating to the position of the Dominions.*

20. *University of Birmingham, Austen Chamberlain Papers.* (The author is grateful to Mr. K. W. Humphreys, Librarian of the University of Birmingham, for permission to consult these.) In 1925 Ramsay Macdonald had called public attention to the difficulty: "The present system of consultation has two main deficiencies . . . It renders immediate action extremely difficult . . . Conclusions reached at and between Imperial Conferences are liable to be reversed through changes in Governments", Cmd. 2301 (1924 – 25), *Correspondence with the Governments of the Self-Governing Dominions with regard to consultation on matters of Foreign Policy and General Imperial Interest,* No. I.

21. *Public Archives of Canada, Sir Robert Borden Papers.* See also Sir Robert Borden, *Memoirs,* Vol. II, 841 – 43.

22. The rejection was less categorical than sometimes represented, being couched in terms of its immediate impracticability. The final paragraph read as follows: "As naval forces come to be developed upon a considerable scale by the Dominions, it may be necessary hereafter to consider the establishment for war purposes of some supreme naval authority upon which each of the Dominions would be adequately represented." *Public Archives of Canada. Sir Robert Borden Papers.*

23. Admiral Sir Frederick Dreyer, *The Sea Heritage* (London, 1955), 240.

24. Brigadier J. H. MacBrien to Sir Robert Borden, July 14, 1919. *Borden Papers.*

25. Admiral Sir Reginald Bacon, *Life of John Rushworth, Earl of Jellicoe* (London, 1936) 425 – 26.

26. *Austen Chamberlain Papers.*

27. Ollivier, *op. cit.,* Vol. II.

28. Amery, *My Political Life,* Vol. II, (London, 1953) 252 – 53; 273 – 75. Cooke, *op. cit.*

29. Cmd. 2083 (1924). *Correspondence with the Self-governing Dominions and India regarding the Development of the Singapore Naval Base,* Nos. 1, 3, 12, 13.

30. *Public Archives of Canada, Arthur Meighen Papers.* Memorandum of May 10, 1926.

31. *Public Archives of Canada, Arthur Meighen Papers.*

32. *Canadian Naval Archives,* Governor General to Secretary of State for Dominions Affairs, June 27, 1927. The author is extremely grateful to the Canadian Naval Authorities and to Mr. E. C. Russell, the official Canadian Naval Historian, for permission to quote from these papers.

33. *Canadian Naval Archives,* File 4000, 100/1A. Commodore Hose to Canadian Minister of National Defence, Colonel Sutherland, June 1, 1933.

34. H. Duncan Hall, "The Commonwealth in War and Peace", *The British Commonwealth at War,* ed. W. Y. Elliott and H. Duncan Hall (New York, 1943) 68.

35. Lord Hankey, *Diplomacy by Conference,* (London, 1946) 132.

36. *Foreign Relations of the United States, 1927,* Vol. III, 102 – 03, Bingham to Hull, T. 292 of May 18, 1937.

37. *Official History of Australia in World War II,* Paul Hasluck, *The Government and the People 1929 – 41* (Canberra, 1952), 56.

38. This summary is based on: Hasluck, *op. cit.,* 56 – 72; Major-General Kirby and others, *The War in the Far East,* Vol. I, 17 – 18; J. D. Scott and R. Hughes, *The Administration of War Production,* (London, 1955), 58 – 60; H. Duncan Hall, *North American Supply,* (London, 1955), 6; Viscount Templewood, *Nine Troubled Years,* (London, 1954) 210; C. M. van den Heever, *General J. B. M. Hertzog,* (Johannesburg, 1946), 270 – 71; *Official History of New Zealand in the Second World War 1939 – 1945;* F. L. W. Wood, *The New Zealand People at War; Political and External Affairs,* (Wellington, 1958), 48, 50, 54 – 55, 58, 66 – 67, 72, 91 – 92.

39. For Germany see D. C. Watt, "Der Einfluss der Dominions auf die britische Aussenpolitik vor München 1938", 8, *Vierteljahresheft für Zeitgeschichte,* 1959. For Italy, especially the role of Australia, see D. C. Watt, "Gli accordi mediterranei anglo-italiani del 16 aprile 1938", *26, Rivista di Studi Politici Internazionali,* (1959). On the last fatuous South African intervention see also D. C. Watt, "Pirow's mission to Berlin in November 1938", 12 *Wiener Library Bulletin* (1958).

40. Hall, "The Commonwealth in War and Peace", *op. cit.,* 13.

41. K. G. Feiling, *Life of Neville Chamberlain,* (London, 1946), 400.

42. Feiling, *op. cit.,* 408.

43. Though they reserved to themselves the right to complain. As Sir Joseph Ward wrote in 1929 prior to a gentle complaint on inadequate and over-hasty consultation,

"His Majesty's Government in the United Kingdom act in such matters not only on their own behalf but in a very real sense as the agent or trustee of His Majesty's other Governments." F. L. W. Wood, *op. cit.,* 16.

The rise of the Labour party, paralleled by the decline of the Liberals, has been perhaps the major development in twentieth-century British political history. Yet the Conservative party has been in one way or another the controlling party in office substantially more than double the time of either rival group. The Conservative record appears to bear out Samuel Huntington's con-tention—in an American Political Science Re-view *article (June 1957) concerned mainly with American issues—that the conservative ideol-ogy is a "positional" one, responding again and again to a specific social situation, meeting a specific historical need. By that reading, there should be no surprise that the Conservative tra-dition in Great Britain could accommodate to the substantial changes that have taken place since 1945. As the "intellectual rationale of the permanent institutional prerequisites of human existence" it accepted the welfare state, for ex-ample, and has struggled to define contempo-rary approaches to a changing social order. W. L. Burn's article, suggesting some of the re-formulations that became evident after 1945, was first given as a paper in a series of lectures designed to commemorate the fiftieth anniver-sary of A. B. Dicey's famous* Lectures on the Relation between Law and Public Opinion in England during the Nineteenth Century. *The volume of articles, edited by Morris Ginsberg, was entitled* Law and Opinion in England in the 20th Century *(London, 1959, copyright, the Lon-don School of Economics and Political Science).*

5

The Conservative Tradition and Its Reformulations

W. L. BURN

It may be worth while to consider the hypothetical but by no means improbable figure of a staunch Conservative meditating on the election results in January 1906. He had anticipated defeat for his party but never a defeat so catastrophic as this. The agony of the moment has endowed him with power to see into the future. What he sees towards the end of that survey is no more alluring than the dismal present. Neither the monarchy nor the Church of England seeks or welcomes his partisan support; the Acts of 1918 and 1928 have virtually established universal adult suffrage; the hierarchical structure of society has been fatally damaged and government by deference has come to an end.

With these guides it would not have been impossible for him to foresee much that has, in fact, happened in the intervening fifty-odd years; even though he might have been tempted to foresee, as well, a good deal that has not happened. He might well have foreseen the House of Lords deprived of its veto and reduced to the possession of a short suspensive power; the disestablishment of the Church of Wales; the complete independence of most of Ireland and of parts of what he knew as the British Empire; the scarcely challenged right of secession of those Dominions which remain in the Commonwealth; allegiance to the Crown no longer the essential symbol of imperial unity; taxation deliberately conceived in part for social rather than fiscal ends, penal in its incidence and all-embracing in its range, adding a vast burden to life and an additional terror to death. Such a man, one can suppose, would have found particularly unattractive the idea of his grand-daughter going, completely unabashed, to draw an allowance for her second and subsequent children. Altogether he would have found if he had lived for another half-century, and can be credited with foreseeing in 1906, such a disintegration and proletarianisation of society as he understood it as to transform it into a mob, and such a weakening of the national will as to leave it purposeless and helpless. What one cannot credit him with foreseeing is a Conservative and "allied" vote of 13.7 millions against a Labour vote of 13.9 millions in 1951 and of 13.3 millions against 12.4 in 1955.

It might be said, of course, that by 1951 or 1955 the Conservative Party, or Conservatism, had ceased to exist; that the votes were given to candidates or to a body masquerading under such names, attracting the woman who was tired of standing in queues and the man who had voted Labour in 1945 because he hoped thus to get a council house and voted Conservative in 1955 because he had not got one. The burden of such suggestions is that the party in question (though the criticism is levied from time to time against all parties) has abandoned its tradition in order to gain votes, has sold its soul for the sake of office.

One would have more respect for this opinion if it were not a little jaded, if it or its like had not been heard so often before. It was urged with the utmost bitterness when Wellington and Peel decided in 1829 that Roman Catholics must be allowed to sit in Parliament. It was urged again, in the eighteen-fifties, after the protectionist wing of the Conservative Party had acquiesced in the abolition of agricultural protection. Anthony Trollope, brought up in a Tory household, became a Liberal and even contested an election in that interest. Some of the reasons which led him to do so may be surmised from a passage in one of his novels, *The Bertrams,* published in 1859. Writing there of a year about 1845, he observed sardonically:

> "At that time we had not thoroughly learnt by experience, as we now have, that no reform, no innovation—experience almost justifies us in saying, no revolution— stinks so foully in the nostrils of an English Tory as to be absolutely irreconcilable to him. When taken in the refreshing waters of office any such pill can be swallowed. This is now a fact recognised in politics and it is a great point in favour of that party that their powers of deglutition should be so recognised. Let the people want what they will—Jew senators, cheap corn, vote by ballot, no property qualifications or anything else, the Tories will carry it for them if the Whigs cannot. A poor Whig premier has none but the Liberals to back him, but a reforming Tory will be backed by all the world except those whom his own dishonesty will presumably have disgusted."

Without the least difficulty one could find the same accusations of dishonesty and duplicity made at later dates; over the parliamentary reforms of 1867–68;

over the establishment of the Irish Free State; over the more recent grant of independence to the Sudan and its consequences for the southern Sudanese.

Sometimes a mild dose of historical fact is useful to abate feverish judgment. The utilitarians had been among the strongest exponents of parliamentary reform in the eighteen-twenties and thirties. It was a utilitarian of the next generation, Robert Lowe, who proved himself the foremost opponent of the next instalment of parliamentary reform but, again, within a very short time, when his views had been overridden, he was serving under Gladstone as Chancellor of the Exchequer. The most notable of Disraeli's critics in the same conflict had been Lord Salisbury, then Lord Cranborne, the author of that bitter article in the *Quarterly Review* of October 1867 on "The Conservative Surrender"; but he accepted office in the next Conservative ministry. Much of the legislation carried by Liberal governments between 1906 and 1914 would have been abhorrent to Gladstone; and one cannot be certain that Keir Hardie, if he were alive now, would be a welcome recruit to a Labour Cabinet. The maintenance of domestic peace can exact heavy sacrifices from individual consciences and the line which divides duplicity from magnanimity is not always clear. Sometimes, indeed, it is obscured by the magnanimity of those who have been foremost in accusations of duplicity. Although the article on "The Conservative Surrender" had described some of the writer's late colleagues as "showing a freedom from scruple surpassing all former example" it went on to add this:

> "It is the duty of every Englishman and of every English party to accept a political defeat cordially, and to lend their best endeavors to secure the success, or to neutralise the evils, of the principles to which they have been forced to succumb."

We may have found here something which is fundamental to the Conservative tradition, but before we consider that possibility there is another point to be made. There have to be taken into account what the Prayer Book calls "the changes and chances of this mortal life," operating with a range which can confuse the individual mind and benumb the individual conscience. It would be fair to say that the England which Dicey surveyed in his *Law and Opinion* was an England at peace, economically prosperous, with a stable currency. In the fifty-eight years from 1901 to the present this country has been engaged (counting the last year and a half of the South African War) in a major war for the whole or part of fourteen years. In addition to the years of active hostilities there have been those when war was deemed near or imminent, to be prepared for or averted by expensive rearmament. Those years it is scarcely possible to designate arithmetically since the subjective element in judgment is necessarily so strong; but if one put them at a score one could not be guilty of exaggeration. This is not to argue that the years of war or threatened war were revolutionary in the sense that they constituted the direct and sole cause of what, but for them, would never have come into existence. Even that stern economist Hicks Beach did not see the cost of the South African War in isolation. What disturbed him was the conclusion that the national willingness to spend lavishly on the war was only part of a national willingness to spend lavishly—by his standards—on anything.

"There is no party or section of party" (he complained in introducing his budget in April 1901) "that is in favour of economy for economy's sake."[1]

If super-tax had not been included in the budget proposals of 1909 to meet in part the increasing expenditure on naval construction it would probably have come in another budget, for other reasons. If a partial enfranchisement of women had not been enacted in 1918 it would almost certainly have been enacted before much longer. It may be that the fact or probability of major war merely accelerates the operation of factors already existing. But it is the acceleration which is important here; the explosion of a train of events, with vast and continuing consequences on national life, even though the train had been laid much earlier.

Again, Dicey's England was one in which ideas could come slowly to their fruition, nurtured in country-houses not yet dependent on half-crowns from visitors and in universities not yet semi-nationalised institutions endeavouring to cram every possible student within their walls; suffering changes of emphasis and range, but neither the progeny nor the victims of economic catastrophe. That melancholy string of problems—unemployment, full employment, overemployment, deflation, inflation, the balance of payments (which even the most irresponsible of politicians have not been able to avoid noticing for the last forty years)—were not the problems to which Dicey directed his mind.

At bottom he assumed an England (perhaps an upper middle-class England) which was in control of the situation; which would be able to take its time and gradually absorb or transmute or reject the ideas presented to it. Since his day there has been less time to spare; action has been taken, perhaps has had to be taken, without full consideration of its consequences and its implications. This has to be said, not exactly in defence but perhaps in mitigation of such changes in the tradition or policy of any political group as may otherwise seem merely time-serving, inexplicable save on the basis of the most material and cynical considerations. If one studies the activities of groups with far narrower objectives than a political party can possibly have it becomes clear how even those objectives and the methods used to attain them have changed from time to time.[2] When one comes to deal with national parties one is tempted to ask, with Matthew Arnold:

> ". . . wherefore try,
> To things by mortal course that live,
> A shadow durability,
> For which they were not meant, to give?"

This is obviously a temptation which must be resisted here. But the warning is worth remembering; the more so because the tradition of a political party has a good many facets. As viewed by an opponent it presents a picture as depressing as one's passport photograph, something repellent or, at the best, the subject of apologetic and reluctant recognition. As viewed by those included in it, it has a decidedly more attractive appearance as the extension into national politics of the behaviour of a pleasant and homogeneous family group. To some, the Conservative tradition would be fittingly embodied in "hard-faced" businessmen entertaining each other on expense allowances: to others it echoes still with the romantic idealism of Young England. And occasionally the points of view are changed with embarrassing consequences. The parliamentary debates on the Television Bill in 1954 provided some amusing instances of this. In the debate in the House of Commons on March 25, 1954, for instance, arguments from the Conservative benches were tinged with a sentimental egalitarianism. "The question," said one Member, "is whether we are seriously to maintain that a nation where we have National Service for our young people and where we have adult suffrage cannot trust the people to choose between one form of television service and another." But from Mr. Herbert Morrison came the lament that the Conservative Party was no longer a party of "aristocratic culture": it was evidently a long time since Bagehot had written of "the finest brute-votes in Europe." Almost as entertaining as the efforts of anti-Conservatives to keep Conservatives within the bounds of a particular tradition are the efforts of Conservatives to forget those parts of their own tradition which have become unfashionable: at least it is difficult to remember reading much in the way of Conservative analysis or exposition of Conservatism as it existed in the days of its ten-year dominance between 1895 and 1905.

There are two elements in or two characteristics of the Conservative tradition which appear to be worth special remark. The first is the claim that the Conservative Party is a *national* party. Obviously this is a claim which any party must make under a system of universal adult suffrage: it is not easy to conceive of a party explicitly seeking the favours of the electorate on the ground that it represents a narrow, sectional interest. Even so, this claim is

very firmly established in the Conservative tradition. It was made by Disraeli
in his Crystal Palace speech of 1872.

> "The Tory party, unless it is a national party, is nothing. It is not a confederacy of no-
> bles, it is not a democratic multitude; it is a party formed from all the numerous
> classes in the realm—classes alike and equal before the law, but whose different
> conditions and different aims give vigour and variety to our national life."

Eighty-five years later, at the Brighton conference in October 1957, Mr. Macleod said:

> "If we are not a national party, representing both trade unionists and employers, we
> are nothing."

If this were merely said in imitation of Disraeli it would still be enough to support the argument advanced. But it was surely much more than imitation;
rather, the deliberate application to a contemporary problem of traditional language and a traditional way of thought.

It is relevant in this connection to notice the number and length of the periods since 1901 when the Conservatives have formed part, and usually the predominant part, of a coalition. It would be technically correct to describe Balfour's ministry as a coalition. About the coalition ministries of 1915 – 16 and
1916 – 22 there can be no doubt. The exact moment at which the National government, formed in 1931, ceased to be "national" in more than name admits of
argument which it is unnecessary to pursue here. Although the present government is supported by a few National Liberals and Liberal-Conservatives it
would be pedantic to describe it as a coalition; but Sir Winston Churchill's government of 1940 – 45 was a coalition in a perfectly simple and satisfactory
sense and his anxiety to extend its life after hostilities were over will not have
been forgotten.

The fact that the Conservative Party has formed part of so many coalitions
makes it the more difficult to follow the track of the Conservative tradition,
pure and undefiled. Can the Catering Wages Act of 1943, for example, be
properly described as a Conservative measure? There is also the point to be
made that to some Conservatives this anxiety to take part in coalition government was repellent. Readers of the late L. S. Amery's *My Political Life* will
recollect his repeated fears that the Conservative Party should be led into or
remain in a coalition constructed on the negative basis of anti-socialism.[3]
Even so, one would be justified in noticing a tendency (to put it no higher) on
the part of the Conservatives to enter coalitions and the reluctance of some of
them—as in 1922—to leave them. Nor can this tendency be wholly explained
by the existence of extreme "emergencies": the recurrence of a particular
combination of symptoms in a patient may establish the diagnosis of a particu-

lar disease although each of the symptoms, in itself, is capable of some other explanation. At all events there is ground for considering the possibility that this tendency on the part of political Conservatism has a fairly close relation to the emphasis in the Conservative tradition on its "national" quality and range. And this emphasis, in its turn, may be due in part to the fact that the Conservative Party has a very long experience of the responsibilities and anxieties of office. It is equally arguable that the Labour Party, as its experience of office and of the chance of office has increased, is much more of a "national" party than it was as a minority in the twenties.

The second major characteristic of the Conservative tradition is the importance deliberately given in it to non-political elements. One must necessarily read with some caution such expositions of political philosophy as occur in electioneering pamphlets but, with this warning, it is interesting to look at *The Right Road for Britain,* published by the Conservative and Unionist Central Office in 1949.

> "Conservatism proclaims the inability of purely materialist philosophies to read the riddle of life, and achieve the necessary subordination of scientific invention and economic progress to the needs of the human spirit. . . . Man is a spiritual creature adventuring on an immortal destiny, and science, politics and economics are good or bad so far as they help or hinder the individual soul on its eternal journey."

The same theme has been urged by too many Conservative thinkers of eminence to allow us to dismiss it as merely propagandist. It would be easy to multiply quotations from Burke and more useful to note some more recent examples. Thus we have Lord Percy (Lord Eustace Percy as he was then) writing in 1935:

> "Conservatism finds the motive force of human progress, not in the compulsory authority of the State, but in the individual's conscience and sense of duty. It is the individual human heart that is shaken by the wind of the Spirit. Many of the greatest crimes and the greatest failures of history have been due to the attempt to realise the highest human ideals through political authority." [4]

We have Mr. Kenneth Pickthorn beginning his booklet, *Principles or Prejudice,* with the statement that "politics do not really matter quite so much as is generally assumed in public discussion" and going on to remark that to most people immediate personal relations, to a few eternal values beyond this world and this life, are more important than politics. [5] In *The Case for Conservatism* Lord Hailsham argued that "Conservatives do not believe that the political struggle is the most important thing in life" and asserted at the end of the same paragraph that "the man who puts politics first is not fit to be called a human being, let alone a Christian." [6] Finally, we have Mr. T. E. Utley saying, in the first of a series of articles published in the *National Review* in 1948, that:

> "The great dividing line in British politics has always been between those who regard politics as supremely important and those who conceive it to be the handmaid of religion, art, science and society. The Left are in the first category. Conservatives are in the second." [7]

There may be some exaggeration here. Not all Conservatives, certainly not all Conservatives at all times, have been in the second category. Bonar Law was not, nor that redoubtable fighter, L. S. Amery; though the one had very few personal interests and recreations outside politics and the other very many. Still, this does not greatly affect the argument that part of the strength of Conservatism comes from its appeal (whether made deliberately or not) to non-political or even anti-political elements in society.

This appeal was symbolised in the career of the late Earl Baldwin. Mr. G. M. Young quotes this tribute to him from an anonymous correspondent of *The Times,* writing at the end of the parliamentary session of 1925:

> "He has brought into public life a pleasant savour, freshness and health. It is the fragrance of the fields, the flavour of apple and hazel nut, all the unpretentious, simple, wholesome, homely but essential qualities, suggestions and traditions of England that Mr. Baldwin has substituted for the over-charged, heavy-laded, decadent atmosphere of our post-war days." [8]

The quotation, not forty years old, may seem incredibly "dated." Yet it is scarcely to be doubted that Baldwin made a contribution of capital, perhaps of vital, importance to British political life. That, however, is by no means the whole story. In the domestic field Baldwin was a highly accomplished, though not infallible, politician. Was he deliberately seeking to cloak his political ambitions in the more appealing trappings of the simple Englishman? Or was he essentially so much of the simple Englishman that he could make his appeal to his countrymen in no other way? The doubts cannot be resolved here but one thing is plain: so far as his success was the result of his ability to create an "atmosphere" conducive to national peace and unity it was necessarily limited in its range. Economic problems, still less international problems, could not be "solved" by the creation of an atmosphere.

This is a special illustration of the point which Lord Percy made:

> "This dualism, this belief in a *civitas dei* distinct from the political State, is the essential strength of Toryism, but it is also the reason why its political action seems often to be so unsatisfying." [9]

The Conservative, therefore, is placed in a position of peculiar difficulty. He

may well be indifferent to much of the action of the political State, even hostile
to political action generally. But his sense of responsibility to the nation as a
whole makes it impossible for him to withdraw to an "ivory tower." In practice
he deals with his difficulty empirically: unless his deepest feelings and convictions are challenged he puts up with a great deal that he dislikes and fears.
If he is a Conservative of the hopeful kind he can comfort himself that the
worst is over, that henceforth things will improve. If he is of a more sceptical
turn he has the consoling reflection that things might have been much
worse—and probably, after a breathing-space, will be.

Naturally there have been occasions when the Conservative Party has acted
in a more heroic and even in a desperate way. The supreme example of these
is its policy towards Ulster. The speech which Bonar Law made in Belfast on
April 9, 1912, has often been quoted but it is worth quoting again if only as a
reminder of the intensity of a distant passion.

> "I say to you with all solemnity: you must trust to yourselves. Once again you hold the
> pass for the Empire. You are a besieged city. Does not the picture of the past, the glo-
> rious past with which you are so familiar, rise again before your eyes? The timid have
> left you, your Lundys have betrayed you, but you have closed your gates. The Govern-
> ment by their Parliament Act have erected a boom against you, a boom to cut you off
> from the help of the British people. You will burst that boom. The help will come and
> when the crisis is over men will say of you in words not unlike those used by Pitt 'You
> have saved yourselves by your exertions and you will save Europe by your ex-
> ample.'" [10]

One did not need to be very old, in the England of 1912−14, to be aware of the
dangerous tensions behind that irrecoverable façade. And there were other
moments when the Conservative Party turned, as it were, to bay. Appealing to
Anglican sentiment and acting through the House of Lords, it was strong
enough to oblige the Liberals to abandon the anti-Anglican Education Bills of
1906 and 1908. But it is more to the point to remember those legislative measures which the Conservative Party, whether through the House of Lords or
otherwise, could have stopped or seriously delayed; and did not. There was
the Trade Disputes Act, 1906. Every year nowadays, almost every week,
provides evidence of the vast significance of this measure and when it was
under discussion it might well have seemed sufficiently offensive to many
Liberals, as well as to most Conservatives, to merit challenging in force. But
the Conservatives, under Balfour, did not contest its third reading in the Commons and it was passed without a division by the Lords. The progress of the
Old Age Pensions Bill of 1908 was accelerated by the use of the closure but
the opposition to it, as Halévy says, was feeble and timid and an amendment

by the Lords which sought to limit its operation to a period of seven years was evidence of no more than a fear of coming down on one side or the other of a particularly difficult fence. The National Insurance Act of 1911 was subjected to a delaying amendment in the Commons but passed its second reading in the Lords without a debate. The Act of 1912 which accepted the principle of a minimum wage for miners was virtually unchallenged by the Conservative opposition; although the fact that it did not settle a national minimum wage but allowed of district agreements may have made it somewhat more acceptable. By and large, the Conservatives accepted the social reforms of 1906 – 14 with notable ease; in contrast with their resolute opposition to certain constitutional reforms. It was not to be expected that they would oppose in principle or even seriously contest in detail those further social reforms which have more recently come to constitute the so-called "Welfare State."

One cannot avoid noticing, at this point, the charge that the guiding rule in Conservative policy was not tradition or principle but expediency. Expediency, of course, is the word one attaches to those acts of one's opponents which they describe as flexible. But the charge can be put thus: that the Conservative Party in the years 1906 – 14 showed itself willing to challenge the Liberals on issues such as those provided by education and licensing Bills, Ulster and tariff reform, where it would expect a considerable amount of working-class support or at least be in little danger of working-class hostility; but shrank from opposing legislation which was or was thought to be ardently desired by the mass of working-class voters.

Even the most fanatical Conservative could scarcely reject this charge absolutely. But it is equally difficult to accept it as providing a single, satisfactory explanation. The Conservative challenge extended to the Parliament Bill and although the attack on the powers of the Lords proved less popular than Liberal politicians imagined, the defense of those powers was not an obvious path to popularity with the electorate. On the other side, the National Insurance Act was not initially so popular with the working-class that Conservative opposition to it could not reasonably have been prolonged on grounds of expediency alone. But it is perhaps more to the point to remember that a certain bias in favour of action for the benefit of the working-class and its organisations already existed as one element in Conservative tradition. It does not follow that this bias had not itself come into existence from motives of expediency and it is easy to over-estimate the quality and even the amount of Tory support for Factory Acts and Tory opposition to the Poor Law (Amendment) Act of 1834. Nevertheless, the bias was there even before Disraeli's last ministry, whose legislation so much strengthened it. A Conservative who modified or abandoned his opposition to the Trade Disputes Bill of 1906 could recall the Conspiracy and Protection of Property Act and the Employers and Workmen Act of 1875 and console himself with the belief that his action was not inconsistent with Conservative tradition. At the same time he could justify his more obdurate opposition to Home Rule or at least to the inclusion of Ulster within the jurisdiction of an Irish parliament by arguing that such policies were not comprehensively acceptable to the nation at large.

In other words, conservatives who demanded of policy that it should be truly national could accept as proof of its attainment of such a standard the probability or the fact that it would be or was comprehensively acceptable. The consequence has been Conservative acquiescence in measures which have originally been those of other parties, even measures initiated in the face of violent Conservative protests. There are instances which could be quoted to the contrary, such as the denationalisation of the steel industry and the partial denationalisation of the transport industry; but they have to be set against Conservative acquiescence in the nationalisation of a larger number of industries. On balance the scales appear to come down decisively on the side of acquiescence.

Although it was part of the Conservative programme in 1949 to restore the University constituencies and to hold elections in them immediately after their restoration, this proposal was abandoned when a Conservative government came into office. Mr. McKenzie's industry and acumen have recently shown us how often such Conservative organisations as the National Union have pressed for a fundamental reform of the Second Chamber [11] : it is within our knowledge that no such reform has been undertaken by a Conservative government unless we are prepared to consider the Life Peerages Act, 1958, as the tentative beginning of such fundamental reform in the powers as well as in the composition of the House of Lords. And perhaps one does not need to go very far from the field of fact into that of speculation to be convinced that a referendum of Conservative voters would have rejected the Homicide Act of 1957. In any event, what has been notably lacking in the Conservative tradition is any large-scale and comprehensive attempt to put the constitutional clock back or to create a different kind of constitution, weighted in favour of the rights of property and the easier maintenance of the *status quo*. Such an attempt might logically have demanded the establishment of a "written" constitution with provision for judicial review of legislation. The nearest approach to it was the Conservative desire [12] to exclude certain "organic" matters from the scope of the Parliament Bill of 1911. This was not achieved and it can be taken that the attempt to achieve it—perhaps a sudden improvisation of policy rather than part of a tradition—has been abandoned. It is notable that a report drawn up by a strong group of Conservatives, inside and outside Parliament, and published in 1946 under the title, *Some Proposals for Constitutional Reform*, began with the categorical statement:

> "We are agreed that the problems of government by which this country is faced today can be solved within the framework of the existing Constitution."

It may be argued that this tradition of acquiescence has been violated in at least one major instance, by the passing in 1927 of the Trade Disputes and Trade Unions Act. On this Mr. G. M. Young has said:

> "With the laying of the Trade Disputes Bill, the Disraelian make-believe rolled away like a morning mist and revealed the Conservative Party armed and accoutred to keep the Unions in their places and arrest the growth of the Parliamentary Labour Party. The Conservatives were, in fact, determined to make a party triumph out of what, rightly viewed, was a national victory, and Baldwin put himself in their hands." [13]

The extent to which the Conservative Party (or the government of the day) was thus "armed and accoutred" was, in fact, much slighter than would be realised by anyone who had read Mr. Young's words but had not read the text of the Act. It is perfectly true that the Act substituted what is called "contracting-in" for the payment by trade unionists of the political levy for the more onerous process of contracting-out provided by the Trade Unions Act of 1913; and that it excluded from legalised picketing such picketing at or near a persons's house or place of business as might intimidate him in the sense of creating in his mind a reasonable apprehension of injury to himself, his family, his property or his business. It is also true, however, that the Act did not deprive trade unions of the immense advantage they possessed in the immunity from actions for tort conferred upon them by section 4 of the Trade Disputes Act of 1906 except in so far as they might be engaged in an "illegal" strike; defined as having an object other than or in addition to the furtherance of a trade dispute within the industry concerned *and* as being "designed or calculated to coerce the Government either directly or indirectly by inflicting hardship on the community." So far as such "illegal" strikes were concerned persons furthering them were made subject to the ordinary law of conspiracy, and picketing in the course of such strikes was deprived of the protection afforded to it, on certain conditions, by section 2 of the 1906 Act. It is to be observed, moreover, that the 1927 Act, being primarily directed against one rare species of strike, was not the occasion for any civil litigation during its existence and only afforded ground for one criminal conviction, subsequently upset on appeal. [14]

If, as Mr. Young suggests, it was the design of the Conservative Party "to keep the Unions in their places" the means they chose were not notably comprehensive or effective. If the party violated its tradition of acquiescence the violation was hardly extensive. But it is more important to remember that since its return to office in 1951 the Conservative Party has made no attempt to re-enact, with or without modifications, the 1927 Act or to interfere with the legal position and powers of trade unions. The refusal of successive Conservative governments to initiate legislation which could be construed as unfavourable to the trade union movement has provoked considerable criticism among rank-and-file Conservatives. The excesses or alleged excesses of pickets during the provincial omnibus strike in the summer of 1957 appeared to be viewed, not perhaps with indifference but without deep concern, by the government; and requests by "back-bench" Conservatives for an inquiry into offenses committed, convictions secured and punishments inflicted remained isolated and ineffectual. One would probably be justified in associating this apparent complacency on the part of the government towards public disorder not merely with an anxiety to court the support of trade unionists but also with another form of acquiescence—acceptance, to a marked degree, of the opinions of those penal reformers who seek a milder criminal law, more mildly administered, and eliminate retribution from among the ends of criminal justice. It was formerly part of the Conservative tradition that the Conservative Party was *par excellence* the party which regarded it as the first duty of a government to maintain law and order and that a Conservative government could be trusted to do so, even if it had to employ harsh methods. The current trends in criminal statistics provide no evidence of such ability on the part of a Conservative government: the speeches and writings of some of its members give an impression of them as waiting helplessly to be told by commissions and committees what they ought to do. More than any other party the Conservatives reflected, for good or bad, the instinctive impulse. Perhaps for this reason they have changed more quickly than any other party as they have grown more thoughtful and decorous, as their instincts have become atrophied.

It may be prudent to return from these speculations to more concrete consequences of what has become the Conservative tradition of acquiescence. Mr. Pickthorn has given us this succinct and acceptable definition of a Conservative:

". . . a man who believes that in politics the onus of proof is on the proposer of change." [15]

It follows that once a change has been accomplished such a man throws the onus of proof on the proposer of further change, whether that further change is an extension of what has already been done or a reversal of it. The vast social and technical developments of the last half-century, comparatively few of them directly willed or planned by politicians, have left a great deposit or accumulation of change which it has become the Conservative tradition to accept.

What it accepts includes the subordination of the individual to the political State. To enunciate such a truism is merely to begin, not to conclude, the argument: Conservative tradition is not obliged to admit that such subordination must be in itself an evil. It is, of course, a danger since it may threaten the existence of those non-political values which Conservatives traditionally prize. Even so, those values have never been immune from danger and never will be. To admit that is not to decry the need, in Conservative opinion, for their due protection. But how are they to be protected? There is no simple, single nostrum for universal application: at least for universal application by a party which claims to draw its support from all classes and to be especially conscious of its national responsibilities. Mr. R. A. Butler stated the problem when, in a speech in the House of Commons on October 31, 1957, he said that it was the duty of the government "to strike a just balance between the claims of the citizen and the community as a whole in an era in which the nation must be equipped with the resources of a fully competitive economy." [16] But to state a problem is only, at most, the first step towards its solution and a critic of contemporary Conservatism might think that a little of the ability which it displays in stating problems could well be used in finding solutions to them.

One such partial solution was propounded over forty years ago by Lord Hugh Cecil in his book on *Conservatism* (1912).

"When, therefore, it is said that the State must act for the common good, that proposition must be subject to the reservation that State action must not in any case be immoral, and that to injure innocent people is immoral."[17]

The essence of this solution is the enforcement on the State of the obligation to observe certain standards of conduct—standards which are still reasonably easy of description and definition. Even as between private persons they do not command obedience spontaneously: means have to be devised and sanctions applied to ensure obedience to them. Those means are supplied in large part and in the ultimate analysis by the courts of law. How far have these means been brought to bear, at the instance of Conservatism, upon the State?

The answer must be, until recently very little. We are all aware of the vast legislative and quasi-judicial powers delegated to and possessed by Government Departments. It can scarcely be argued that, save in a context irreconcilable with Conservative tradition, those powers have been consistently exercised or perhaps could be exercised in such a way as to accord with Lord Hugh Cecil's criteria. This was a matter which called for examination and action by Conservatives. But no Conservative government took effective action to implement the report of the Committee on Ministers' Powers (the Donoughmore Committee) which reported in 1932 and although a little—a very little—was done by the Administration of Justice Act and the Limitations Act of 1933 to implement the report of the Crown Proceedings Committee of 1927 it was a Labour and not a Conservative government which initiated the Crown Proceedings Act by 1947. Lawyers of the older fashion still regard as the fatal defect of that Act the retention of the rule relating to discovery by the Crown; but no Conservative government has modified or abrogated it. The inquiry into the Crichel Down proceedings, though it may since have become part of the Conservative tradition, was forced upon the Conservative government of the day.

It may well be that the root of the Conservative difficulty in defending non-political values lies in its reluctance to examine their implications. Let us consider shortly the question of private property. Is there, in the Conservative tradition as it exists today, any coherent theory, any studied and comprehensive defence, of the right of private property? There are partial defences and we can look at one of them, Lord Hailsham's in *The Case for Conservatism*. It is modest in length, only occupying six pages [18] in a book of 314 pages. It repeats and accepts the conventional arguments in favour of private property but it makes two reservations: Conservatives do not defend every particular kind or sort of property; and there are cases "where the rights of private owners, although themselves perfectly legitimate, ought not to prevail against the public interest." Of two kinds of property recognised by the law is one to be regarded as the less defensible (and therefore the most susceptible to attack) than the other? Is a fried-fish-and-chip shop in Balham to secure a higher degree of protection than a kind of property which Lord Hailsham appears to find socially undesirable—ground-rents in Cardiff owned by a limited company in London (presumably a limited company with its registered office in London)? And who is to assess the nature and quality of the "public interest" which Lord Hailsham assumes ought to prevail against the legitimate, though compensated, interests of private owners? Is it a District Valuer? Is it the Lands Tribunal? And, indeed, on what scale ought compensation for the expropriation of private interests to be paid? To say [19] that "proper compensation should be paid" is, in effect, to say nothing.

The difficulties in the way of being usefully precise were illustrated during the debate in the House of Commons on February 21, 1958, on the second reading of a private member's Bill, the Compensation (Acquisition and Planning) Bill, which was carried in spite of the lack of government support. It appeared from that debate [20] that Conservatives accepted as fully as did Labour members the principle that the interest of the individual should not be allowed to stand in the way of the interest of the community. What the Government did not accept, what no Conservative government since 1951 has accepted, was the principle that the individual interest is of so much importance to society that its owner ought to receive compensation at ordinary market rates for its destruction or for injuries which reduce its value.

Yet the Conservative conscience is not insensitive to the claims of property. If it has no comprehensive defence to offer it has a partial substitute for it, embodied in the phrase, "a property-owning democracy." We can turn to Lord Hailsham for an interpretation of this.

"According to Conservatives, the aim of every man may legitimately include the possession of enough private property to own, if he so desires it, a house and garden, to bring up a family including the provision of a slightly better education than the *table d'hôte* afforded by the State, to indulge a reasonable hobby or leisure-time occupation and to end in his old age with a little more than the State pension, however generous." [21]

It is fair to say that Lord Hailsham does not explicitly describe more ambitious aims as illegitimate. It is perhaps not unfair to say that the Conservative ideal has become the man who is buying with the assistance of a building society or a local authority the house he lives in; who runs a car (perhaps secured by a hire-purchase agreement); who is able to send his son to a cheap public-school or at least to procure him extra tuition for the admission examination to a grammar school; who follows some inexpensive hobby; and who will not, when he retires, be wholly dependent on his old age pension. Few Conservatives would regard these modest aims as unworthy or decline to recognise their realisation as being within the Conservative tradition. But some might well question the degree of stability and permanence afforded by such an existence: very much at the mercy of changes in the bank-rate and the rate of interest on mortgages, or changes in purchase-tax, petrol duty and hire-purchase regulations; always at the mercy of schemes for compulsory acquisition and purchase. Lord Salisbury regarded it as the primary duty of Conservatism to give a sense of confidence: the degree of confidence possible in the conditions noted cannot be a very high one.

It is sufficiently clear that property has become far less important as part of the Conservative tradition than it formerly was. Almost entirely divorced from the exercise of political rights, it has come to be regarded as something in the nature of a cushion which will at least give its possessor a slightly better position than that of someone who is wholly dependent on the provisions made for him and his family by the State. A man so favoured, though he is unlikely to be able to do without the allowances, benefits and pensions offered to him by the State or its agents, will be able to supplement them.

It is a temptation, at the end of such a survey as this, to enlarge upon recent developments, despite the danger of losing one's sense of proportion and of seeing as a turning-point what may in a few years appear to be no more than one of the sinuosities of politics. Even so, some of the legislative measures recently passed or now under discussion demand a brief notice. The Housing Repairs and Rents Act, 1954, and the Rent Act, 1957, represented attempts to make the ownership of house property economically viable. The Life Peerages Act, 1958, may or may not be the beginning of an effort to reform the powers as well as the composition of the House of Lords. In the Commons on October 31, and in the Lords on November 27, 1957, the Government announced its acceptance in principle of a considerable number of the recommendations made by the Franks Committee on Administrative Tribunals and Enquiries[22] ; and the County Agricultural Executive Committees have been deprived of the disciplinary powers conferred on them by Part II of the Agriculture Act, 1947.

These developments, with the possible exception of the Rent Act, are modest; certainly not such as can properly be described as revolutionary. They do not justify the suggestion that Conservative policy has become reactionary (using that word in a neutral or even in a favourable sense). They scarcely justify the more moderate suggestion that Conservative policy has ceased to be fundamentally acquiescent. What they may represent is a consideration of the problems created by continued acquiescence. There had been built up by collectivist legislation a mass of new vested interests: the interest of the tenant of a privately owned house protected by the Rent Restriction Acts; the interest of the agricultural tenant largely protected against dispossession by his landlord and not ill-protected against increases of rent by the Agriculture Act, 1947. Indeed, it is significant that neither landowners nor tenant-farmers were enthusiastic about the removal of the disciplinary powers of the County Agricultural Executive Committees: many of them regarded the existence of these powers—especially as they became increasingly ineffective—as a cheap obligation to bear for the reward of guaranteed prices. It was open to the Government to continue the full protection afforded to such interests and to create new ones. This they have declined to do. Their action, though limited to a narrow range, perhaps justifies the suggestion that, although the Conservative tradition in the last half-century has been largely one of acquiescence, it still contains elements which allow of an occasional check to that process.

NOTES

1. Lady Victoria Hicks Beach, *The Life of Sir Michael Hicks Beach, Earl St. Aldwyn,* Vol. II, p. 138 (2 vols., London, 1932).

2. To cite only one instance, Henry Carter's *The English Temperance Movement* (London, 1933) explains the several and sometimes incompatible objectives of temperance reformers, ranging from "partial abstinence" (abstinence from the use of spirits as distinct from beer and wine) to statutory regulation or prohibition of the sale of all intoxicating liquors.

3. *e.g.,* Vol. II, pp. 226, 235 (3 vols., London, 1953-55).

4. Quoted, R. J. White, *The Conservative Tradition,* pp. 32 – 33 (London, 1950).

5. *Signpost Booklets,* p. 3 (London, 1943).

6. Pp. 10, 11 (Penguin Books, 1947).

7. Vol. 130, No. 781, p. 197 (March, 1948).

8. *Stanley Baldwin,* p. 101 (London, 1952).

9. R. J. White, *op. cit.,* p. 33.

10. Robert Blake, *The Unknown Prime Minister,* p. 129 (London, 1955).

11. R. T. McKenzie, *British Political Parties,* pp. 223-226 (London, 1955). There remains the question whether, at any given moment, a Conservative cabinet or the National Union has the better claim to be regarded as the representative of Conservative tradition. Neither has an exclusive claim, but, on the grounds of constitutional organisation and historical fact, the cabinet has the better.

12. Embodied in Lord Lansdowne's amendment of July 4, 1911, to the effect that no Bill which affected the Crown or the Protestant succession, which made provision for Home Rule in Ireland or which raised "an issue of great gravity on which the judgment of the country has not been sufficiently ascertained" should become law "unless and until it has been submitted to, and approved by, the electors in a manner to be hereinafter provided by Act of Parliament."

13. G. M. Young, *op. cit.,* pp. 124-125.

14. *R. v. Tearse* [1945] K.B. 1.

15. *Principles or Prejudices,* p. 5.

16. *Parliamentary Debates (Commons),* 1956-57, Vol. 575, cols. 401 *et seq.*

17. Quoted, R. J. White, *op. cit.,* p. 85.

18. Pp. 97 – 102.

19. P. 102.

20. *Parliamentary Debates (Commons),* Vol. 582, cols. 1541 *et seq.*

21. *Op. cit.,* p. 99.

22. The Government did not, however, accept the recommendations of the Franks Committee regarding the appointment of members of Tribunals and of Inspectors. It proposed to keep these in the hands of the Ministers concerned, subject to consultation with the new Council on Tribunals in the one case and the Lord Chancellor on the other.

Throughout its history, the Labour party, like many modern political parties, has been characterized by friction and sometimes confusion about ultimate aims and proximate means. By and large, the mainstream of the party has been reformist, seeking to improve economic and social conditions by parliamentary means, paying lip service to the ultimate creation of a socialist commonwealth, but dedicated in action to the gradual achievement of specific and limited goals. A minority of the Labour party, in their own view more dedicated socialists than the majority, have in one form or another demurred. Disillusioned by the slow progress of parliamentary action, they have criticized gradualism— "Labourism" as it has come to be called—and demanded a root-and-branch attack upon the ills of society. Often their strictures have been more apparent than their prescriptions for action, but their attitudes raise questions about the viability of a major party that this article by implication and the subsequent essay directly attempt to address. Richard W. Lyman's piece has two purposes. It makes clear how divided opinion was, especially in the nineteen-thirties, about whether parliamentary tactics could lead to significant change in the social order. And it demonstrates as well how much the controversy continued after the thirties by an examination of subsequent orthodox and left-wing interpretations of Labour's experience. Richard W. Lyman is Professor of History and President of Stanford University. He is the author of The First Labour Government, 1924 *(London, 1958). His essay is reprinted from the* Journal of British Studies, *V (November, 1965), 140–52.*

The British Labour Party: The Conflict between Socialist Ideals and Practical Politics between the Wars

RICHARD W. LYMAN

The purpose of this paper is to set forth, somewhat arbitrarily, a composite view of the British Labour Party's history between the Wars, to be labelled the orthodox Labour interpretation, and then to set against it a contrasting view which has been expressed by several left-wing writers within the Labour Party. This examination of conflicting opinions can scarcely be dignified with the title historiographical inquiry. In the first place, there are other more or less coherent interpretations of Labour Party history in this period besides the two sketched herein, most notably a Communist view, expressed in such works as Allen Hutt's *The Post-War History of the British Working Class*.[1] Secondly, as Stephen Graubard has recently said in relation to the Fabian Society, much of the Labour Party history in this period is in fact autobiography.[2] Finally, as will soon become distressingly apparent, the interpretations that most writers have given of Labour between the Wars have been influenced by, connected with, even in some cases identical to the same authors' views on Labour today. History used to be called "past politics"; in this case it cannot entirely escape becoming "present politics."

I

According to the orthodox view, the Labour Party was emerging from its infancy in the 1920s, having established its claim to be considered a major contestant for power as recently as 1918. As Francis Williams puts it:

> With the acceptance of the new constitution and the endorsement of the international policy contained in the Memorandum on War Aims and the domestic programme con-

tained in *Labour and the New Social Order,* the Labour Party finally established itself. The formative years were ended. Now at last it was an adult party certain of its own purpose; aware also at last of what it must do to impress that purpose upon the nation. [3]

This "adult party" went on to make electoral progress, particularly in 1922, '23, and '29, which, though incomplete, far exceeded any prewar accomplishments. It even held office twice as His Majesty's Government. Granted, the interwar Labour Governments were something less than triumphs. But in each case, it is argued, Labour was hampered by inexperience, by lack of a clear majority in the House of Commons, by the increasing weariness and conservatism of some of its leading figures, and (especially in 1930 – 31) by a world economic crisis beyond the control of *any* British Government. At that, both minority Governments enjoyed significant successes, such as Ramsay MacDonald's conduct of foreign affairs and John Wheatley's Housing Act during the first Labour Government, and Arthur Henderson's foreign policy during the second. Williams even dares to praise the second Labour Government's efforts to help the jobless: "In normal times," he writes, "these schemes would have represented a notable offensive against unemployment—the greatest indeed ever made by any British Government." [4]

On the other hand, according to the orthodox view, Labour learned from its failures. After the General Strike of 1926 there were no more general strikes (indeed very few strikes of any kind); after the two minority Labour Governments there were no more minority Labour Governments (not as yet, anyhow). More than that, following the traumatic defeat and "betrayal" of 1931, Labour set about defining its program and reinforcing its socialist determination, so as to be ready to take over at last when the British electorate should have come to its senses and overthrown the "National" Coalition—which ought to have happened in or about 1940, but understandably got delayed until 1945. Labour then swept to power, backed by the superb political machine which Herbert Morrison had built while the Tories were not looking, and the ensuing Labour Government proceeded to put into effect the program prepared in the wilderness. Even the normally modest Clement Attlee, recalling his book, *The Labour Party in Perspective,* says, "In considering the future, I set out the programme which I thought a Labour Government in power should carry out. In 1945 I had the pleasure of seeing that programme implemented." [5] There was no more of the unseemly fumbling of the interwar Governments, no more feeble imitation of the senior parties, no more doubt as to what the right socialist reading of Britain's economic tea leaves should be. The only reason why this did not lead to " 'the complete political extinction of the Tory Party, and twenty-five years of Labour Government,' " as Aneurin Bevan demanded, [6] was the bad luck of happening to inherit the postwar era of austerity. The electorate, mistaking wartime privation for socialist planning, reacted against both and sent Labour back to the wilderness, where the Party languished until 1964.

II

The left-wing is somewhat different. It has been ably expressed in such recent books as Ralph Miliband's *Parliamentary Socialism* and Michael Foot's biography of Aneurin Bevan. The failures of the 1920s are, of course, more frankly faced and labelled in this version; indeed, they are if anything exaggerated. But more important, the causes of these failures are seen, not as the result of inexperience or a few personal shortcomings, and still less of outside forces beyond British control. [7] Failure came, according to the Left, as the inevitable result of a more fundamental flaw in the British Labour movement, the error of Gradualism; or, if one gives it a slightly different emphasis, of Labourism; [8] or, if one wishes to become really unpleasant about it, MacDonaldism. Miliband even has a chapter entitled, "MacDonaldism Without MacDonald," thereby showing in one phrase what he thinks of Messrs. Attlee, Morrison, Ernest Bevin, *et al.* in the 1930s.

Gradualism was wrong, it is argued, because it assumed that the development of socialism could take place within the context of the ordinary political struggle of the Ins and the Outs, the traditional party parliamentary game. Gradualists imagined that socialism could be achieved by instalments, each instalment being accepted with no more serious obstruction on the part of the Conservatives than Labour oppositions generally gave to Tory governments. Each instalment would then remain, unharmed by interludes of Tory rule, and ready to serve as the foundation on which the next Labour government would resume construction of the socialist commonwealth. The Gradualists failed to recognize that socialism is not just an extension of state activity for the sake of providing more social services and an increased role for the government in economic life; it is not, as one bitter phrase put it, "merely capitalism plus the National Health Service." It is not just that the players must be different; the very rules of the economic, political, and social game must undergo sweeping alterations. Socialism by instalments, then, merely serves to warn the capitalist enemy, to give him time in which to prepare his defenses—and worse yet, his counterattack. [9] The Left argues that failure to see this, on the part of Labour Party leaders, weakened them at critical moments. It made them too quick to accept half a loaf, too confident that the other half could be acquired at the next turn of the political wheel.

But that is not all. Gradualism is also accused of having weakened Labour's appeal to the public, by removing its distinctiveness. Thus in 1935, especially, it became easy for the wily Stanley Baldwin to steal Labour's clothing and so win the general election. Since both parties proclaimed their faith in the League of Nations, and Labour's socialist message was allegedly blurred by love of compromise and parliamentary good manners, the electorate was left with no very compelling reason to evict the Government. To borrow an expression from mid-twentieth-century American politics, the Left charges the official leadership in the interwar years with "me-tooism" vis-à-vis the Conservatives. Finally and ironically, assert the critics, all this compromising did not save the Gradualists from the effects of Tory misrepresentation and manipulation of the electorate's fears and prejudices in 1924, 1931, and 1935.

III

It is time to look critically at these two interpretations, and first at some flaws in the orthodox view. For one thing, the failures in the 1920s not only owed a great deal to the failure to define the Party's economic program and policies—this the orthodox, safely post-Keynesian, will admit freely enough. But difficulties also stemmed from an excessive concern to appear respectable, so that the electorate would understand that Labour was indeed "fit to govern." The wound that Winston Churchill administered to Labour by suggesting in the early 1920s that they were *not* thus fit was indeed a lasting one. As late as 1936, when Hugh Dalton was lamenting in his diary the vacillations of the Party over rearmament, it was in those words that he recorded his exasperation: " 'Plenty of "consultation." Awfully wearisome. We *are* unfit to govern.' " [10] It was not only Ramsay MacDonald, with his love of Court Dress and his dislikes of "The Red Flag," who was guilty of paying too much heed to such considerations. One sees the lengths to which the Labour trimmers would go demonstrated in the struggle that it took to get nationalization of the coal mines—the oldest of socialist proposals in Britain—included in the immediate program which the Parliamentary Party Executive drafted in February 1929 in expectation of a Labour government. [11] It can be argued that concern to appear respectable played some part in the biggest failure of all, concerning unemployment. True, most Labour people clung to fiscal orthodoxy mainly from an honest reluctance to challenge the supported experts in an esoteric field. But there was also a failure to recognize that one could not very well hope to supplant capitalism while taking all one's financial advice from the banking and brokerage community. Perhaps a little of the inverse snobbery so beloved of the Left might have proven useful as a corrective to a surfeit of deference to Montagu Norman and his friends.

The orthodox interpretation also errs in taking too cheerful a view of Labour's recovery from the 1931 disaster.[12] It is claimed that the Party quickly set about providing itself with the program and the socialist determination that made possible the successful legislation of 1945 – 50.[13] This view greatly exaggerates the continuity between proposals developed during the 1930s and those actually carried out in the later 1940s. Probably most people would agree that one of the most important achievements of the 1945 Government was the establishment of the National Health Service. Yet where in the documents laboriously ground out of the Party Conferences of the 1930s does this great scheme appear? The 1934 program, *For Socialism and Peace,* promises a State Health Service, and refers the reader to a National Executive Subcommittee Report bearing that title, and published as Appendix VI to the 1934 Annual Report. Following this lead, one encounters a document less than three pages long, making no pretensions to finality, setting forth only the most general outlines of a scheme, and warning not only that the service must needs be developed "by stages," but also that even the first stage could not be achieved immediately by a Labour Government. A more detailed report was promised for the next year's Conference. Dr. Somerville Hastings remarked, "The scheme is only in embryo [appropriate metaphor for an M.D.], and I do want to urge the Executive to carry on with what is admittedly a very difficult task."[14] Apparently the difficulty proved too great, or other matters too pressing; no further report was presented before the War.[15]

A similar tale could be told of most other aspects of the 1945 Government's work. As Arnold Rogow puts it: "In 1945 the policies and programme of the Labour Government were, to a large extent, inherited from the war time, Conservative-dominated Coalition Government."[16] This was especially true of the planning machinery. As for nationalization, everyone is familiar with Emanuel Shinwell's bland admission: " 'We are about to take over the mining industry. It is not so easy as it looks. I have been talking about nationalisation for forty years but the implications of the transfer of property have never occurred to me.' "[17] If one prefers to bypass Shinwell, with his record of fairly consistent eccentricity, there is the sober acknowledgement of Robert Brady that "with the partial exceptions of transport and steel, all of the nationalization, or semi-nationalization programs [of the 1945 Government] were based squarely on findings, and in large part on recommendations, which had been made by Conservative-dominated fact-finding and special investigating committees."[18]

The orthodox view tends also to paint a misleading picture of a steady and inexorable march towards power, once Labour had recovered from the immediate shock of 1931. According to Shinwell, for example, "The high expectations of the Party after the election of 1935 that within three or four years the Baldwin-Chamberlain combination would have failed in both economic and international affairs, and that another general election would bring victory to the Labour cause, was now to be frustrated by war." [19] Even G. D. H. Cole, not unduly disposed to overestimate the strength or unity of Labour between the Wars, makes the same point by implication: "The [wartime] Electoral Truce was from the first widely disliked by Local [Labour] Parties which saw themselves deprived of the chance of seats they hoped to win. Its effect was inevitably unfavorable to Labour, which had been the attacking party and was still seriously under-represented in the Parliament elected in 1935." [20] The continuing disunity of the Party is largely discounted as the persistent nagging of a tiny minority—the Socialist League and its friends—who are regularly voted down by the solid sense of the trade union delegates. Yet here is the view of R. H. Tawney, generally a cheerful and kindly man, as relayed by Sidney Webb in February 1934:

> Tawney said that the most serious thing was the total absence in the Labour party of any *common* mind—everyone insisted on his own particular views, magnifying all the differences. Cole was hopelessly uncooperative, and changeable at that. The younger intellectuals mostly supporting Stafford [Cripps]. The rank and file of Labour Conference impatient with the National Executive, which was itself incompetent and had no leadership. He agreed that we must not trouble about the next election, and look only to seven years hence. [21]

Certainly "the next election" did turn out to be a disappointment. Some recovery from the depths of 1931 was inevitable, but to wind up with only 154 seats "was a poor total," as Dalton said. [22] Nor was there much sign of forward movement in the later 1930s. David Butler, analyzing the by-elections, argues quite convincingly that Labour was, if anything, *losing* ground electorally after 1933. [23] It is at the very least extremely doubtful that Labour was headed for victory, had the expected election of 1940 not been postponed five years by the War.

The orthodox version of Labour's interwar history, then, errs on the side of overoptimism, underrates the disunity and blurred vision of the Party, puts too much emphasis upon extraordinary factors as the explanation for Labour's limited achievement in this period. But is the view from the Left more accurate or helpful?

IV

Underlying the left-wing interpretation there are two unresolved questions, which confronted the Left politicians at the time and have faced historians sympathetic with the Left ever since. First, how can one achieve a mandate for revolutionary change in a profoundly unrevolutionary society? And second, even if such a mandate is forthcoming, how can the cumbersome processes of parliamentary democracy, created to safeguard individual rights and to tame autocratic power, become the effective instruments for carrying out that change? [24] To Michael Foot or Ralph Miliband or Raymond Williams it is distasteful, even perhaps immoral, for Labour to accept the role of a mere political party. They require a more exalted view than that. For them, Labour exists as a social movement, which aims at a fundamental reordering of society. It must be revolutionary in every sense but that of requiring violence at the barricades. From this it follows, for the Left, that Labour cannot afford to accept the conventional limits upon the activities proper for a British political party. To have done so was to have played the enemy's game. Indeed, the situation was worse than that, for the enemy, meanwhile, felt free to ignore these same conventions whenever it suited him; Labour, it is argued, has always behaved far more tamely in opposition than have the Tories. [25] Repeatedly, the moderate leadership of the Labour Party is castigated by the left-wing historians for excessive devotion to parliamentary methods and established canons of political propriety; indeed, this is the central thesis of Miliband's book.

Yet the critics, too, are committed democrats, and this does limit their freedom in suggesting alternative paths which Labour could have followed. Since Miliband has addressed himself to this question more directly than most—it is to his credit that he thus recognizes its importance—his retrospective advice deserves consideration. He is discussing the shortcomings of Labour's attack on Chamberlain's appeasement policy in the later 1930s:

> There were many things the Labour leaders could have done. They could, to begin with, have embarked on an unremitting campaign of meetings, demonstrations, marches, rallies and petitions, all designed to mobilize a body of public opinion sufficiently strong to force the Government on to different courses, or to force changes in its leadership, or to sweep it out of office. Secondly, they could have used, indeed abused, their parliamentary opportunities to harass the Government, to obstruct its business, to refuse to participate in that sedate parliamentary minuet which was the Government's best guarantee against effective challenge. They could, thirdly, have sought to mobilize their industrial strength and used that strength as a means of pressure upon the Government . . . And they could also have sought to bring about a grand alliance of all those who opposed the Government so as to break the frozen political mould in which Britain was imprisoned.
>
> Of course, all this might have failed. The point is that the attempt was not made. There were parliamentary debates: there were manifestoes, declarations, pamphlets, meetings, and even half-hearted 'campaigns'. There was, in other words, little more than the traditional routine of Labour politics. [26]

In this quotation the essential barrenness of the left-wing case becomes quite clear. Consider its four main suggestions in order. The first closely approximates the Party's actual behavior in the 1930s, as the concluding paragraph of the quotation unintentionally makes clear; the difference is that "an unremitting campaign of meetings, demonstrations, marches, rallies and petitions" sounds very fierce, while "parliamentary debates . . . manifestoes, declarations, pamphlets, meetings, and even half-hearted 'campaigns' . . . little more than the traditional routine of Labour politics," sound feeble and futile. The contrast is more one of adjectives than of substance. No genuine devotee of revolutionary strategy and tactics could find anything very interesting in Miliband's first recommendation.

His second might at first glance appear more promising. But just how was the Labour Party, 154-strong, to have "refused to participate" in Parliament without being hammered by the cloture or dragooned by fresh tightening of the rules of procedure? Would it have been better for the Parliamentary Labour Party to have emulated the Foxite Whigs of an earlier day and simply withdrawn from Westminster? To ask the question is virtually to answer it. The point is clear: either organized parliamentary obstruction becomes a revolutionary act or it stops shorts of that, and ends in futility. In any case, the British public showed no sign of wanting a breakdown of Parliament added to their sea of troubles in the Nazi era. There is no evidence that they would have supported a party which resorted to such a strategy.

Miliband's third point, that Labour could have called on the trade unions to use their "strength as a means of pressure upon the Government," is no more realistic. Chastened by the humiliations of the General Strike, husbanding their strength through the ordeal of the depression, convinced that progress was more likely to be had by collaboration than by all-out war against employers and the Government, the British trade unions were not available for such adventures as Miliband suggests. This is quite aside from the question whether political strikes are not rather dubious tactics for a democratic party.

Finally, there is Miliband's clinching argument: Labour "could also have sought to bring about a grand alliance of all those who opposed the Government so as to break the frozen political mould in which Britain was imprisoned." This is, in short, the Popular Front, which was certainly not without vocal advocates in the Britain of the 1930s. Whether Labour ought to have been more ready to collaborate with nonsocialist opponents of the Government may still be debated. But what is interesting in the present context is the flagrant contradiction between Miliband's fourth point and his previous three. Labour, he argues, ought to have adopted an all-out, raging, tearing campaign with no holds barred and scant regard for constitutional propriety; it ought to have behaved with the parliamentary manners of a Parnell and the industrial restraint of a militant syndicalist; and then it ought to have turned around and invited the wholehearted collaboration of the Churchillite Tories, the Samuelite Liberals, the nonparty moderates of the Five Years Group, and so on, in a Popular Front. In fact there was no practical hope of breaking "the political mould in which Britain was imprisoned" until the Tory critics of appeasement reached the point of being willing to come out in open opposition to the Chamberlain Government. This the Labour leadership understood, and said, at the time. [27] They understood also that neither Eden nor Churchill would find any appeal in a policy of Parnellism in the Commons and political strikes in the defense industries. Without the Tory dissidents, what is left of the Popular Front? It is hard to take seriously the suggestion that the National Government might somehow have wilted had Labour been willing to add the Communists and the dwindling I.L.P. at one end, and Herbert Samuel's little band at the other. [28]

The problem for the Left, in short, was to find an escape from Gradualism without losing sight of parliamentary democracy. It was never solved by the Labour Left politicians of the interwar years, and it has not been solved by their scholarly adherents since. The nearest that Sir Stafford Cripps, Harold Laski, and the rest ever came to a solution was in the years immediately following the 1931 debacle. This defeat suggested to them that any future socialist government, even though duly elected with a majority in Parliament, would meet desperate, last-ditch resistance, of an unconstitutional nature, from the defenders of the old regime. To counter this, Labour would have to resort to strong-arm methods of its own, in self-defense. Otherwise the people's will would be frustrated. [29] There is no doubt that to Cripps, at least, this pessimistic answer to the question, "Can Socialism Come by Constitutional Methods?" [30] was painful; it is most unlikely that he saw it as a means of reconciling loyalty to the democratic faith with advocacy of dictatorial powers for a future Labour government. But this was nevertheless the outcome, and it is hardly surprising that Tory propagandists had a field day with Sir Stafford's speculations about the necessity of the next Labour government's resorting to rule by ministerial decrees and perhaps prolonging the life of Parliament so as to ward off capitalist vengeance at the polls. Interestingly enough, Cripp's views did find partial expression in the paragraph on parliamentary government at the end of Labour's 1934 manifesto, "For Socialism and Peace." As several speakers pointed out at the time, however, the Party was careful to hedge its commitments concerning the possible need for special powers. [31]

The whole argument may have now a rather unreal air about it in the light of the calmness with which Britain took the Labour victory of 1945. [32] But it was highly significant of the division of opinion in the Party in the 1930s. To the Left, it was only natural to expect a crisis, not only because Labour had been the victim of considerable crisis-manipulation before, but also because they intended a Labour victory to represent more than an ordinary change of government. It was to be a revolution, bloodless (they hoped), but nevertheless fatal, in the very short run, for the existing order of society in Britain. Why should the titled, the property-owning, and the privileged *not* resort to desperate measures, if Labour meant business, and its business was the eradication of these elements in society?

But to the orthodox majority, it seemed equally self-evident that all the speculation about future resistance to a Labour victory was jeopardizing the chances for that victory in the first place. The delegate from the Penryn and Falmouth Divisional Labour Party, a young man named A. L. Rowse, asked the Conference in 1934, "Why should we go about the country giving everybody the impression that the moment there is a Labour majority declared in the country there is going to be a first-class crisis? It is very bad propaganda and tactics." [33] Politicians are normally the last people in the world to borrow trouble. And the orthodox majority in the Labour Party of the 1920s and '30s were in this, as in most other respects, normal politicians.

Is this, then, the nub of the "conflict between socialist ideals and practical politics"? Hardly, for both sides at the time were intensely preoccupied with what they took to be "practical politics," and not least the "practical politics" of winning a following for their respective points of view within the Labour Party. The conflict seems to have concerned issues of strategy and tactics to be used for attaining the socialist millennium, more than the shape of the millennium itself. Perhaps it is significant that, when Labour finally did come to power in 1945, it was that most outspoken member of the left wing, Aneurin Bevan, who carried through the most successful and, American Medical Association views to the contrary notwithstanding, one of the least ideological of the Government's achievements, the National Health Service. It will be interesting to see how Michael Foot, in his second volume, interprets this triumph of political pragmatism.

NOTES

1. Allen Hutt, *The Post-War History of the British Working Class* (London, 1937).

2. Stephen Graubard, review of A. McBriar, *Fabian Socialism and English Politics*, in *A.H.R.*, LXIX (1963), 116–17.

3. Francis Williams, *Fifty Years March* (London, 1949), p. 284.

4. Williams, *Fifty Years March,* p. 336. Cf. Elie Halévy, *L'ère des tyrannies* (Paris, 1938), p. 204: "Bizarre ironie! Le parti qui était censé détenir la clef du problème [of unemployment] se trouvait incapable de la résoudre. Je sais, naturellement, quelle était leur excuse: ils ne pouvaient rien faire parce qu'ils n'avaient pas la majorité absolue. Mais n' étaient-ils pas, au fond de leur coeur, ravis de ne pas l'avoir, parce que les responsibilitiés du pouvoir les épouvantaient?"

5. Clement Attlee, *As It Happened* (London, 1954), p. 87.

6. Quoted in Michael Foot, *Aneurin Bevan,* I (London, 1962), 505.

7. The Labour Left, like the Tory Right, has generally tended to minimize the importance of such forces, from the days when it pictured Lloyd George as losing the peace in 1919 almost singlehandedly to those when it imagined that Mao Tse-tung and Gen. DeGaulle would tamely follow a British example in nuclear disarmament, were Britain to set one.

8. A word given currency by the title of T. A. Rothstein's *From Chartism to Labourism* (London, 1929), and revived by the New Left more recently.

9. See Arnold Rogow, *The Labour Government and British Industry, 1945 – 1951* (Oxford, 1955), esp. chs. vii-viii, for an effective analysis of the Conservative and business community response to the socialist threat in the later stages of the third Labour Government.

10. Hugh Dalton, *The Fateful Years* (London, 1957), p. 88.

11. Hugh Dalton, *Call Back Yesterday* (London, 1953), pp. 182-83.

12. Clement Attlee, in *The Labour Party in Perspective* (London, 1937), p. 59, goes about as far as one can go: "While the immediate shock was severe, the general effect on the Party was salutary. It led to a re-examination of its fundamental position. It caused a reaffirmation of its aims and objects."

13. See, e.g., G. D. H. Cole, *A History of the Labour Party from 1914* (London, 1948), pp. 278 – 79. "The Party Executive had made up its mind that such vagueness [as had characterized previous programs] would not do, and that the coming years of opposition must be devoted to working out a clear and concise policy which the Party would be pledged and able to translate into legislation when its chance came. This was unquestionably wise; and in fact the Policy Reports which were put forward at every Conference from 1932 onwards did serve as the foundation for the third Labour Government's legislative and administrative programme in 1945; so that the main difficulties over policy then arose in fields which had been surveyed inadequately, or not at all, or where the situation had changed so greatly as to make the programmes devised before 1939 no longer workable in the post-war world" (p. 279). The concluding words do provide an escape hatch, but the emphasis is clearly on the relevance of the planning of the 1930s to the post-1945 policies; discrepancies between the two are made to seem the exception rather than the rule.

14. Labour Party, *Report of the Annual Conference,* 1934, pp. 214 – 15. A pressure group within the Labour movement, the Socialist Medical Association, had prepared a more detailed scheme, published in 1933 as *A Socialized Medical Service.* But this differed significantly from the N.H.S. as finally enacted; see the summary of the S.M.A. proposals in Harry Eckstein, *The English Health Service* (Cambridge, Mass., 1958), pp. 107 – 08.

15. See *A National Service for Health* (London, Labour Party, 1942 – 43). J. and S. Jewkes, *The Genesis of the National Health Service* (London, 1961), p. 3, point out that it was "not until the publication of the Government's White Paper on Health Services in 1944 that the vital switch of policy was made from the idea of the public provision of a *minimum* service to the provision of the *best possible* Health Service for all." Italics in original.

16. Rogow, *Labour Government and British Industry*, p. 2.

17. Quoted in *ibid.*, p. 155. See also Emanuel Shinwell, *Conflict Without Malice* (London, 1955), pp. 172 – 73.

18. He proceeds to enumerate these. Robert Brady, *Crisis in Britain* (Berkeley, 1950), p. 41. As a crude measure of the distance between Labour's program in the 1930s and the policies actually carried out in 1945 – 51, see Attlee's comments on coal in *Labour Party in Perspective*, p. 186: "The internal price of coal need not be affected by the world price. It is a matter for decision as to how much coal we should sell abroad. . . . The Coal Board will get the best prices that it can, whether in competition or, preferably, by international agreement, but, whichever it is, there is no reason why it should affect the wage of the miner." It is significant also that when Charles Mowat, in "The Approach to the Welfare State in Great Britain," *A.H.R.*, LVIII (1952), 55 – 63, wishes to cover the interwar years, he does not discuss Labour Party programs and reports, but rather such books as those of Eleanor Rathbone, or Sir John Boyd Orr's *Food, Health, and Income* (London, 1937), and then moves on to the crucial contribution of Britain's experience in World War II.

19. Emanuel Shinwell, *The Labour Story* (London, 1963), p. 162.

20. Cole, *History of the Labour Party*, p. 399.

21. London Library of Political and Economic Science, University of London, Sidney Webb to Beatrice Webb, Feb. 4, 1934, Webb Papers, II 3 (i), item 94. Quoted by kind permission of the Passfield Trustees.

22. Dalton, *The Fateful Years*, pp. 74 – 76.

23. D. E. Butler, *The Electoral System in Great Britain, 1918 – 1951* (Oxford, 1953), p. 184. See R. B. McCallum and A. Readman, *The British General Election of 1945* (London, 1947), pp. 266 – 67, for a suggestive analysis of the conditions prerequisite to Labour victory, most of which materialized as a result of the War.

24. The latter dilemma is eloquently stated, in another context, by Peter Gay in the preface to his *The Dilemma of Democratic Socialism: Eduard Bernstein's Challenge to Marx* (New York, 1952).

25. Robert Dowse, "The Parliamentary Labour Party in Opposition," *Parliamentary Affairs*, XIII (1960), 520 – 29.

26. Ralph Miliband, *Parliamentary Socialism* (London, 1961), pp. 233 – 34.

27. See the National Executive's manifesto issued on May 1937 entitled "The Labour Party and the Popular Front"; relevant passages are quoted in Cole, *History of the Labour Party*, p. 354. It is clear that the attitude of the Labour leadership would have changed had a major Tory breakaway been likely—see Dalton, *The Fateful Years*, ch. xiv.

28. Yet after the War Cole could still say, in discussing not the Popular Front but the narrower United Front of Labour, Communists, and I.L.P.: "Even a strictly limited unity for the purpose of the common struggle agaisnt Fascism might have made a vital differ-

ence to the course of events." What this difference might have been he does not disclose. Cole, *History of the Labour Party*, p. 291.

29. See Harold Laski, *The Crisis and the Constitution* (London, 1932), and *Democracy in Crisis* (Chapel Hill, 1933).

30. Title of Sir Stafford Cripps's pamphlet, reprinted in Christopher Addison *et al.*, *Problems of a Socialist Government* (London, 1933).

31. See *Report of the Annual Conference,* 1934, pp. 149 – 50.

32. But see Rogow, *Labour Government and British Industry*, esp. ch. ix, for evidence suggesting that the triumph of Gradualism may have been more apparent than real, and that Laski's fears of the 1930s may have been closer to the mark than his opinion towards the end of his life.

33. *Report of the Annual Conference,* 1934, p. 162.

Overlapping the previous article and using some of its material, the present selection moves on to investigate the contemporary condition of the Labour party in the light of its past. The conclusion takes issue with a substantial body of critics, among them scholars as well as "practicing" politicians, who have seen in the divisions within the party auguries of disintegration and displacement. The author concludes that the party's variety was probably an element of strength as it rose to power in the twentieth century, and that its future success may indeed depend upon its continued appeal to a broad spectrum of the electorate rather than to a strictly working-class constituency. Henry R. Winkler is University Professor of History and Senior Vice President for Acadamic Affairs at Rutgers University. His article, originally the Taft Lectures in History at the University of Cincinnati, was first published in Han-Kyo Kim, ed., Essays on Modern Politics and History Written in Honor of Harold M. Vinacke *(Athens, Ohio, 1969). It is reprinted by permission of the Taft Fund of the University of Cincinnati and of the Ohio University Press.* [1]

7 The British Labour Party in the Contemporary World

HENRY R. WINKLER

I | At Home

During the past two decades, the Labour Party has been by far the most successful of all the major western Europe parties professing the ideology of democratic socialism. In Germany, the Social Democratic Party exists in name, but it has long since, for all practical purposes, abandoned even lip service to socialist ideas. In France and Italy, social democracy has been challenged by parties of the extreme Left—and has seemed unable to meet the challenge with cohesion, let alone success. In country after country, no viable political alternative has emerged to challenge the parties of modernized conservatism—Christian Democrats, Tories, Gaullists—parties that have been so prominent in the western world since 1945.

Yet in Great Britain, a Labour Party came into office for six years after a sweeping victory in 1945 and, after years in the wilderness during the fifties and early sixties, once again assumed control, with a House of Commons majority of almost a hundred seats. What has been the character of this party? What have been some of its problems? Why has it been successful? How do we explain its transformation from a narrow sectarian group into a national organization appealing—unevenly, to be sure—to more than a working-class constituency? How, in other words, do we assess the process by which the Labour Party became domesticated? How did it prepare for its contemporary exercise of power, however limited that power may have been in practice? Let me first concentrate on the home front, on internal issues, and then turn to foreign policy and international questions.

The contemporary Labour Party is almost exactly fifty years old. Its roots go back, of course, much further, to the political reforms of 1867 and 1884 which gave the franchise to manual workers but hardly provided guidance about how that franchise might be used. For decades, the defense of working-class interests had oscillated between industrial and political action, between trade union activity to improve the standards of labour and tentative efforts to collaborate with the dominant national parties in the hope that similar improvements might thus be fostered through conventional political channels.

By 1900 the trade union movement had come of age. Unskilled as well as highly-trained workers were organized in a series of societies more or less combined under the umbrella of a Trades Union Congress. And by that time, some at least of the leaders of Labour had become disillusioned with the effort to work through the existing political parties. For a time, the Liberal Party, a loose coalition with a radical wing of some strength, looked like a possible home for the working class. But by the end of the nineteenth century, for reasons almost all concerned with the special interests of particular groups in the Liberal Party, it seemed clear that middle-class Liberals at the local level were not ready to share office nor to formulate policies in cooperation with the increasingly impatient young leaders of the Labour movement.

But though the Labour Party was formed in 1900 (it was originally called the Labour Representation Committee and took the name Labour Party only in 1906), it was hardly an important force before the First World War. It had come into existence as a coalition of trade unionists and socialists. But some of the trade unions looked upon it with suspicion, and some of the moderate socialists, such as those in the Fabian Society, were not at all sure that independent political action was the answer to Labour's needs. Only the socialists of the small Independent Labour Party, founded in 1893 to send workingmen to Parliament, repeated some of the incantations of a nineteenth-century socialist dogma without making any considerable impact upon either their allies or the country as a whole.

From the beginning then, the Labour Party was a coalition of elements quite as disparate as the constituent forces of an American political party. And the disparity was at least as sharp between those who called themselves socialists as it was between them and the supposedly less profoundly dedicated leadership of the trade union movement. Sometimes its prewar experience has been analyzed in terms of the conflict between socialist ideals and practical politics. But a number of careful scholars—among them Philip Poirier, Henry

Pelling, Frank Bealey—have demonstrated in recent years how oversimplified such a formulation really is. [2]

Before the First World War the parliamentary position of the fledgling Labour Party was an exceedingly difficult one. Dependent upon the Liberals for most of its seats in the House of Commons and upon the trade unions for much else, limited by its leaders' commitment to parliamentary action and by their need to support piecemeal reform, the Labour Party remained a tail wagged by the massive Liberal bulldog of Prime Minister Herbert Henry Asquith and his chief lieutenant for domestic questions, David Lloyd George. Its parliamentary representatives hardly concerned themselves with any conflict between socialist ideals and practical politics. Rather they sought by compromise to make whatever gains were possible for the working class and above all to prevent their fragile party from being crushed in the Liberal embrace. For example, in order to gain Liberal support against a serious threat to Labour Party financing, the Party's secretary, a handsome, eloquent young Scot, James Ramsay MacDonald, felt compelled to strike a bargain in which he pledged his support for the contributory features of Lloyd George's new Insurance Bill, even though they were vehemently opposed by some members of his party. There was little question here of socialism, of course. The concern was with the survival of the parliamentary party and with the achievement of some fairly limited gains, mainly for the rank-and-file of trade unionists, whose leaders, but not necessarily themselves, supported the Labour Party.

Such ideological—as opposed to tactical—conflict as did exist came mostly within the ranks of the Fabian Society and especially of the Independent Labour Party. Philip Poirier, in a paper which so far as I know has not been published, [3] has shown how a growing minority became disillusioned with the policies pursued by MacDonald, flirted with continental schemes of direct action, became infatuated with alternatives to parliamentary action, and in some cases even wanted to sever their connection with the parliamentary party. From almost the beginning of its existence, then, the Labour Party did face the dissatisfaction of some of its constituent elements because its leaders' definition of the socialist future appeared to contain so little commitment to socialism in the intervening present. Yet I think it is clear that the socialist critics, however vehement their strictures, remained a vocal and even substantial, but not very effective minority throughout these early years. Those who wished to disaffiliate from the Labour Party or to jettison parliamentary politics in favor of direct action were at least logically consistent. But the rather ill-defined socialist touchstone of most of the disaffected hardly served as a serious criterion of action in the prewar state of democratic policies.

I have spent so much time on this early period because it seems to me that here we have the clue to the complex character of the Labour Party throughout its history—now as well as in 1900. Beyond this, I think that here we have the clue to its survival and its success. In contrast to the Labour Right, who have seen the millenial demands of the all-out activists—those who believed themselves alone to have imbibed the pure mother's milk of socialism—as a danger frightening away all moderate supporters of Labour; and in contrast to the Labour Left, who have seen "gradualism" as the main enemy threatening the soul of a future Socialist Commonwealth, I tend to see the tensions and the struggles within the Labour Party as contributing ultimately to its triumphs, rather than being responsible for the limited character of its accomplishments. How does one justify this paradox? Let me try, in the first place, by turning to the Party's history between the two World Wars.

Both the Labour Left and the Right can find arguments for their positions in that history. A tiny minority group before 1914—almost a coterie—the Labour Party became the official Opposition in the early twenties. Electoral progress was steady, and the Party even held office during two brief terms in 1924 and 1929 – 31. Ramsay MacDonald as Prime Minister in both these Labour Governments captured the imagination of many of his countrymen—and many foreigners—with his striking thatch of silver hair and his equally silver tongue. In the nineteen-thirties, after MacDonald had broken with the Party over how to cope with the Great Depression, Labour slowly made a comeback. In that decade foreign affairs, after the advent of Hitlerism in Germany, became the touchstone of all policy. Although Labour suffered from a kind of schizophrenia on international questions in the era of appeasement, it nevertheless presented the only viable non-Conservative alternative to policies that even some Conservatives—Winston Churchill is of course the prime example—regarded as disastrous. And, once Churchill came to power in 1940, the leaders of the Labour Party became his chief lieutenants in the governance of England. Altogether an interesting, if somewhat puzzling, history. How has it been interpreted by those in the Labour Party to whom their history is, after all, part of the contemporary struggles within the Labour movement?

In the years before 1918, the conventional interpretation has gone, the Labour Party was, to be sure, a confederation of disparate groups. But once the war itself had opened up new possibilities, Sidney Webb and Ramsay MacDonald and Arthur Henderson—the so-called architects of the new party—had responded by working out an effective new constitution. No longer was the Party a mere coalition of pressure groups, but now it was able to forge ahead on a new basis, attracting members directly and finding a new cohesion and a new unity. Of course, there remained the cleavage—or at least the differences—as between the great trade union phalanx and the more socialist-minded brethren from the constituency parties. But such differences as appeared were minor and relatively unimportant, and in any event, usually reflected the instability of tiny splinter groups. The Party was clearly now committed to socialism, for did not Clause IV of the new constitution define the Party's aims as "the common ownership of the means of production, distribution and exchange"?

Richard Lyman [4] once used Francis Williams' book, *Fifty Years' March,* [5] to illustrate the orthodox interpretation. Williams, who was made a life peer in 1962 and died in 1970, had been a distinguished editor of Labour's *Daily Herald* between the wars and after 1945 served as Adviser on Public Relations to Prime Minister Clement Attlee. In his view:

> With the acceptance of the new constitution and the endorsement of the international policy contained in the Memorandum on War Aims and the domestic programme contained in *Labour and the New Social Order,* the Labour Party finally established itself. The formative years were ended. Now at last it was an adult party certain of its own purpose; aware also at last of what it must do to impress that purpose upon the nation.

Now to continue with Lyman's paraphrase of Williams, the adult party made a series of electoral gains in the twenties, even holding office for two brief periods in 1924 and 1929 – 31. Of course, the interwar Labour Governments were hardly impressive. But in each case, Labour was hampered by inexperience, by lack of a majority in the House of Commons, by the increasing weariness and conservatism of some of its leading figures, and (especially in 1930 – 31) by a world economic crisis beyond the control of any British Government. Even so, there were significant successes, like those of Arthur Henderson at the Foreign Office, and in any case Labour learned from its failures. After the General Strike of 1926 there were no more general strikes; after the two minority Labour Governments there were no more minority Labour Governments. More than that—we are still following Francis Williams—after the traumatic defeat and "betrayal" of 1931 (when Ramsay MacDonald became Prime Minister of a "National" Government) Labour set about defining its program and reinforcing its socialist determination, so as to be ready to take over at last when the British electorate should have come to its senses and overthrown the "National" Coalition. Finally in 1945, Labour swept to power—but let me defer 1945 until I have noted the sharply conflicting interpretation of the Labour Left and briefly commented on both these neat formulations.

The left-wing interpretation of the interwar years and what followed is, as I say, different from that presented by a Francis Williams. Argued in a volume of interesting essays called *Towards Socialism* [6] and sponsored by the New Left

Review, outlined by Michael Foot in the first volume of his able biography of Aneurin Bevan, [7] put most cogently by Ralph Miliband in his book entitled *Parliamentary Socialism,* [8] this view emphasizes all that has been wrong in the earlier history of the Labour Party. Like the Socialist critics before World War I, these left-wing authors have been impatient with a leadership which accepted the necessity of compromise and of trimming, but which, above all, by operating as a mere political party, really rejected, in their view, the socialist aim of a fundamental reordering of society. By such lights, the interwar history of the Labour Party is almost disastrous, the tale of missed chances and opportunistic goals, one in which excessive devotion to parliamentary methods led to the effective rejection of most of what socialism stood for. Here is a quotation from Miliband, which will serve perhaps to indicate the flavor of this kind of argument.

> [The Labour Party's] accent, after the defeat of 1931 [he writes], had been on 'education and organization.' But it had deliberately refused to further that education by the organization, outside Parliament, of a militant movement in defence of working-class interests. To erase the stigma of the Labour Government's performance in 1931, it would have had to embark, after 1931, on something like a permanent crusade, in deed as well as in words, as a result of which it might have hoped, come an election, to do substantially better than ever before. But instead of the massive effort of which there had been so much talk after the catastrophe of 1931, there had only been the routine of speeches and of meetings, of eminently reasonable wage negotiations and of equally reasonable conciliation of employers and of the Government, of polite parliamentary debates and of equally polite representations to Ministers, with the occasional rally or demonstration, all suggesting that Labour had good intentions and even remedies—much less that it had an angry cause. [9]

In this view, the failures of the twenties and the thirties are emphasized and are attributed to an inevitable weakness of majority policy, its sin of gradualism, its commitment to parliamentary procedures, its mistake of "Labourism" in place of socialism.

Now it seems clear that the orthodox version is over-optimisitc, that it papers over the cracks and the contradictions within the Party, and that it overemphasizes accident and exceptional circumstances in explaining Labour's failures between the wars. Indeed, most official Labour Party histories, like most memoirs of participants in that history, read like campaign documents or anniversary brochures rather than like serious dissections of the problems and accomplishments of the past. Whether it is in Francis Williams' *Fifty Years' March* or in Clement Attlee's *As It Happened* [10] —the latter surely one of the most reticent memoirs in recent times—one gets little of the dilemmas, the uncertainties, the muddle of Labour Party policies and performance in the interwar years.

On the other hand, the left wing has been better at saying what was wrong than at providing alternatives. They have hardly suggested other paths that Labour might have followed, whether in international affairs—about which I shall want to comment later—or in the achievement of revolutionary change in a profoundly stable society. And, of course, their failure to suggest such alternatives in turn stems from their own commitment to democracy, which leaves them frustrated by its limitations, impatient of its slowness, but still unwilling to go all the way in rejecting its principles and even its procedures as they have developed in Britain. It follows, therefore, that their demonstration of what was wrong in the twenties and the thirties is rather more effective than their relatively vague suggestions as to what might have been done differently.

I would like to suggest that the very divisions implied in the two positions I have so sketchily summarized, far from being a detriment to the emerging Labour Party, were a positive advantage. Of course, splits occurred and constituent elements fell away. By 1932, for example, the Independent Labour Party had become so alienated from the mainstream of Labour thinking that it finally disaffiliated and found its own independent way to political oblivion. Yet when one considers the really massive breaks in party continuity in modern British politics—the Tories over the Corn Laws in 1846, the Liberals over Irish Home Rule in 1886—one finds the Labour Party no more, and probably considerably less, subject to disruption than its competitors for public support in modern times.

Samuel H. Beer, whose *Modern British Politics: A Study of Parties and Pressure Groups* [11] is in my opinion the most brilliant American writing on British politics since the pioneer work of A. Lawrence Lowell, has argued persuasively—but not persuasively enough to persuade me—that what happened after 1918 was that the Labour Party, while it continued to be a coalition, became something more. He sees in the 1918 Constitution a genuine turn to ideology, a commitment to the establishment of a "Socialist Commonwealth." But I am struck by much of the evidence he adduces to support his conception of such a "socialist commitment." He notes the "huge mass party utterances"—conference debates, party programs, parliamentary speeches—that reflect not only responses to particular circumstances and special interests, but also a unified doctrine, even, as he puts it, "a system of thought."

Now I would argue that if this had really been the case, if this "system of thought" had been anything very much more than a rather vague series of changing plans fixed in a matrix of anticapitalist rhetoric and socialist aspiration, then the appeal of the Labour Party would have been considerably less effective than in actual fact it was. It is interesting that when Professor Beer seeks statements to epitomize the "socialist commitment" he turns to Bruce

Glasier and to Robert Blatchford, both essentially pre-1919 propagandists, as often as he turns to the major leaders of the Labour Party, whose platform oratory hardly seems enough to pin down the precise character of the "socialist commitment." I am not really taking issue with Professor Beer. I am merely arguing that the idea of a "socialist commitment"—which could be generally accepted because it was so vague and tackled so few of the hard questions of definition—the idea of a "socialist commitment" does not tell us much about why the Labour Party—whatever its vicissitudes in the interwar years—managed to remain the second major party in Great Britain and to maintain the potential for power so dramatically exercised during the Second World War and after 1945.

The reason, let me repeat, seems quite clear. Rather than appealing only to that obvious minority of the electorate to whom socialism was an attractive doctrine, the Labour Party, like the American Democratic or Republican Parties, attracted a relatively wide spectrum of the population. For the intellectual Left, there were the theoretical formulations of a thoroughgoing socialist system of values and promises of "socialization" of essential services—which in practice meant nationalization of certain basic enterprises. For the organized working classes, there were promises of reforms to meet the demands of the trade unions—which in practice meant gradualist legislation within the framework of existing institutions. For the middle classes, most of whom would presumably have been frightened by a thoroughgoing socialism, as much as for the underprivileged groups in society, a somewhat rudimentary (rudimentary until the experience of World War II) vision of expanded social welfare services was held out. And, although I am not concerned with international questions for the moment, in a certain sense this eclecticism—inadequate though it may have been in practice—can be similarly seen in the tightrope balancing of Labour on questions such as that of rearmament. Weak though Labour's policy might have been in the Hitler era, it had the enormous advantage—I am not defending it—of avoiding the dangers of too one-sided a commitment either to the Left or the Right or even the Center, and thus the advantage of preserving the Party as a national rather than a sectarian group. In the United States, it has been argued, the very similarities of the two major parties—their substantial agreement on most fundamental questions—has preserved a modest choice within a framework of continuity. So in Great Britain—where the political terrain is so different—nevertheless the very all-things-to-all-men character of the Labour Party made it a possible alternative for many undoctrinaire voters, and so made it possible for the Party to grow and eventually to prosper. After all, the Liberal Party, which might have been expected to fill the role of a respectable alternative to Conservatism, had collapsed in the sequel to World War I. While the Labour Party did not become a second Liberal Party, it did in fact attract many who might have supported a unified Liberal Party as well as many socialists who found the Liberal version of politics inadequate.

The importance of this broad base to the fortunes of the Labour Party became quite apparent during the Second World War. When Winston Churchill became Prime Minister in the dark days of 1940, he set up a War Cabinet of five members. Two of them were Labour Party leaders, Clement Attlee and Arthur Greenwood. In addition, a considerable sprinkling of other Labour Party officials filled a series of crucial offices. In the course of time, Attlee, Ernest Bevin, and Hugh Dalton became the leading figures in the administration of home affairs, Attlee as Deputy Prime Minister, Bevin as Minister of Labour and National Service, Dalton as President of the Board of Trade. Churchill was immersed in the grand strategy of the war. As a result, the representatives of Labour had the opportunity to gain invaluable experience of government. Equally significant, they had the opportunity to commend themselves to the future electorate as men of good sense, good will, and genuine ability.

The sweeping Labour victory of 1945, won in an election held soon after V-E Day, came nevertheless as a dramatic shock. It was not a repudiation of Winston Churchill. It was an expression of hope that a fresh new group of men might attack the many problems of postwar Britain with greater imagination than the tired old team who seemed to dominate the Conservative Party. Whatever the reasons, the Labour Party, with a huge parliamentary majority of 146, took office pledged to implement a program of reform that had been outlined in its electoral manifesto, *Let Us Face the Future.* And, as Samuel Beer has noted, "to an extent unprecedented in British history," the actions of the Government reflected the promises of this party program. [12]

On the surface, the most radical legislation pushed through Parliament by the new government had to do with public ownership. Between 1946 and 1949, the Bank of England, the fuel and power industries, inland transport by road, rail, air, and canal, iron and steel were all nationalized. To Americans, looking at the British scene from a distance, this legislation appeared to herald a drastic policy, striking at the very heart of established relationships of ownership and power. In actual fact—and here I emphasize once more my central theme—"nationalization" in practice made relatively little change in the industries concerned. It was accompanied by generous compensations for the owners. It was confined, with one exception, to industries that could be regarded as public utilities rather than as primarily producers of manufactures for private profit. And it was implemented by the establishment of a series of national governing boards, mostly independent of serious parliamentary control and certainly a far cry from the "social ownership"—that is, "social management"—envisaged by the Labour Left. The hesitancy with which the Labour leaders approached the nationalization of iron and steel—the one industry slated for nationalization that could hardly be defined in conventional terms as a public utility—and the violent reaction to the proposal from a heterogeneous opposition merely emphasize how moderate, almost how uncontroversial, was the bulk of the nationalization scheme. Whether it was successful is not my point here. I simply want to emphasize that it reflected a fairly widespread consensus, and that it did not go far beyond that consensus. Indeed, the bulk of the services nationalized had already long been under substantial public control.

Even more widely acceptable to a general public were the social service measures of the Labour Government. Richard Titmuss, one of the architects of the famous Beveridge Report on social security, has indicated the main areas of public (or publicly supported) social and welfare services. [13] He lists them as:

1 Education from the primary school to the university.

2 Medical care, preventive and curative.

3 Housing and rent policies.

4 Income maintenance (including children's allowances, old age pensions, public assistance, and schemes for unemployment, sickness and industrial injuries benefits).

5 Special services in kind for dependent groups, the old, deprived children, unsupported mothers and various handicapped classes.

The Labour Government expanded sickness, unemployment, and retirement benefits and provided maternity grants, widows' pensions, and death grants in the National Insurance Act of 1946. It passed an Industrial Injuries Act in the same year and also a National Assistance Act to cover the destitute not properly provided for by National Insurance. In education it proceeded to try to implement (though resources were desperately scarce) the provisions of R. A. Butler's Education Act of 1944. Its Rent Control Act of 1946, Housing Acts of 1946 and 1949, Children's Act of 1948 helped flesh out the skeleton of services listed by Professor Titmuss. And finally, its National Health Service Act of 1946—perhaps the single most important piece of legislation passed by the postwar Labour Government—nationalized almost all hospitals (nursing homes were excepted) and established a free and comprehensive medical service.

Like nationalization, the social welfare state appears on the surface to be extreme, radical, a full-fledged acceptance of the views of the Labour Left. Yet increasingly it was the Left that became frustrated by the administration of the social services and found them less than utopian. Why? For a clue, let me turn once again to Richard Titmuss. He has pointed out that "The principle of universality applied in 1948 to the main social welfare services in Britain was needed as a major objective favouring social integration; as a method of breaking down distinctions and discriminative tests between first-class and second-class citizens. But equal opportunity of access by right of citizenship to education, medical care and social insurance is not the same thing as equality of outcome. It is only a prerequisite—though a necessary one—to the objective of equalizing the outcome." [14]

And what tended to happen was this. The higher income groups made the better use of the National Health services; they received more special attention; occupied more of the beds in better equipped hospitals; had better maternity care; received more psychiatric help than members of the unskilled working classes.

In housing, state subsidies to owner-occupiers of many kinds of houses were on the average greater than the subsidies received by most tenants of public housing schemes.

In education, scarce resources allowed—even until today—only a relatively small proportion of young people access to good secondary and university programs. Immense sacrifices in earnings and labour foregone were called for from parents and children living in poor conditions, so that more often than not, despite the principle of universality, it was the middle-class youth who benefitted. There was a vast difference between universality in theory and in practice. Fundamentally, the advent of the "Welfare State" in Britain did not lead to any significant redistribution of wealth and income in favour of the poorer classes, although the services for all were improved. And this in turn helps explain both the frustration of the Labour Left and the overall success of the Labour Party.

That success was called seriously into question after 1949, of course. All that I have been noting—nationalization, social service schemes—took place against a backdrop of problems that have led a group of young writers to label the period from 1945 to 1951 the "age of austerity." Its symbols were the end of Lend-Lease and the negotiation of an American loan on particularly onerous terms, the terrifying fuel crisis of 1947 and the convertability crisis of the same year, the balance of payments crisis in 1949. Above all, its major symbol was Sir Stafford Cripps, courageous, ascetic, a bit bloodless, bringing in successive sacrificial budgets as Chancellor of the Exchequer, fostering the export drive at the expense of the domestic standard of living, swallowing the bitter pill of devaluation despite opposition from both Left and Right. And, as the difficulties of governing a country whose resources were simply stretched too thin became apparent, the Labour Party seemed to come apart at the seams.

When the Party, in the election of 1950, retained its majority in the House of Commons by a bare six seats, the stage seemed set for an all-out clash. The explosion was not long in coming. Hugh Gaitskell, the moderate ex-university teacher who succeeded Stafford Cripps as Chancellor of the Exchequer, had to cope with a mounting rearmament bill during the Korean War. Among other steps, he put charges on dentures and spectacles obtained under National Health. Aneurin Bevan, the stormy and able Welsh petrol of the Labour Left, not only protested; he resigned as Minister of Labour in April, 1951, and was soon followed by Harold Wilson, the President of the Board of Trade, and by John Freeman, Parliamentary Secretary to the Ministry of Supply. The occasion for the split was dentures and spectacles; the reasons were much more deeply rooted. The Left believed that the spirit had gone out of the drive to create a socialist Britain. They bitterly opposed the policy of consolidation pursued by Attlee and advocated by Herbert Morrison and increasingly by Hugh Gaitskell as the champion of the new right wing of the Labour Party. Morrison and Gaitskell, in turn, regarded the Bevan position (he was often supported by Harold Wilson, Richard Crossman, Tom Driberg, Ian Mikardo, and Barbara Castle—and it is interesting that not only Wilson, but also Crossman and Castle were influential in the recent Labour cabinet) as unsound and unrealistic. They were determined to smash it. There were other issues—a struggle for the succession to Attlee, first between Bevan and Morrison, then between Bevan and Gaitskell, and genuine difference of views on matters of rearmament and defense policy. Although Bevan and his friends made their peace with their colleagues, the Labour Party that fought the election of 1951 was out of heart and badly confused in the face of a well-mounted Tory revival. The Labour majority of six was transformed into a Conservative majority of seventeen, not a comfortable margin but a workable one.

Defeat opened the floodgates to further bitter and acrimonious conflict. The struggle for the succession eventually found Gaitskell triumphant, backed as he was by the leaders of the most powerful trade unions connected with the Labour Party. But during the course of the struggle the Bevanites coalesced as a strong faction, challenging the parliamentary leadership of the Labour Party on a host of issues. At first the issue was rearmament, the Bevanites convinced (rightly as it turned out) that Britain was overcommitting herself, the Gaitskellites insisting on a policy more closely attuned to that of the United

States. As the years rolled on, controversy over general rearmament gave way to struggle over German rearmament and once again, in 1954, Bevan resigned, this time from the "shadow cabinet." Crisis followed crisis, each one more or less patched up, but each revealing what seemed to be irreparable cleavages within the Labour Party. When the Conservatives won a second election in 1955, this time by a majority of 59 seats in the Commons, there were predictions of a breakup of the Party—and even a little flutter of hope among Liberal supporters.

After the election, Hugh Gaitskell won the leadership of the Party in relatively easy fashion, and a reexamination of Labour policy was undertaken. Unofficially, in 1950 a group calling themselves Socialist Union published *Twentieth Century Socialism* and a year later C.A.R. Crosland continued the revisionist dissection of older ideas. Crosland in particular was much impressed by John Kenneth Galbraith's analysis of the "mixed economy." His essay on *The Future of Socialism* [15] raised serious questions about the effectiveness of nationalization as about many other traditions of British socialism. Arguing that the transformation of capitalism made it necessary for socialism to change its character, he wrote eloquently—but it must have sounded strangely to those brought up on the slogans of the past—of such things as liberty and gaiety in private life, of cultural and amenity planning, of the declining importance of economic problems. Clearly his revisionist dream, which Gaitskell shared, emphasized the reformist element in Labour Party policy, not its millenarial aspect.

All this came to a head in 1956, when Gaitskell, perhaps tactically less skilful than Attlee had been, tried to bring the Labour Party Constitution into line with the policies that had actually been pursued since 1949. He proposed to amend Clause IV by changing the phrase having to do with "the common ownership of the means of production, distribution, and exchange." After all, nationalization had been tried and the brave new world had not emerged. Surely, then, "socialism" meant something broader and more flexible and should be so defined. But Party tradition and the opposition of the Left were stronger than Gaitskell's logical inferences from Labour Party history. The revisionist attempt was given up. And the Party's principles were, as one observer has put it, if anything even more ambiguous after than before this abortive attempt at clarification.

Once again I have spent a considerable time in recapitulation because the Clause IV upheaval illustrates the point I have been emphasizing. Throughout the decade of the fifties, "With almost compulsive iteration, the same battles are fruitlessly fought out again and again through the same cycle of renewed confrontation, bitter strife, and temporary and indecisive compromise." [16] Two opposing conceptions of the meaning of socialism created at least two different factions. The Bevanites in some ways took over the role in the fifties that the Independent Labour Party had played in the twenties. There was, in other words, an essential continuity, if not on precise issues, then on the mode of division over matters of basic philosophy. The Bevanite struggle should have split the Labour Party wide open. Disheartened by unprecedented electoral defeats—1959 was soon added to 1951 and 1955—the Party by most continental standards, for example, should have been headed for oblivion. But it refused to collapse.

Part of the reason was personality. Gaitskell, learning to become an able tactician, solidified his position both among the trade unions and the constituency parties. Bevan and Harold Wilson both came into the "shadow cabinet." The former, in what turned out to be the last years of his life, deserted his own rebellious minority to support the Party leadership on virtually every issue. Part of the reason was accident. Anthony Eden's disastrous handling of the Suez affair in 1956 solidified the Labour Party behind Gaitskell and gave it a unifying issue. "Law not War" became the watchword of a revived leadership. For a moment the Labour Party became the spokesman for all those who were repelled by what they considered to be British aggression in the Middle East. Not that the country as a whole opposed the Suez operation. It did not. Popular jingoism, even in the Labour Party, was heated and widespread. But Labour was able to capitalize on the domestic effects of Suez—its evidence of the weakness of the British Government in the face of American pressure, its inability to hold down gasoline prices, the obvious collapse of the Conservative Prime Minister. And part of the reason, in the early sixties, came to be the ubiquitous economic difficulties suffered by the country. To be sure, Eden was replaced by a much more formidable opponent and for a time the euphoria of Harold Macmillan's early leadership tended to conceal the basic problems. "I'm all right, Jack" went hand in hand with "You never had it so good." But in the winter of 1962–63, unemployment rose alarmingly and the familiar routine of power cuts and electrical failure seemed to demonstrate that not a great deal had changed since Labour's "age of austerity."

In such circumstances, Gaitskellite moderation again began to seem an attractive alternative to the similar moderation of Macmillan or his successor, Sir Alec Douglas-Home. Revisionism was a coherent doctrine as developed by Anthony Crosland and Roy Jenkins. It was a doctrine that made sense to many in the middle classes who might have been Liberals if there had been the slightest chance of the Liberal Party's being effective. But at the same time, the continued existence of older "socialist" commitments, while it did not really satisfy many left-wing intellectuals such as R. H. Crossman or Ian Mikardo, nevertheless gave them a forum—and a hope—within the ranks of Labour. And, it goes without saying, both revisionists and fundamentalists elicited support from different groups within the working class itself. The precarious balance in the Labour Party somehow was maintained. I would argue that in some ways because of this, rather than in spite of it, Labour once again prospered.

This, then, has been the background of the most recent Labour Government. In 1963, Hugh Gaitskell, at the age of 56, suddenly succumbed to a rare disease. And his successor, not surprisingly if my analysis here has any validity, his successor was not the Gaitskellite George Brown nor the equally Gaitskellite James Callaghan, but Harold Wilson, a man of the Left, the ally of Aneurin Bevan. An able speaker and an outstanding administrator, Wilson had been a bright young prodigy in Clement Attlee's cabinet. That he came from modest circumstances and had clawed his way to the top was an advantage among many Party members who rather resented the middle-class intellectuals in the Party's leadership. Though he had resigned office at the time of Bevan's first quarrel with Gaitskell, he had quickly found his way back to the fold. When the election of 1955 had revealed how inadequate was the Party's electoral machinery, Wilson headed the committee assigned to make inquiry and suggest remedies. His decisive election as Leader appeared to make possible the best of several worlds. He was a socialist of the Left, to be sure, but from the beginning he emphasized that change in leadership did not mean change in party politics. In a curious way, he took on the mantle of Gaitskell, emphasizing more vigorously the importance of science and education in the modern technological world, but clearly giving the impression that he was eclectic, open to new ideas, not particularly doctrinaire.

The mistakes of the Tories—and mishaps such as the sordid Profumo affair—combined with the reinvigoration of Labour to turn the electoral tide in 1964. Perhaps the Tories, like Labour in 1951, were simply too tired to give effective leadership any longer. The Labour Government of 1964 had only a four-seat margin in the House of Commons, a margin that made the conduct of legislative business, under constant harassment, a wearing and dispiriting experience. Finally, in 1966 a second election swept Labour again into real power, this time within a margin of about a hundred seats. I am told by a good friend in the Ministry of Labour that on election night the Prime Minister and his closest confidants were appalled by the margin of their victory. Wilson had hoped for a majority of thirty to thirty-five seats, big enough not to be threat-

ened by the Tories, narrow enough so that all wings of Labour would feel compelled to maintain party discipline. With a margin of one hundred he had few
sanctions with which to threaten recalcitrant followers, certainly not the possibility that Labour would be thrown out of office soon if they kicked up their
heels too vigorously.

Yet the position was ticklish. I have dropped a number of names during the
course of this paper—George Brown, James Callaghan, Roy Jenkins, Anthony
Crosland on the Right of the Party; Richard Crossman, Barbara Castle, Wilson
himself on the Left. Every one of those names, in the early years of office, was
on the list of the Labour cabinet, along with others representing virtually every
shade of Labour opinion. Disagreements persisted, we can be sure, in the cabinet as they so clearly persisted among the rank-and-file in the House of
Commons.

Indeed, once again there was evident what I suggested above—the kicking
up of various heels within the Labour Party. The Vietnam war, commitments
east of Suez, the German question, the pay freeze, devaluation—the issues
read very much as they did at an earlier time. Even Harold Wilson, who had
seemed to many as unflappable, calm, and unperturbed by problems as Harold Macmillan, occasionally lost himself and struck out at his Party critics like
his predecessors. Indeed, in early 1967, he gave a public tongue lashing to his
supporters which many felt would leave almost irremediable scars. And subsequent quarrels seemed to bring the party close to dissolution.

Perhaps. But I would suggest that the evidence is against such an interpretation. Throughout the years, the history of the Labour Party has been the
history of tension among its various elements. The issues have changed somewhat, the alliances have often been modified, but the struggle over how far and
how fast to move has been pretty much a constant. Consistently, these nagging and fundamental differences have arisen over the course of the years as
the Labour Party gradually came to replace the Liberals as an alternative to
the Tories in the governing of Great Britain. Increasingly, the Party's appeal
had to be made, if it were to maintain its commitment to parliamentary democracy, to a broader sector of the country than to the working class alone. For
many, this clearly indicated a refinement and a redefinition of the ideas and
the ideals of the Party. For others, a smaller group, it made imperative an even
more passionate dedication to the undiluted faith of the fathers of socialism.
And at no time, not even in the halcyon years between 1945 and 1948 or at
present, has this difference really been reconciled.

To many observers, this has seemed a handicap, a difficulty that will eventually break up the Labour Party. Again and again, in the public press—some-

times with considerable satisfaction—the pundits have predicted dire things for the Party. Yet those of us who have tried to apply the lessons of American political life to the admittedly different environment of Britain may be forgiven if we are not impressed by the doom-singers and prophets of disruption. For us, the multiparty, dedicated to a host of functions and serving a variety of constituencies, is no unfamiliar institution. For us, therefore, the very heterogeneity of the Labour Party, its ability to encompass such disparate views, seems an element of strength, not of weakness. And if this assessment is correct, then Labour's future does not depend, as so many correspondents write and as the historian Henry Pelling has recently implied,[17] on the ability of one man, Harold Wilson. Instead the Labour Party, like the Conservative, is likely to remain, *because of* its very character, one of the twin rocks upon which parliamentary democracy so firmly rests in the Great Britain of today.

II | Abroad

In the first part of this essay I tried to suggest that the very heterogeneity of the Labour Party, its conflicting interpretations of what constituted socialism and what to do about it, may well have been an explanation of the Party's growing strength rather than an indication of divisive weakness. I was concerned mainly with domestic issues and internal politics, leaving aside foreign policy until now. To a certain extent, I should like to use the Labour Party's attitudes on international questions further to illustrate the theme I emphasized above. I propose to try to see what happened to the foreign policy positions of the Labour Party as it gradually became transformed from a tiny propagandistic coterie into one of the major political parties in one of the major countries of the world. And perhaps a survey of what happened will help in understanding something about the international role of the Labour Party in the world of the present.

As in domestic affairs, the background out of which the Labour approach emerged is of some relevance. Before the First World War, working-class interest in foreign affairs was sporadic and slight. The workers newly enfranchised in 1867 and 1884 inevitably directed their political attention much more toward domestic issues than toward the obscure complications of external relations. Despite the enormous increase in British productivity over half a century, despite, indeed, the undoubted rise in the standard of life of the "average" worker, millions on the land or in the drab industrial slums continued to live in squalor and poverty. Of necessity working-class organization was primarily concerned with the "condition of England question." The new unionism, sweeping through the ranks of unskilled and semi-skilled labour toward the end of the century, dramatized the urgency of the struggle for economic and social advancement. But the very urgency of that struggle, in turn, made it certain that even when they turned to political action the unions would give but short shrift to questions of international import.

In similar fashion the socialist societies whose establishment paralleled that of the new unionism were largely occupied with a thoroughgoing criticism of the contemporary social and economic environment. Both the Social Democratic Federation, Marxist in its inspiration, and the Independent Labour Party, deeply rooted in a nonconformist tradition, worked to arouse the social conscience of their time to an awareness of the intolerable conditions hidden behind the superficial facade of industrial society. Until about the turn of the century, there is little evidence that either group paid more than lip service to an internationalism which, if genuinely embraced, might have led to a modest comprehension of foreign policy issues and their relation to domestic problems. Not even the Fabian Society, select, small, and exclusively intellectual, lifted its eyes far beyond the horizon off the British shores. Ambivalent on the issue of imperialism that came to a head during the Boer War, the Fabians tended to be silent on other international questions until the First World War made imperative some stand on the most crucial issues of the time.

In large measure, the prewar Labour Party inherited this indifference to the world of diplomacy and foreign policy. Understandably, the new party found virtually all of its energies absorbed in the struggle to defend workers' rights through the medium of Parliament. Occasional pronouncements by Party leaders on foreign affairs only served to emphasize how little attention they usually attracted. This is not to say that the Labour Party had no international outlook before 1914. Enough students have written about the "internationalism" of Labour's background to make it unnecessary to stress the point, but it is wise to keep this conception in proper perspective. The Labour Party and some of its constituent societies were indeed members of the Second International. On occasion it joined with its fellow-members in denouncing imperialism and colonial exploitation, branding militarism, and stressing the international solidarity of the working classes. But the legend of socialist solidarity, to be broken so irreparably when the European armies marched in 1914, even before 1914 represented an aspiration rather than a reality of international life. Certainly there is little evidence of any genuine temper of working-class internationalism among the rank-and-file of the Labour movement. Its presence among the leaders of the Labour Party can perhaps be more plausibly related to the myths of Labour solidarity than identified as a fundamental motivating force within the Party before 1914.

I am inclined to think that the heritage the Labour Party received from the Liberal tradition of the nineteenth century was much more important than the influence of socialist internationalism. The prewar internationalists of the Labour Party tended to be vague, imprecise, never really sure whether to support a policy of collaboration by sovereign states or to advocate the absorption of competing nationalisms in some broader world sovereignty. Their uncertain position almost exactly paralleled that of a minority of dissident Liberals who were moved in the years before 1914 to reject the imperial and diplomatic maneuvers of their own party as they had opposed those of the Tories. In both cases, the "liberal" protest—a kind of cry of conscience—stands out more clearly than any proposals for an alternative policy.

Perhaps the most instructive example of the essentially liberal character of much of the influence molding Labour's international attitudes is to be found among the currents of pacifism that ran so strongly in its ranks both before and after the First World War. Of course, there was an element of doctrinaire "socialist pacifism" in evidence before 1914. This element became more vocal and extended its sway in the first few years after the conflict. But "socialism" and opposition to "capitalist-inspired" struggles were not really the crucial determinants of the pacifism of the bulk of Labour's supporters. Labour pacifism was deeply rooted in the ethical soil of nineteenth-century English liberalism. Labour pacifists in the early twentieth century, like their Liberal fellows, came to their view of the evils of international conflict more frequently by way of Biblical injunctions and moral precepts than through a systematic socialist analysis of international society.

Taken together, these two elements in the prewar background of Labour—the indifference of the mass of its supporters to international questions and the essentially liberal attitudes that shaped whatever attitudes were in evidence—were of considerable influence in determining the course taken by the Party after the First World War. The very lack of interest in foreign affairs, which made the cataclysm of 1914 so totally unexpected to all but a tiny minority, bred compensating extremism once the war was over. Seen in retrospect, the international policies pursued by the British and other governments appeared mean and sordid, particularly to men who had paid so little attention to them in the past. As a result, when those who had opposed the war (and some who had not) hammered home the moral that no capitalist government could be trusted, that international cooperation was a chimera until most states became socialist, and that working-class solidarity across national boundaries was the only hope for a peaceful world, they found substantial support for their millenialism even among those in the ranks of Labour to whom socialism was hardly a crucial issue. At the same time, the more immediately optimistic idealism characteristic of the liberal strain in British society played its role in gradually persuading the Labour Party of the advantages of patiently strengthening international institutions by a program of "practical" cooperation among the nations. What I have called in one of my articles a "League of Nations policy" was in the long run negotiable because it offered an alternative to doctrines of class war with which the British socialist was uncomfortable, however much he may have been attracted to them in his period of temporary disillusionment. And that alternative in turn was based on more congenial conceptions of international morality, pacifism, and collaboration that represented a return to the liberal heritage upon which Labour's approach to foreign policy had in part originally been built.

In broad sweep, then, Labour's views on foreign policy can be described in terms of the rather variegated appeals I found in the formulation of domestic issues. But, for the moment, I am more concerned with the development of an official position on international questions, since I am myself convinced that what happened in the nineteen-twenties placed its imprint on all subsequent Labour positions. The 1914 war, as Carl F. Brand has commented, "ended whatever sense of detachment from world affairs existed in the Labour Party." [18] By the end of the war, the Party had become the leading British advocate of a generous peace of reconciliation. Although there were differences of emphasis within its ranks, the Party was able to reach something like a consensus on its rejection of any programs of conquest and annexation and on its support for a permanent international organization to ensure the durability of the peace. Actually, the consensus came about slowly. At the beginning of the war the Independent Labour Party remained consistent with Labour's prewar views, emphasizing the British Government's share in the responsibility for the convulsion and demanding from the very start the early negotiation of peace. The trade union majority of the Labour Party, on the other hand, joined with the Fabian Society in supporting the war and by implication, at least, the view that it must be fought to a finish. Nevertheless, these sections of the Labour movement eventually reached sufficient agreement to support a *Memorandum on War Aims* that may, without serious exaggeration, be labelled the first major pronouncement on foreign policy in the history of the Labour Party. The *Memorandum,* which preceded both Lloyd George's important statement of war aims in January, 1918, and President Wilson's Fourteen Points, became the platform upon which the Labour movement carried its case to the country in the last year of the war. By then, Labour's official leaders were unquestionably the foremost political force behind the drive for a moderate peace. In effect, they pleaded for a generous reconciliation with the enemy, whether as a result of negotiation or after he had been defeated. Since they were convinced that a League of Nations was fundamental to such a reconciliation, many of them came to believe that President Wilson's views were close to their own. When the Armistice was finally achieved, therefore, they looked forward with some hopefulness to the forthcoming conference called to discuss the "preliminaries" of peace.[19]

Needless to say, it is doubtful that this official position reflected the attitudes of Labour's rank-and-file. For a moment, at least, the Labour Party's leaders were out of step with most of their followers. To a country flushed with victory, warnings that peace must be built upon more than punishment hardly seemed worthy of attention. But by the time the Versailles Treaty was drawn up, the situation had begun to change. When the character of the proposed settlement became known, despair ran through almost every quarter of the Labour movement. The reaction was perhaps epitomized by Will Dyson after he had heard that Clemenceau, leading his fellow delegates down the Hall of Mirrors at Versailles, had stopped and said, "Curious! I seem to hear a child weeping." Dyson sketched the picture in a powerful cartoon. The weeping child, with the Peace Treaty at its feet, wore a band above its head entitled "1940."

As time wore on, words like "mockery," "barefaced swindle," "sheer and unadulterated brigandage" were used almost constantly to characterize the Treaty. Even when the Labour Party began to propose modifications of the peace settlement, its proposals were so extreme that they seemed designed to build a propaganda case rather than in the hope of any immediate success. Certainly, very few among the Labour leaders settled down to work within the system devised at Paris for the achievement of their ultimate aims. What is striking about the Labour response is not so much its dissatisfaction with many of the specific terms of the Versailles Treaty, but rather the air of hopelessness and rejection that permeated virtually all the movement's pronouncements in the immediate aftermath of 1919. Even in the case of the League of Nations, which it did not repudiate entirely, Labour insisted that until it was so revised as to be a different organization it could have no real value and merited little support.

And yet, despite the bitter spirit of repudiation that marked the immediate aftermath of the war, by the end of the twenties Labour had somehow managed to arrive at a responsible foreign policy, responsible in the sense that the Party came to accept the institutions of the international world in which it lived and sought to promote its hopes for European stability and security through those institutions. I have written about the twenties and thirties elsewhere, and this is not the place to repeat the details of my analysis. [20] For my purposes here it will be enough to note that what I have termed the "gradual development of a temperate, coherent, and even widely accepted foreign policy" was the resultant of a number of influences. Partly it reflected the simmering down of postwar emotions, the "second look" at policy after disillusionment burned itself out. Partly it was a response to the conscious and thoughtful efforts of a small group of able men, above all the dull and dedicated Arthur Henderson, to work out a policy based upon realistic international cooperation in place of what they held to be the anarchy of prewar international politics. And partly it was a reaction to two brief terms of office. In 1924, Ramsay MacDonald made a sparkling reputation as an international conciliator and earned the first great political triumph of any Labour minister. Between 1929 and 1931 Arthur Henderson demonstrated how patient goodwill might pay dividends in the relaxation of various tensions. Some years ago in an essay in *The Diplomats,* I wrote of Henderson as follows:

> . . . at a time when the British people felt themselves secure and most British leaders were unwilling to make any sizable commitments in Europe, he had some sense of the real difficulties faced by the beneficiaries of the Versailles system on the continent . . . he collaborated fully in trying to erect a genuine structure of international guarantees through the League of Nations in order to make disarmament possible. . . . His policy of appeasement, the development of the League, and then disarmament came closer to being one of effective collective security before 1930 than any within the realm of serious possibility. Seen in the light of the 1920's, it was a thoughtful, perceptive, and practicable line of approach. . . . By 1932, all the basic assumptions of the campaign which was supposedly to culminate in the progressive reduction of armaments had disappeared. It was now time for rigid resistance to the demands of an importunate German nationalism—and time also for equally firm support of France and the European order. . . . To change a way of thinking overnight, however, was difficult, and there were few who saw the issues clearly. If Henderson did not have the insight of a Winston Churchill after 1932, he had at least . . . opened up to Europe some of the avenues for a constructive approach to the problem of an enduring peace. [21]

In August, 1931, the second experiment in Labour Government was shattered by the Great Depression. Ramsay MacDonald, in one of the most astounding shifts in modern British politics, took over the Prime Ministership of a National Government whose Opposition was his own former party. For nine years, until well after the outbreak of the Second World War, that Government was in actual fact controlled by the Conservative Party whether the Prime Minister was Ramsay MacDonald or Stanley Baldwin or Neville Chamberlain.

Step by step, during the thirties, the hopes for a durable peace became more and more illusory. The economic crisis undoubtedly stimulated the determination of Italy, Japan, and Germany to rewrite the terms of Paris and redraw the frontiers of 1919—by arms if necessary. The Japanese invasion of Manchuria was the first major attempt to change the *status quo* by force. When the League of Nations was ineffective in dealing with the seizure of Chinese territory, the way seemed open for a wholesale attack on the established order. Soon the festering nationalism of German National Socialism became the chief touchstone of international relations. Faced with a Nazi threat to its own territory, the Soviet Union—for a brief period at least—shifted from its dogmatic isolationism and emerged as the advocate of "collective security" against aggression. Meanwhile, Fascist Italy moved toward an uneasy partnership with the Nazis in the Rome-Berlin Axis. When Hitler abandoned the League and openly announced a program of large-scale rearmament, the Western Powers should perhaps have acted. But France was ideologically divided and defensively minded, the United States aloof from European affairs. Leadership fell, almost by default, to Great Britain. But here too there were factors that blocked a firm stand against the Nazi menace. Fear of war, pacifism, mistrust of the Russians, the hope that "appeasement" of legitimate demands would satisfy Germany—all played their part. Particularly after 1935, the dictators won victory after victory. Italy's seizure of Abyssinia, the German reoccupation of the demilitarized Rhineland, Franco's triumph in the Spanish Civil War, the *Anschluss* with Austria, the seizure of the Sudetenland, the end of Czech independence, the turn upon Poland—the catalogue is familiar and depressing.

In Britain, from about 1933 to 1939, an impassioned debate was waged over the respective merits of appeasing the dictators or of uniting with other nations to resist their attacks upon the European order. The advocates of appeasement were, as we know, the formulators of British policy. Their policy was a failure. It did not prevent the use of force against Austria or Czechoslovakia or Poland. It was characterized, as a friendly critic, Professor W. N. Medlicott, has noted, by "a depressing lack of initiative, foresight, and quick thinking."[22] It made the mistake of ignoring the Russians almost completely, whatever may have been the purposes of the Soviet Union during those years before the war.

But was Labour's position any more realistic? Did Labour in the nineteen-thirties have a viable alternative to the policies of Simon and Hoare, Eden and Chamberlain? Many observers have felt the Labour Party did not, that the ambivalences and differences so manifest in conference resolutions and parliamentary statements reflected not only indecision but a basic unwillingness to face the possibility that collective security might—indeed almost certainly would—mean the need to use military force to bring the aggressors in Europe to heel.

Now much of this is true. Reginald Bassett has shown how little Labour really differed from the dominant Conservatives on Japan's Manchurian invasion at the level of proposals for effective policy. [23] Protests and calls for collective action appeared in large numbers, but at no time were they translated into more than emotional gestures. For a time after 1931, the leader of the battered Labour Party was George Lansbury, and Lansbury was a Christian pacifist. Labour was at one with Conservatives—as for that matter with American policymakers—in not even contemplating military sanctions. And as crisis followed crisis, Labour's foreign policy, certainly until 1935 and perhaps until 1937, was marked by confusion. It gave the clear impression that the Party was being torn apart by cross-purposes, perhaps like most groups in Great Britain during those difficult years. The nadir was undoubtedly reached in the Party's conference at Hastings in 1933. There a resolution supposedly committing the Party to resist war by a general strike marched along with a "League of Nations policy" including the use of collective sanctions. It is true that 1933 witnessed the high point of pacifist sentiment in the Labour Party and that subsequent conferences laid greater stress on the prevention of war by the positive organization of peace. But that a war resistance resolution could be accepted by the very conference that also supported the collective system illustrates the deep fissures in the Labour movement.

Even after 1935, Labour's uncertainties on international issues were clear. Let me cite just one example. While peace talks were going on at Paris in 1919, many within the British Labour movement came to support the view that German Austria should be permitted to unite with the new German Republic. The position, perhaps most cogently put by the distinguished journalist H. N. Brailsford, was in the circumstances of 1919 a liberating one. The people of Vienna and its environs, cut off from the markets and resources of the old Hapsburg monarchy, might well have been better off within the Weimar orbit. But such an *Anschluss* in 1938, when Germany was Nazi and Austria at least quasi-Fascist, held out doom and disaster for many hundred of thousands, including the Austrian Socialists with whom British Labour had had close affiliations. Labour opposed the *Anschluss*, to be sure. But there was always the nagging feeling that it was after all proper for Germans to be united with Germans, that the *Anschluss* should somehow have been carried out years earlier, that it was at any rate too much to contemplate risking the danger of war to prevent it. The failures—at least the missed opportunities—of the twenties are reflected in the hesitations and rationalizations of the thirties.

Similarly, the issue of British rearmament after 1933 must be seen as it actually was and not as the myths of party polemics have made it seem. The authority of Winston Churchill, for example, is frequently cited to illustrate the irresponsibility of Labour's position. Here is Churchill on Labour in 1934: "The Opposition are very free-spoken, as most of us are in this country, on the conduct of the German Nazi Government . . . . But these criticisms are fiercely resented by the powerful men who have Germany in their hands. So that we are to disarm our friends, we are to have no allies, we are to affront powerful nations, and we are to neglect our own defenses entirely." [24] That is a caricature of Labour policy, but it has somehow come down as revealed truth, made plausible because down to 1937 Labour did in fact vote to amend the arms estimates proposed by the National Government. Senator Jacob Javits of New York once remarked, during the course of a television interview, that the only way to indicate Congressional disapproval of certain Administration policies might be in the vote on particular appropriations. He was not suggesting that all the appropriations were unnecessary or undesirable. He was reflecting on how certain kinds of criticism might most effectively be made. So it was with Labour in the thirties. The leaders of the Party were not pacifists, although when they voted against the arms budget they surely pleased the pacifists among their followers. But absolute pacifism, as the reality of the Nazi threat became more apparent, steadily diminished in importance. The Labour leaders did not trust the National Government, they did not believe that it was willing to pursue a policy of cooperative resistance to Fascist aggression through the League, they suspected that the Government was eager to make a deal with the Fascists—and consequently they voted against the armed services budgets. They knew that those budgets would be passed overwhelmingly, but they were using their votes to register disapproval of the Government's international policy. It was a technique, incidentally, that had a long and well-recognized history in Parliamentary tactics. But, of course, such a position cried loudly to be misinterpreted and misrepresented, so that eventually such Labour leaders as Walter Citrine, Ernest Bevin, and Hugh Dalton were able to demonstrate, as the German menace grew greater, the self-defeating character of the negative vote on the estimates.

I do not want to outline the history of Labour's approach to foreign policy in the thirties. I think I have written enough to indicate how badly divided that approach often was—and I have not even mentioned the tensions occasioned by Stafford Cripp's campaigns for the united front and the Popular Front. But in addition to disagreement and disunity there was also a developing unity and consistency. In many popular accounts, Ernest Bevin is the hero of this saga. Most undergraduate students of twentieth-century Britain can recite the story of the 1935 Labour Party Conference at Brighton. They can picture Bevin lumbering up to the platform, after George Lansbury's emotional soul-searching over force and collective security, ruthlessly to destroy the basis of Lansbury's position. Lansbury, with all his faults, and they were many, was beloved in the Labour movement. He had taken the leadership of the Party in the dark days after 1931 and had done his best to help pull it from the abyss. But his Christian pacifism seemed more and more irrelevant to the younger men who were becoming increasingly impatient with an appeasement policy that they regarded as acquiescence in evil. Bevin objected, as he inelegantly phrased it, to Lansbury's "hawking his conscience around from body to body," asking to be told what to do with it. The performance was brutal and there were protests, but the job was done. Soon Lansbury resigned the leadership. Clement Attlee succeeded him, and by 1937 Labour finally gave up its unrealistic posture on arms and on foreign policy and increasingly stood for effective action. The search for alternatives to force was seen to be an illusion. And in September, 1939, the Labour Party that entered the war was a united party, accepting the conflict in the certainty that it now had to be fought to a victorious end.

I would agree that most of this is accurate, though I think it over-dramatizes the role of Ernest Bevin. Actually the policy finally accepted by the late thirties was pretty much the policy hammered out under the leadership of Arthur Henderson in the twenties. That, in turn, was why I spent so much time on the twenties. For in foreign affairs after 1931, it is my own feeling that Hugh Dalton, who had served as Henderson's Under-Secretary, was much more clear-minded and realistic much earlier and much more consistently than was Bevin. I think Dalton did more to educate the Labour Party to the facts of international life in this period than did Bevin. He wrote effectively, he spoke indefatigably, and he was convinced, from the beginning of the thirties, that to think of collective security without rearmament was wishful thinking. Much more than Bevin he emphasized that theme, until the concrete lessons of Abyssinia and the Rhineland and Spain began to convince others that the loud-voiced and blustering Dalton was right.

The war itself is almost a blank so far as Labour's international policies are concerned. To be sure, Labour issued pronouncements outlining its postwar aims in general and even in concrete detail. But once the Party's leaders entered into Winston Churchill's coalition government, they came to be more and more responsible for domestic affairs and tended, whatever their own views, to follow Churchill's lead on the many and involved issues of wartime diplomacy. Not that there were no problems. The Labour Party, for example, was almost torn apart on the issue of the Government's policy in Greece and in

Italy. But in a sense, so long as the war went on in Europe, the Labour ministers could give no effective lead for an independent policy. The continuity of British policy was symbolized at the Potsdam Conference in July, 1945. By that time the Labour Party was in opposition, since an election had been set after the collapse of the German armies. When Labour won that election, Clement Attlee continued at Potsdam, merely changing his role from that of Leader of the Opposition to that of Prime Minister.

Continuity or not, for the first time after 1945 the Labour Party in theory had the opportunity to pursue an independent international policy. In 1924 and in 1929 – 31, the Labour Governments had been minority governments, dependent upon the Liberals and thus restricted in what they could undertake to do. Now, with a clear and substantial majority in Parliament, perhaps the situation might be different for Ernest Bevin, the new Foreign Secretary. Leonard Woolf, the veteran Fabian expert on foreign affairs, had already issued a call that Labour's foreign policy "must be founded uncompromisingly on Socialist principles." Bevin, to be sure, and his successor, Herbert Morrison, carried out an astonishingly widespread program in international affairs. Yet despite this, there was not much difference between Bevin, the conservative Laborite, and Anthony Eden, the liberal Conservative. Indeed, in a debate in the House of Commons on August 20, 1945, Bevin agreed that in the wartime coalition he and Eden had never differed on any important question of foreign policy. [25] Like Arthur Henderson, in other words, Bevin pursued a middle-of-the-road policy. And like Henderson, Bevin as a policymaker had elicted a very varied set of judgments.

The areas of choice for the new Labour Government were, of course, limited. It should be remembered that there is a vast difference between foreign policy statements when a party is out of office and foreign policy when it assumes the responsibility of government. In the case of Labour, foreign policy programs enunciated by the Party's National Executive before 1945 reflected the fact that Labour was an opposition party. After 1945, policies were developed by the Foreign Secretary in consultation with the Cabinet and the permanent officials of the Foreign Office. And, as Matthew Fitzsimons has pointed out, "This policy, in turn, required the support of the Parliamentary Labour Party, which could express its dissatisfaction and press for modifications but could not openly oppose Bevin's policy without overturning the Labour Government and jeopardizing Labour's domestic program as well. But even more important, Great Britain was "now a power with world interests, not a world power." [26] Year by year, the overwhelming strength of the United States and the growing might of the Soviet Union became increasingly evident. British policymakers were forced to recognize how narrow were the parameters of choice in their foreign policy.

My own feeling is that the most successful long-run international actions between 1945 and 1951 were in the field not of foreign policy, strictly speaking, but of colonial affairs. The freeing of India, made inevitable I think by the impact of the Second World War, was nevertheless a generous and imaginative policy that owed much to Clement Attlee's firmness and almost as much to Lord Mountbatten's tact. Partition was tragically accompanied by several hundred thousand communal murders, yet it is hard to escape the conclusion that no other solution could have avoided the bloodshed of the transition. India, Pakistan, and Ceylon entered a Commonwealth no longer restricted to governments largely made up of white British stock. In the Gold Coast, Sierra Leone, Gambia, Mauritius, Nigeria, liberal constitutions were granted, and in East Africa, despite complicated tensions among blacks, whites, Arabs, and Indians, constitutional progress was promoted. In most cases, the constitutions were first steps on the road to independence. I am not suggesting that these steps were evidences of Labour's generous spirit. Partly they were a response to the pressures for self-government felt in the colonial holdings of all the imperial states. Partly they simply reflected a necessary reduction of commitments by an overextended nation. Nor am I suggesting that success was invariable. Rhodesia, Cyprus, Guinea, Nigeria, even perhaps Ghana may be taken to illustrate the other side of the coin. Yet looking back to the late forties and comparing the British accomplishment with, say, that of Belgium in the Congo, one is tempted to give high praise for the strategy by which devolution was carried out in most cases.

These accomplishments may be most readily placed under the rubric of imperial policy. But it is on other grounds—always excepting India—that the postwar Labour Government's reputation as a great success in foreign affairs is usually based. I myself tend to demur somewhat from that judgment. A bit earlier I compared Ernest Bevin's middle-of-the-road policy with that of Arthur Henderson. Just as prewar Labour writers used to regard Henderson as the greatest Foreign Secretary of the twentieth century, so postwar spokesmen have transferred the mantle of greatest to Bevin. To be sure, on the surface Bevin's policy seems to stem naturally from the temperate, even cautious internationalism that Henderson persuaded the interwar Labour Party finally to accept. But it is increasingly my conviction, as I look back at the years between 1945 and 1951, that Bevin's tragic flaws of personality, his growing inability to accept criticism, the narrowness of his vision of international cooperation made much that appeared to be successful in the long run mistaken and self-defeating for Great Britain.

Most striking, of course, was his extraordinary mishandling of the Palestine mandate. One need not be a Zionist enthusiast nor a hundred and fifty percent American patriot to see that Bevin allowed his emotion to get the better of his judgment in a situation that was at best appallingly complex. James G. Mac-Donald's impression of Bevin in 1945 is revealing, however much one discounts MacDonald's own biases. "His bitterness against Truman was almost pathological," MacDonald wrote. "It found its match only in his blazing hatred for his other scapegoat—the Jews, the Israeli, the Israeli Government." [27] This was hardly a proper outlook from which to think through a balanced and coherent Palestine position. In a sense, it was Bevin's bumbling lack of sensitivity that impelled him to pursue what a delegate at the 1945 Labour Conference had already called "a traditional Conservative policy of power politics in Palestine." [28] The charge was, as a matter of fact, correct. And the irony of it was that the policy no longer worked. The British were, for all practical purposes, driven out, and the Israeli state that Bevin was certain could not come into being actually was forged in the fires of war. And yet—not surprisingly—no matter how incompetent was Bevin's policy, it was a popular one in Great Britain, popular at least until its failure became clearly manifest. It seems clear that if Bevin—let us say the Labour Government—had been more generous, more liberal, more patient even, in its response to terrorism and bloodshed, it would have faced much more popular opprobrium. The very fact that the "socialist" party did not act as socialists might, on the basis of countless propaganda statements, have been expected to act, ensured that even in failure the Palestine policy would not bring political disaster to the Party. But that it was a failure, there can be no doubt.

It is upon Bevin's European policy, however, that his reputation really rests. Faced with Britain's inability to keep the Soviet Union out of the Mediterranean, the assessment goes, he called in the Americans, whose Truman Doctrine protected British interests at the same time that it accomplished even broader purposes of western defense. He seized brilliantly upon the vague suggestions of George Marshall's Harvard speech to forge a Doctrine upon which to build the cooperative economic recovery of most of non-Communist Europe. As the cold war became increasingly threatening, he was a pioneer in shaping the defense of western Europe, by fostering the Brussels Treaty for western military union and then by promoting the more extensive North Atlantic Treaty Organization. Virtually all of these policies—perhaps the retreat from Greece is the exception—were in the mainstream of traditional British foreign policy. They were based on the view that security required military strength and that military strength required military allies. Although there was much lip service given to the United Nations, in actual fact it was the United

States to which Bevin looked for both military and economic support. The very fact that Europe recovered spectacularly and that eventually the cold war relaxed into a kind of cold truce appears to be a testimony to Bevin's prescience and his skill.

Yet once again, I have nagging doubts. We have recently had a spate of books—written by responsible scholars, not hysterical crackpots—that have questioned whether in fact the so-called cold war was not the result of mistakes and miscalculations on both sides. For a change, not the motives but the judgments of western statesmen have been analyzed—and the possibility, at least, is raised that Bevin's inflexibility, along with that of both Truman and Stalin, may have made the conflict of interests—a conflict that of course existed—between the East and the West, more rather than less dangerous to the security and the healthy development of all the states of Europe. Clearly, much of this is conjectural and will remain so for a long time. But it is no longer as easy to swallow all the black-and-white certainties of the late forties and early fifties as it was for most of us at that time.

In any case, I suspect, the greatest single lost opportunity of the forties will increasingly come to seem to be the refusal of the Labour Government—and on this, as on most issues of foreign policy, it had the support of most Conservatives—to merge Britain, economically at least, in Western Europe. I know, of course, all the arguments that appeared valid to Labour then—and to many Conservatives—as they have appeared to many within the Labour Party to this day. Relations with the Commonwealth; tariff policy against areas outside the emerging Common Market; safeguards for British and Commonwealth agriculture; short-run effects on sterling; socialist planning versus the potentially restrictive policies of a European Union; all of these raised deep-seated and valid problems. But in the long run, it seems clear, Britain was going to have to pay a high price for the choice of a supposedly special relationship with the United States and with the Commonwealth, both of which were likely to become chimerical with the passing years. As the Common Market emerged, and as it later took on the stamp of Charles DeGaulle's limited vision of a united Europe, the unfortunate consequences of the Labour Government's decisions in the early stages of European Union were to become increasingly apparent.

However one may sum them up, Bevin's policies did not command universal support within the Labour movement. He was, to be sure, in the mainstream of a middle-of-the-road internationalism supposedly building upon the work of his Labour predecessors who had taught the Party the meaning of international responsibility. But to some within the Party, needless to say, moderate internationalism and Bevin's close collaboration with the United States appeared to be almost mutually exclusive. The issue of rearmament, in particular, created a crisis that was perhaps more real than the controversy over spectacles and false teeth I noted earlier. It appears to me that the supporters of Aneurin Bevan were correct, that Great Britain could not afford the scale of rearmament urged upon her by the United States—especially after the outbreak of the Korean War—and reluctantly accepted by Clement Attlee's Government. But whatever the merits of the argument, in foreign and defense policy, as on domestic issues, the Labour Party seemed to speak with many voices. And the differences persisted much more bitterly when Labour went into opposition after the election of 1951.

I commented at some length about the searing—and tedious—conflict that raged within the Labour Party throughout the fifties and into the sixties. In part, perhaps in large part, it was a struggle for the succession, a quarrel over the direction in which British socialism was headed. But it was also, as I noted, a quarrel over foreign policy, a quarrel that reminds one of the controversies that wracked the Party in the years following the First World War. First rearmament and the Korean War, then German rearmament, then British production of the hydrogen bomb, then the broader question of an "independent nuclear deterrent," as it was euphemistically called—each raised fundamental questions that, in characteristic fashion, threatened irreparable divisions and resulted in none. Soon after Hugh Gaitskell had succeeded to the leadership at the end of 1955, he opened the way for Aneurin Bevan to become reconciled with the Party. The result—it seemed to many Americans an odd one—was that Bevan, who had opposed on the international front much that Gaitskell had supported, became the shadow foreign minister on the Labour front bench.

In a way, it was Conservative blundering that made this possible. I have the feeling that the pros and cons of the Suez crisis of 1956 were much less clearcut than either American journalists or Secretary of State Dulles considered them to be. But I am also certain that Anthony Eden, who by now was Tory Prime Minister, mismanaged the Suez affair appallingly. He gave Labour an opportunity to rally to the defense of a United Nations position, to denounce the Anglo-French ultimatum, to call for censure of the bombing of Egypt and the use of British troops. In actual fact, several studies have suggested that there was a substantial rank-and-file nationalist support of Eden's actions. [29] After a time, Labour's leaders thought it wise to soft-pedal the Suez issue. But my point is that Suez enabled the various factions of the Labour Party to act in concert and thus to begin again the never-ending process of reknitting the rather ravelled fabric of Labour politics, of maintaining the precarious balance so characteristic of the Party.

When Harold Wilson succeeded Hugh Gaitskell as leader of the Party, its official position on international affairs hardly changed at all. Indeed, though Wilson in his own way had been a Bevanite, an article that he wrote for the *Atlantic Monthly* [30] a few months after taking over in 1963 might well have been written by Gaitskell or, for that matter, by Ernest Bevin. He emphasized that the Labour Party's approach to overseas affairs was conditioned by its loyalty to three groupings: the Western alliance, the Commonwealth, and the United Nations. And it seems to me significant—to go back now to the argument that I began to develop in the first part of this paper—that with respect to none of the three loyalties was Wilson categorical to the point of irreversibility. Opposed to neutralism as he was opposed to German nuclear weapons, he threaded a narrow path between too much dependence upon the Americans and a totally unrealistic pretension of total independence. By most Englishmen, beyond a doubt, his position was accepted as the practical one, just as after he came into office in 1964, his foreign policy was so regarded. Neither of his Foreign Secretaries, Michael Stewart and George Brown, showed himself to have the tough fiber of Ernest Bevin, but on the whole they pursued Ernest Bevinite not Aneurin Bevanite policies.

Wilson, himself, with singular lack of success tried, to a certain extent, to play the role of mediator in the attempt to bring the Vietnam war to an end. But, much to the fury of the Labour left, he made no bones about his Government's ultimate, if reluctant, acquiescence in American policy. Thus, a measure of continuity was again discernible, though once more there was restlessness and more than restlessness over Vietnam, over military commitments east of Suez, over Rhodesia, over a number of other questions.

I have very deliberately avoided writing about the recent years in any detail. It has seemed to me more useful, since I am a historian of the earlier twentieth century, to go back and to comment, even if only in general terms, about the background that may help place contemporary policies into focus. Labour's international stance has been, on the whole, what most observers would, I think, regard as temperate and responsible. It came into existence as the Labour Party reached maturity and the possibility of having to take office. As it emerged, it reflected the "taming" of some of the more extreme notions of earlier socialist pioneers. It was more frequently a broadly liberal foreign policy than it was a socialist foreign policy. Arthur Henderson, Ramsay MacDonald, Ernest Bevin, Clement Attlee, Hugh Gaitskell, Harold Wilson—on the whole this is a roster of middle-of-the-road practitioners whose international positions, with obvious differences of emphasis, might well have been those of Austen Chamberlain, or Anthony Eden, or Harold Macmillan. But of course, just as the positions of the more moderate Conservatives have been on occasion challenged by their "backwoodsmen"—the reactionaries who have pined for the good old days of empire and have wanted little nonsense about international cooperation—so has the position of the moderate Labour Party leadership by its dissidents on the left—internal critics whose disgust over the policies of the center have again and again caused some observers to believe that the existence of the Party itself was being threatened.

If what I have had to say in this analysis has any merit, however, the Party's internal controversy over foreign policy, like its quarrels over domestic issues, is paradoxically an element of strength rather than of weakness. Despite the seeming contradictions, despite a great deal of public mud slinging, despite even abstentions and withdrawals from Party discipline, British electors of various persuasions somehow have managed to find something for almost anyone in the foreign policy of the Labour Party. As a result—to conclude with what I have been arguing all along—the Labour Party, like an American political party in a totally different environment, manages to have a breadth of appeal that explains, I believe, its viability as an alternative to Conservatism in the politics of modern Britain. Whether in present circumstances viability can be equated with effectiveness on either the domestic or the international stage is, I think, still an open question.

NOTES

1. This paper in slightly different form, was delivered on April 19 and 20, 1967, at the University of Cincinnati as the Taft Lectures in History. Harold Vinacke honored me by being present at both lectures, and it seemed appropriate therefore to offer this essay as my thanks for all that I learned from him about being a scholar—and much more.

2. Philip Poirier, *The Advent of the Labour Party* (London: 1958); Henry Pelling, *The Origins of the Labour Party, 1880–1900* (London: 1954); Frank Bealey and Henry Pelling, *Labour and Politics, 1900–1906. A History of the Labour Representation Committee* (London: 1958).

3. "The British Labour Party: The Conflict between Socialist Ideals and Practical Politics before 1918," American Historical Association Annual Meeting, December 28, 1963.

4. "The British Labour Party: The Conflict between Socialist Ideals and Practical Politics between the Wars," *Journal of British Studies,* V (November 1965), pp. 140–152.

5. London: 1949.

6. Perry Anderson and Robin Blackburn, eds., *Towards Socialism* (London: 1965).

7. Michael Foot, *Aneurin Bevan. A Biography. Volume One: 1897 – 1945* (London: 1963).

8. Ralph Miliband, *Parliamentary Socialism: A Study in the Politics of Labour* (London: 1961).

9. *Ibid.*, p. 230.

10. London: 1954.

11. London: 1965.

12. *Modern British Politics*, p. 179.

13. "Goals of Today's Welfare State," in *Towards Socialism*, pp. 355 – 356.

14. *Ibid.*, p. 357.

15. London: 1956.

16. Beer, p. 227.

17. *A Short History of the Labour Party* (2nd. ed., London: 1965), pp. 129 – 133.

18. Carl F. Brand, *The British Labour Party. A Short History* (Stanford, California: 1964), p. 59.

19. Henry R. Winkler, *The League of Nations Movement in Great Britain, 1914 – 1919* (New Brunswick, New Jersey: 1952); Arno J. Mayer, *Political Origins of the New Diplomacy, 1917 – 1918* (New Haven, Connecticut: 1959).

20. "The Emergence of a Labor Foreign Policy in Great Britain, 1918 – 1929," *Journal of Modern History*, XXVIII (September, 1956), pp. 247 – 258; "Arthur Henderson," in *The Diplomats, 1919 – 1939*, ed. by Gordon A. Craig and Felix Gilbert (Princeton, New Jersey: 1953), pp. 311 – 343.

21. *The Diplomats*, p. 343.

22. W. N. Medlicott, *British Foreign Policy since Versailles* (London: 1940), p. 249; F. S. Northedge, *The Troubled Giant: Britain Among the Great Powers, 1916 – 1939* (New York: 1966).

23. *Nineteen Thirty-One: Politican Crisis* (London: 1958).

24. Winston S. Churchill, *The Gathering Storm* (London: 1948), p. 117.

25. Parliamentary Debates, House of Commons, 413 (August 20, 1945), col. 312.

26. M. A. Fitzsimons, *The Foreign Policy of the British Labour Government, 1945 – 1951* (Notre Dame, Indiana: 1953), pp. 25, 29.

27. David Leitch, "Explosion at the King David Hotel," in *Age of Austerity, 1945 – 51*, ed. by Michael Sissons and Philip French (Penquin Books ed., Harmondsworth, England: 1964), pp. 80 – 81.

28. *Ibid.*, p. 84.

29. For example, Leon D. Epstein, *British Politics in the Suez Crisis* (Urbana, Illinois: 1964), who makes clear, however, that the view that Labour's rank-and-file, unlike its leaders, would have supported military action is not born out by the evidence.

30. The Rt. Hon. Harold Wilson, "Britain's Policy if Labour Wins," *Atlantic*, CCXII (October 1963), pp. 61-65.

There is already a rich literature on the origins and the problems of the system of social security that reached its full growth in the years after 1945. Probably the most impressive single body of work is that of Richard B. Titmuss, who published in the nineteen-fifties and sixties a series of probing analyses of various aspects of the new social institutions. Two of his books that are required reading are the official Problems of Social Policy *(London, 1950) and* Essays on 'The Welfare State' *(new edition, London, 1963). Among the many books dealing with the background of post-1945 programs one of the most revealing is Bentley B. Gilbert's* The Evolution of National Insurance in Great Britain: The Origins of the Welfare State *(London, 1966). In the article reprinted here Kathleen Woodroofe, who teaches at the University of New South Wales in Sydney, Australia, succinctly develops three points. In the first place, she defines what is meant by the phrase "welfare state." She then summarizes the evolution of state control in a number of areas that prepared the way, even before the "origins" of 1906 to 1914, for the social policies of a later period. And she comments upon the criticisms that have been made both of individual features of the social legislation and its administration and of its general assumptions and goals. Her article is reprinted by permission of* The Journal of Social History, *where it appeared in the Summer 1968 issue, pp. 303–24.*

8

The Making of the Welfare State in England:

A Summary of Its Origin and Development

KATHLEEN WOODROOFE

One of the most dangerous habits we have acquired in this age of neon lights and snappy slogans is to tie labels around the necks of highly complex social phenomena. Sometimes it is done with groups of people—the "white-collared" or the "black-coated," the "status seekers" or "The Establishment." Sometimes it is around an entity which smacks of the mystical—the "power elite" or even the "middle class." Sometimes it is around a social system—the "Welfare State" or the "Affluent Society." This habit of reducing a social phenomenon to a slogan is likely to horrify the purist. All generalizations are dangerous, and those expressed in tabloid form are the most dangerous of all. At best, they can tell only part of the story. At worst, they can be untrue and misleading. They may pass into our speech as accepted truths, instead of being recognized as propositions open to discussion and dispute, and, worst of all, the label may remain, even though that which is so labeled has changed its character. Yet despite these dangers, we are unable to discard the labels, and it would be a pity if we tried to do so. Any slogan or catchword which is widely used by people in speaking of their own society must tell us something about that society, for current beliefs about our contemporary world are themselves part of the world to which they refer.

The label "Welfare State" is of recent origin. It was first used by Sir Alfred Zimmern during the 1930's to epitomize the contrast between warfare and welfare—the "guns or butter" of the Nazis—and later, by the Archbishop of

Canterbury who, in 1941, published his *Citizen and Churchman* in which he developed the notion of a "welfare state" of the democracies as opposed to the "power state" of the dictators. The notion held, he argued, only if the state in the democracies fulfilled its moral and spiritual functions in promoting human welfare. The term was soon given a new connotation by the Beveridge Report in 1942 and the legislation of the Labour government which followed it, when the whole concept of welfare was widened from the pre-war concept of a set of social services for the care of people unable to care for themselves—old people, mothers, babies, and children at school—to a new post-war concept of a system of social security, based on the principle which Lord Beveridge summarized as:

> unified universal contributory insurance to ensure at all times to all men a subsistence income for themselves and their families as of right . . . without any form of means test or inquiry about what means they had.[1]

This was in keeping with the mood of the country during the later years of the Second World War, a mood which was summed up in an article printed in *The Times* in 1940 a few weeks after the British Expeditionary Forces had been withdrawn from the Continent and England stood alone against Germany. "If we speak of democracy," *The Times* stated,

> we do not mean a democracy which maintains the right to vote, but forgets the right to work and the right to live. If we speak of freedom, we do not mean a rugged individualism which excludes social organisation and economic privilege. If we speak of economic reconstruction, we think less of maximum production (though this, too, will be required) than of equitable distribution.[2]

This ideal was reflected in much of the new social legislation for education, medical care, and social security which was passed in England from 1945 to 1950.

This development was not confined to England. In 1950, the International Labour Office noted that a "new conception" was transforming the pre-war system of social insurance in many countries. "There is a movement everywhere," one of its reports stated, "towards including additional classes of population, covering a wider range of contingencies, providing benefits more nearly adequate to needs . . . loosening the tie between benefit right and contribution payment, and, in general, unifying the finance and administration of branches hitherto separate."[3] In other words, the post-war quest for a system of social security based on the principles of guaranteed subsistence, comprehensiveness, and universality was transforming, in England and elsewhere, the social service state of pre-war years into some kind of welfare state.

Notice that implicit in these words of Lord Beveridge and the International Labour Office report is a description of the chief characteristics of a welfare state: namely, a state which uses its powers first, to guarantee individuals and their families a minimum income irrespective of the market value of their work or property; second, to narrow down the extent of insecurity by enabling individuals and their families to meet such social contingencies as sickness, old age, and unemployment; and third, to make available to all citizens, irrespective of income, status, or class, an agreed range of social services.[4] Notice, too, that to provide this protection, the state establishes public social services, which aim to provide each individual with the precise form of assistance he needs, and that these services fall into three broad groups. First, there are the social assistance services, such as non-contributory old age pensions, family allowances, housing and national assistance, which aim to bring people of small means up to subsistence level. These are usually financed out of central or local government funds and are subject to a means test. A special genus of assistance in the past has been the Poor Law, which began in England in the sixteenth century as a comprehensive poor relief service based on destitution, and more than three centuries later, was "broken up" into a number of specialist services to attend to the needs of whole sets of people, such as the old, the sick, and the unemployed, as they were separated from the gloomy body of paupers by the Old Age Pensions Act of 1908 and the National Insurance Act of 1911. Second, there are social insurance services, such as national health insurance, unemployment insurance, widows' pensions, and old age contributory pensions. Here the contribution made, rather than need, is the condition on which the services are obtained. And third, we now add social security services to the list. These, seeking to insure security of income, are a type of protection against interruptions of income through sickness, unemployment, accident, or old age. To generalize, perhaps unwisely, one could say that England, in seeking a solution to the problem of poverty, has gone through each of these three stages of assistance, insurance, and security. In so doing, she has gradually created the present welfare state to safeguard her citizens against the most acute forms of social distress.

How then, we may ask, did the welfare state begin?—for it is obvious that it did not spring Minerva-like from the program of the Labour Party in the 1940's, or even from that great surge of social legislation during the first decade of the twentieth century. The taproot of the welfare state can be traced much further down, probably to the sixteenth century when the state's "welfare" activities were confined to keeping the poor alive and not much else, when religious and voluntary agencies in England were unable to stem the advancing tide of pau-

perism, and the growing numbers of "rufflers," "hookers," "bogus sailors,"
"bawdy baskets" and other vagabonds, whom Thomas Harman catalogued
with such worried relish, made it obvious that the problem of pauperism was
now too big to be met by the Church or private charity. The state itself must
step into the breach. It must seek to create employment, and to provide for the
unemployed who still remained; and so the parliament of Elizabeth I created a
system of social security, taking positive, constructive steps to prevent
unemployment by creating work (its most famous measure, of course, was the
Statute of Artificers of 1563) and passing a Poor Law in 1601 to deal with any
residue of unemployment. Here the state was accepting responsibility for
those who couldn't work or who couldn't find work, administering a system of
poor relief based on the parish and financed by a compulsory poor rate levied
on everybody. This marked the beginning of a national system of poor relief directed by the state and incorporating the principle of communal responsibility.
Those poor, it was considered, who, through accident or age, were no longer
able to support themselves, had a definite claim to be protected by the state
and helped by their more prosperous brethren. This principle was made the
basis of poor relief for two hundred years, and a poor law of some kind remained on the statute book until 1948 when the National Assistance Act formally announced its demise.

The Poor Law of England, then, was the seed from which grew the flower of
social security, for as it evolved, the Poor Law contained within itself the embryo of a broad system of social security. By the eighteenth century, it was
providing something more than food and shelter for the starving and the home-
less. Though harsh by our standards, it did provide schools for children in the
workhouse. This was to blossom later into a system of state education. It also
provided better treatment for the sick. This gradually developed into a system
of hospitals for paupers, then into public hospitals, and finally into a national
health scheme. Indeed, the Speenhamland system of 1795, in seeking to gear
wages to the price of the "Gallon Loaf," went far beyond the province of the
Poor Law. Even though its policy of supplementing low wages by an allowance
from the poor rates had disastrous results when put into practice it did take
into account the cost of living, and by offering a guaranteed minimum wage
and family allowances, tried to inject an element of social security into the
wage system. But it was doomed to failure. Especially in the southern counties
where the system was most practised, the results proved unsatisfactory to the
laborers, who were permanently pauperized without receiving adequate maintenance, and to the general body of rate payers whose financial burdens increased without seeming to provide any guarantees against laborers' revolts

such as that which occurred in 1830. Again in the nineteenth century, an attempt was made to distinguish between the "undeserving" and the "deserving" poor, especially the aged poor, and this led to the granting of privileges to the latter both inside and outside the workhouse. The Royal Commission on the Aged Poor in 1896 recommended that in the workhouse, persons of 65 who "by reason of their moral character or behaviour or previous habits" were "sufficiently deserving," should have separate day rooms, extra visits, sleeping cubicles, separate lockers, and larger allowances of tobacco, tea, and sugar. Likewise in 1886, Joseph Chamberlain began to devise a system of work relief to get around the Poor Law so that help could be given the workless without making him a pauper. Later the scheme blossomed into the Unemployed Workmen's Act of 1905 which set up an elaborate system of committees and labor exchanges outside the pale of the Poor Law, so that aid could be given in such a way that the aided did not lose his right to vote.

Thus were England's social services born and bred within the framework of the Poor Law.

Here, then, in this acceptance of communal responsibility for the less fortunate members of society can be found the beginnings of England's welfare state. From then onwards, it is a story, first, of the slow widening of the range of services provided—from the simple "outdoor relief" of the first Elizabethans to the present system of national assistance, from the apprenticing of poor children in the eighteenth century to the provision of a state system of education, and from the care of the sick poor to the environmental health services of the nineteenth century and the National Health Service of today. Second, it is a story of the slow widening of the area of responsibility—from the parish of the sixteenth century, through "a Union" of parishes advocated by the Poor Law Amendment Act of 1834, to the Local Authority of 1930 and, eventually, under the Unemployment Assistance Board of 1934 and the National Assistance Board of 1948, to the nation as a whole. It is also the story of changing opinions about such important matters as the proper role of the state, poverty and the poor, the nature of man, and whether or not social rights should be ranged alongside political and civil rights as the rightful possession of all citizens.

But the Poor Law is not the whole story. The origins of England's welfare state must also be sought later on in history, in the collectivism of the Victorian era. It is only recently that this has been realized,[5] so beguiling is the myth propagated by A. V. Dicey in his hypnotic *Law and Public Opinion in England in the Nineteenth Century,* published in 1905, that the nineteenth century was an age of laissez faire and that it was only in 1865 or "roundabouts" that we can detect the first small beginnings of what he called "anti-laissez faire" or "col-

*when the state
did the welfare state
start? [Essay Q]??*

lectivism." But a closer look at the period shows that the beginnings of the structure and many of the policies of the welfare state occurred much earlier than this. Certainly there were many instances of laissez faire in the first half of the nineteenth century—the most famous, of course, was the repeal of the Corn Laws in 1846—but while the principle of laissez faire was upheld in the external sphere, it was being denied in the internal sphere. Even as the state lifted many of its regulations on commerce, it was imposing regulations on industry, as more and more it was forced to intervene to alleviate the worst stresses and strains of the Industrial Revolution and a rapidly increasing population. In the field of industrial welfare, for example, the government had taken its first step in 1802 by passing the Health and Morals of Apprentices Act to limit the hours of work of apprentices in cotton mills. From this tentative, almost surreptitious beginning, the state had gradually extended its sphere of operation. Then, having admitted the principle that intervention was justified to protect the worker against the worst results of industrial capitalism, the state had to consider the further questions of which workers were to be protected and what kind of protection they should get. At first the state intervened only on behalf of children and women. Men were considered to be strong enough to make a satisfactory contract with their employers without state protection, and when, later, they sought state protection, they were accused of "fighting behind women's petticoats." As for the kind of protection needed, three aspects of modern industry called for attention—at what age should a person be allowed to begin work? for how long should he work? and, under what conditions? For many years, industrial regulation was concerned with these aspects, but later, another question arose—could the state regulate payment for work?—and yet another, what was to happen to the worker who, through accident, sickness, old age, or unemployment, was not able to work? In answering these questions, and putting the answers into operation, there was gradually built up in England an industrial code which, by the first decade of the twentieth century, not only covered hours and conditions of work, but was being extended to the fields of industrial unemployment and social insurance.

Again, in the field of education, the state had been forced to make educational provision for the growing numbers of children able to survive the dangers of the first year of life. The first reaction of the state had been against popular education. Davies Giddy, opposing Samuel Whitbread's Education Bill of 1807, warned the House that education would teach "the labouring classes of the poor" to "despise their lot in life," "render them fractious and refractory," and "insolent to their superiors."[6] Fifty years later, however, the ruling class had begun to realize that a little education, far from being dangerous, could offer protection against social revolution. "The uneducated state of the 'lower orders,' " Andrew Ure pointed out, ". . . is the dark den of incendiarism and misrule . . . which, if not cleared out, will give birth ere long to disastrous eruptions in every province."[7] This fear of social revolution was to grow as the franchise was liberalized, for democracy carried emotional connotations much like those of communism today. "The last time I saw Southey," Thomas Carlyle recalled in 1881, ". . . we sat on the sofa together; our talk was long and earnest; topic ultimately the usual one, steady approach of democracy, with revolution (probably explosive) and a finis incomputable to man; steady decay of all morality, political, social, individual . . . and noble England would have to collapse in shapeless ruin, whether for ever or not none of us could know."[8] The Reform Bill of 1867 produced the same kind of agitated comment. Lord Cranborne (afterwards Lord Salisbury) confessed that he had long "entertained a firm conviction that we are going to the dogs." Carlyle thought "the tug of revolution struggle may be even *near* for poor England," while Disraeli, attacking the Bill of 1866, prophesied the "rule of mobs in great towns and the sway of turbulent multitudes."[9] (This morbid thought, however, did not prevent him from carrying a Reform Bill the following year.) In this situation where democracy, to many, spelled revolution, reasoning such as Ure's carried weight, so that the state which in 1833 had grudgingly granted £20,000 to education for building purposes only, by 1870 was prepared to pass an Education Act to provide a system of state education to supplement the existing voluntary system.

In the field of public health, too, the same process was at work. Originally regarded as a means of protecting the rich against infection, public health had gradually broadened its objectives. The sheer magnitude of the problem of maintaining health in the new industrial towns had forced the government to intervene, and a series of Public Health Acts from 1848 to 1875 empowered central and local authorities to safeguard public health.

But it was not only in fields such as these that state control eddied out in the nineteenth century. In areas less directly related to welfare, the state assumed new powers and responsibilities. In the fifty years from 1825, which Dicey labelled "The Period of Individualism," the government passed Railway Company Acts involving compulsory sale of right of way, Passenger Acts to protect the seven and a half million people who emigrated from the United Kingdom during the first three quarters of the nineteenth century, acts to abolish slavery, to reform the Post Office, to nationalize telegraphs, telephones, and broadcasting, to maintain standards of amenity, safety, and legality in railways, in the mercantile marine, gas and water supplies, food adulteration, and patents, acts to promote arbitration of disputes, to enforce employers' liability, and later, at the beginning of our own century, to create wage boards to set a minimum wage. One could add, too, the so-called "municipal trading" in docks, gas, bath houses, tramways, electric power, housing, slum clearance, hospitals, libraries, museums and other amenities which, from the 1850's onwards, gradually transformed a city such as Birmingham, for example, from an ugly industrial hotchpotch into what one American observer in 1890 claimed to be "the best governed city in the world." [10] No matter into which decade one looks in the nineteenth century, one thing is certain: some interested group can be found ready to use the state for its own ends. Laissez faire and state intervention, despite our tendency to polarize them, can both be seen as an exercise of political power, as instruments to be used by different groups to achieve their individual ends. Sometimes it is the landed oligarch who uses the state, sometimes the industrialist; sometimes, after 1867, it is the urban worker; sometimes, after 1884, the farm laborer. No wonder that the right to vote was sought so assiduously, not for any high-minded philosophical reasons (although these were later invented), but for what it could do. For then as now, it was safer to accept the sad but indisputable fact that you can trust only yourself to work in your own self-interest. The nineteenth century, then, so far from being an age of laissez faire, was a period in which new forms of state control were hammered out. Moreover, intervention was cumulative. The state was a rolling stone which gathered moss, whether in factories, railways, shipping, company finance, education, or religion. Not that the rolling was always unimpeded or the moss gathered green. Laws extending state control always had to be passed in the face of intense opposition, for, despite the thickening statute book, it was still generally believed that the adult citizen should be left free to make what use he liked of his own capacities, and that any attempt on the part of the state to interfere with this freedom must sap individual, and eventually national, strength. Only as a last resort must the state intervene. "State benevolence," Shaftesbury warned, "is a melancholy system that tends to debase a large mass of the people to the condition of the nursery, where the children look to the father and mother, and do nothing for themselves." [11] Behind these words, there lay a firmly held belief that men were pauperized by indiscriminate charity, whether it be private or state charity, a strong dislike of centralization and an even stronger dislike of paying taxes to defray the cost of centralization.

Thus in the Victorian period from 1837 to 1901, often in the face of bitter opposition, some of those social policies began which foreshadow England's welfare state. In the first place, there was a substantial amount of public assistance, although this was given through a comprehensive poor law which, based on the 1834 principle, decreed that the condition of the inmates of a workhouse was to be "less eligible" than that of the lowest-paid laborer, gave assistance grudgingly and at the terrible cost of depriving the recipient of the right to vote and often at the price of separating him from his family. This harsh treatment of the poor was in accordance with the Victorians' conception of poverty and its causes. This was a problem which tended to be ignored. Although there were a few enlightened individuals who pointed to the existence of poverty and the social danger which it entailed, the majority of articulate Victorians tended to shut their eyes to the problem. To them, England's wealth was indisputable. Poverty, when noticed at all, was accepted as a temporary lapse from prosperity, and unfortunate necessity, or as proof of individual indolence, inefficiency or improvidence. It was not until Charles Booth in 1892 published the first of his seventeen volumes on the *Life and Labour of the People of London,* which demonstrated that 30.7 percent of London's inhabitants lived at or below bare subsistence, that a new attitude to the problem was born. Booth, it was clear, had made a scientific investigation not of "the poor" but of "poverty." He had found so startling the extent of poverty that it was obvious that the existing methods for handling it were entirely inadequate. A new solution was necessary. The state itself, he said, must "nurse the helpless and incompetent as we in our own families nurse the old, the young and the sick." [12] Poverty, in other words, was not preordained, part of a "natural" order, or proof of individual aberration. It was not to be exorcized by incantations on thrift and self-help. It was human, explicable, and removable, and if the existing methods for dealing with it were inadequate, unsuitable, or desultory, the state itself must step into the role of provider. But this conception of poverty embodied in Booth's suggestion of what was, in effect, a welfare state, was too novel to be immediately acceptable, and so its effects were not felt until the twentieth century. During the Victorian era, the principles of 1834 still held sway, so that although public assistance was given to those in need, it was given grudgingly and on the harshest possible terms.

In framing social politics other than public assistance, however, the Victorians proved themselves less conservative. By the end of the century they were following Bismarck's lead and passing laws which embraced the new field of social insurance. A Workmen's Compensation Act in 1897 gave employees in certain industries a right to compensation for any accident received at work, and thus prepared the way for an Old Age Pensions Act in 1908 to grant a pension of five shillings a week to those of seventy and over, and a National Insurance Act in 1911 which introduced the principle of compulsory insurance. Likewise in the field of public health, the Victorians from the 1850's onwards broke new ground, for in making vaccination the first free compulsory medical service provided by parliament on a national scale, they created what R. J. Lambert has aptly called "a Victorian National Health Service."[13]

These services rendered by the state were supplemented, then as now, by a spate of services provided by voluntary organizations. Just at the time when Booth's survey was proving the inadequacy of philanthropy in handling mass poverty, private and organized charity was at its zenith. Especially in London, private charities, offering as they did immediate, easy, short-run solutions to the problem of poverty, had spawned to such an extent that many believed the poor had become pauperized as a result. Octavia Hill, whose experiments in housing management and training workers so profoundly influenced succeeding generations of social workers, was convinced that this was so. "I am quite awed when I think what our impatient charity is doing to the poor of London," she told an audience at Fulham in 1889; "men who should hold up their heads as self-respecting fathers of families, learning to sing like beggars in the street—all because we give pennies." [14] "Charity . . . is a frightful evil," agreed Edward Denison, the first "settler" in London's East End; ". . . the gigantic subscription lists which are vaunted as signs of our benevolence, are monuments of our indifference." [15] "Charity infects the people like a silent working pestilence," added C. S. Loch, Secretary of the Charity Organisation Society. "It [has] become an endowment to the hypocrite and a laughing stock to the cynic." [16] These beliefs, however, although they led to an attempt to organize and co-ordinate the various charities, did not lead to a decrease in their numbers. "Doing good" was an activity sufficiently innocuous to be socially acceptable, and so it was a popular pastime of the wealthy and the leisured. It could assuage that sense of personal guilt which lay at the basis of so much of the humanitarianism of the Victoria era. It could create an illusion of purpose in an otherwise purposeless life. Since no training was thought to be necessary, and moreover, the well-intentioned could usually afford the luxury of spurning payment, philanthropy was a cheap, convenient, and often effective way of averting social discontent. To the Lady Clara Vere de Veres of Tennyson's poem, doing good was an avenue of salvation, an insurance on the existing order, an antidote to boredom, and a public expiation of the private sin of living comfortably in a comfortless world. And so private charity remained to supplement the public services provided by the state.

But not only did the Victorian era see the framing of many of the social policies of the welfare state, it saw also the shaping of the apparatus of the modern administrative state. England in the early nineteenth century was a country which might be said to have governed itself. In contrast with France, with its highly centralized system of state administration, England was extremely decentralized. By the 1830's, the central government had shed many medieval and Tudor restraints, and now confined its activities to administering justice, collecting taxes, and defending the realm. There was a great deal of emphasis on "freedom," which meant freedom from any interference by the central government in the affairs of the local communities. Local custom and privilege were very firmly entrenched. Although parliament had never been averse to passing laws, it had never done very much to create those central agencies necessary to enforce them. It preferred to leave administration to the parishes and the local justices of the peace, superintended by branches of the central government, such as the Exchequer, the Treasury, and the Privy Council, which had emerged over the centuries. Now, however, the central government was faced with the problem of towns teeming with new life which had to be po- liced, kept healthy, and protected against the worst forms of exploitation. This required a degree of centralization which ran counter to that deeply felt sentiment so admirably expressed by Mr. Podsnap in *Our Mutual Friend*. "I see what you're driving at," said he. "I knew it from the first. Centralization. No! *Never* with my consent. Not English." And so, in face of opposition such as this, Edwin Chadwick, for example, having succeeded in getting passed his Health of Towns Act in 1848, fought unsuccessfully to save the directive Board of Health which the Act established and on which both he and Shaftesbury served, but the forces of dirt and decentralization proved too strong for him. In 1854, he was driven into retirement, Shaftesbury followed, the Board of Health was disbanded, and the struggle had to begin all over again before further Public Health Acts could be passed in 1866, 1871 and 1875. This battle against de- centralization and non-intervention had to be fought many times before it was won, not only in the area of public health, but in poor relief, industrial regulation, education, and other fields as well. And yet it was fought, in such a way, on such a scale, and with such results that, as Oliver MacDonagh has pointed out, a "revolution in government" occurred, generated by pressures working within the administrative system itself. As it was realized that social evils could not be dealt with effectively by legislation alone, a permanent executive corps of experts was created to enforce the laws passed, to amend them when necessary, to build up a specialized body of knowledge to help them in their work, to delegate responsibility, to experiment and to initiate. From the pressures applied within the administrative system towards centralization, autonomy, delegated legislation, experimentation, and the division and specialization of administrative labor, the "self generating qualities of administration," as Professor MacDonagh calls them, there emerged "the sort of state we recognize as modern."[17] As a by-product of this process, there also emerged a type of civil servant who in these days when the neutrality of the Civil Service is taken for granted, seems alien to us because of his marked lack of neutrality and self-abnegation. Administrators such as Sir Rowland Hill, the originator of penny postage, J. Macgregor and G. R. Porter, joint secretaries of the Board of Trade during the Anti-Corn Law League's violent campaigns, and Chadwick himself were not only civil servants, but social reformers known to have strong political opinions. They were not the kind of men to remain neutral or anonymous when matters concerning their own interests were under discussion; there were programs to be formulated, members of parliaments to be briefed, votes to be canvassed, and newspapers to be kept informed. The nineteenth century, especially the period from 1830 to 1880, was the heroic age of the civil servant when, as Dr. Kitson Clark reminds us, civil servants, far from being neutral, were "most patently closet statesmen" or "statesmen in disguise."[18]

Here, then, in England from the 1830's onwards can be found the social matrix from which the present welfare state emerged. In the early twentieth century, it still bore the marks of its birth. Born in a society fearful of collectivism and centralization, it was yet forced to assume responsibility for increasing numbers of poor whose existence spelled danger to the state. Born in a society less affluent than our own, it sought always to interpret that responsibility in terms of an ideology of scarcity which set great store on public penny-pinching, which assumed that human nature was bad, which took for granted the necessity for a means test to prove destitution, and which claimed that, even if a recipient of relief paid the price in humiliation and loss of civil rights, the help granted him must be minimal, local, and deterrent. "In all large urban communities," said James Stewart Davy, principal officer of the Poor Law Division of the Local Government Board, "you must have test houses where you can have task work for the able-bodied loafer." The work given, he told his questioners, should be both irksome and unskilled, for, he added darkly, "It is the compulsory labour, the discipline and the classification which are the real objects of the pauper's dislikes."[19]

By the first decade of the twentieth century, however, this principle of "less eligibility" was being undermined on all sides. New forces in the electorate, unleashed in 1867 and 1884, had demanded reforms which could not be denied. The reforms, when achieved, indicated a new concept of government which ran counter to the idea that rule should be in the interest of the wealthy. Likewise investigations of poverty made by Booth in London and Seebohm

Rowntree in York suggested a new attitude to poverty and a more effective mode of handling it, while the coming of the Fabian Society, vociferous in its criticism of the existing order and insistent in its demand for change, emphasized the concept of a society whose structure could be manipulated by its members in the interests of all. Sooner or later the forces represented by this new concept of government, this new electorate, this new attitude to poverty, and this concept of a malleable social order had to come to grips with the forces standing behind the Poor Law Amendment Act of 1834. The conflict came at the beginning of the twentieth century and was staged with outward calm in sedate surroundings. The stage was a Royal Commission appointed in 1905 to enquire into and make recommendations about the working of the Poor Law and the relief of distress. It sat for four years and after 159 hearings in which 452 witnesses answered more than a hundred thousand questions, it declared itself unable to agree and issued two reports to prove it. On one side of the stage sat the Poor Law Division of the Local Government Board, supported by the Charity Organisation Society, in the other the four recalcitrants led by that determined socialist, Beatrice Webb. The issue at stake was whether the Poor Law should be "broken up" and its place taken by departments dealing with different aspects of the problem of destitution, and the result was the beginning of a debate on social welfare which was to last for forty years.

The debate was not confined to the theorist. Men of action, too, came to join the fray. In 1906, when, after more than a decade on the back benches, the Liberals came to power, they began to pour into legal mold the philosophy of Lloyd George, then President of the Board of Trade, who saw occurring in England changes which he believed amounted to social revolution. "I believe there is a new order coming from the people of this country," he said. "It is a quiet but certain revolution, as revolutions come in a constitutional country, without overthrowing order, without doing an injustice to anybody, but redressing those injustices from which people suffer." [20] Whether these changes constituted revolution is debatable, but certainly they came without overthrowing order. They did no obvious injustice to anybody, except perhaps to the working man, and they did redress certain injustices from which people suffered. Between 1906 and 1912, school children gained the social right of free meals and medical inspection without fear of their parents' losing the vote; an old age pension of five shillings a week was granted to the needy and deserving of seventy and over; while by the National Insurance Act of 1911, a man could claim a small health insurance benefit for himself and, if he were in certain industries, an even smaller insurance payment if he became unemployed. At the same time, a Coal Mines Regulation Act gave miners a nominal eight-hour day; labor exchanges were created to speed up the movement of labor; local authorities were given power to build houses and plan towns; and members of parliament were, for the first time, paid a salary.

These Acts charted a new course for government activity, and several were designed gradually to overthrow the Poor Law, but because at the time there were no alternative ideas with which to work, nor new insights into the social phenomena of human need and human behavior, many of the ideas and assumptions of the old Poor Law remained to be transferred, often unwittingly, to the new social services. If, for example, poverty was often the outward and visible sign of an inward and spiritual disgrace, then the poor needed to be punished or rewarded. The Old Age Pensions Act of 1908 sought to apply this principle by separating the worthy poor from the unworthy and withholding pensions from those deemed lazy or improvident. Again, since it was assumed that each man was an island, need was conceived in terms of the individual rather than the family or the work group. Accordingly, in 1911, National Health Insurance provided cash benefits during a period of sickness which were the same for a single man as for a man with a family, and thirty-seven years had to elapse before the state grudgingly recognized the fact that sick workers usually had wives and children to support. Thus many of the social services which were born in this period embodied the moral assumptions of the nineteenth century, with the result that tensions were created then which still remain today.

In spite of this, however, the years from 1906 to 1912 saw further approaches to the welfare state. Certainly work on the superstructure was interrupted by the First World War, but it was resumed immediately afterwards, and the country's lawmakers continued to break off further fragments of need from the Poor Law or from uncoordinated activities of voluntary organizations, and to build new services around them. In 1920, pensions were granted for the blind, while in the following year, unemployment insurance was extended to most manual workers, cash benefits for the unemployed were raised, and the period during which benefits were paid was extended. Thus, somewhat timidly, did England's government seek to deal with the poverty and unemployment which beset the country after the First World War. In the following decade, when the cold wind of depression forced the problems once more to the front, the need for more drastic measures was realized, but although an Unemployment Assistance Board was created in 1934, it was only in the 1940's that an attempt was made to set up a unified and comprehensive program of social services to combat, in Lord Beveridge's phrase, the "Five Giants" of Want,

Disease, Ignorance, Squalor, and Idleness which lay across the path of social progress.

The necessity for such a program had long been realized. Despite the various state schemes of assistance and insurance, there were still many people in England who were not covered by them; there was still a means tests; benefits were often inadequate, particularly in respect to unemployment; the duration of benefits was limited; and the provision made was always on the basis of the individual and not the family. It had become clear, too, that a people at war for the second time in twenty-five years would not be satisfied with flamboyant slogans which were not accompanied by social action. The needs of the war machine had involved planning at different levels, and there was a feeling that if England could plan for war, she could and should plan for peace, and that the time to begin was while the war was still going on. The Beveridge report, therefore, was launched in an atmosphere of expectancy, which explains why it was instantaneously a best-seller and its principle of a "national minimum" debated from one end of England to the other. It explains, too, why immediately after the war had ended, the Labour Government passed in quick succession its Family Allowances Act in 1945, its National Insurance and National Health Service Acts in 1946, and its National Assistance Act in 1948 in order to put the Beveridge plan into action to provide for all its citizens protection from the "cradle to the grave."

This system of social secruity was Britain's way of handling the problem of poverty. By government policy and a network of welfare services, she hoped to provide employment for those who were unemployed, to insure her citizens against the major hazards of life, and eventually to give them "a national minimum" of health, wealth and well-being. These were not favors to be dispensed by the bountiful, nor were they privileges to be won by the sycophant. They were social rights to be secured to the citizen, and since to accept assistance no longer meant loss of personal liberty or disfranchisement, social rights were not alternative to political and civil rights as they once had been. Instead, political, civil, and social rights were now embodied in the law of the land; institutions were being fashioned through which they could be realized and guaranteed; and the rights of citizenship were established in their modern form.

How far have the ideals of the welfare state been achieved? Opinions differ. Critics have complained that national assistance does not touch many real cases of need, that not enough money is spent on education, and that the National Health Scheme is too expensive, lends itself to abuse by the patient, and often runs counter to the interests of the doctor. Also, the critic adds, warming to his task, the provision of subsidized housing is fitful, social security provisions are not making the poor better off relatively to the rest of the population, and where living standards have improved, the improvement has been due, not to changes and developments within the social services, but to factors lying outside them.

Some of these criticisms are undoubtedly correct. In a land which boasts that it has a "national minimum," there still remains what Peter Townsend calls a "submerged fifth" of seven to eight million people [21] who, being old, disabled, widowed, or handicapped, live perilously close to the margins of poverty. Despite the Education Act of 1944, more than 70 percent of all children still leave school at 15 or less, and only 6 percent go on to a university and 9 percent to any form of higher education. There is evidence, too, as Brian Abel-Smith has remined us, that the middle classes rather than the working classes are the beneficiaries of England's system of social security, since it is they who get the "lion's share" of the public social service, the "elephant's share" of occupational welfare privileges, and who, in addition, enjoy "hidden social services" provided by concessions in the income tax. [22] Again, where living standards have improved, the improvement has often been due not to the extension of the social services, although they have sometimes mitigated the most acute poverty, but to the maintenance of a high level of employment and to the dramatic increase in the number of working wives from 500 thousand in 1939 to 4 million in 1960. It is these two latter developments, rather than the largesse of a welfare state, which account for the fact that there are fewer poor in the England of the 1960's than there were in the England of the 1930's. Yet granted these criticisms and modifications, there still remains an area in the welfare state in which achievement has undoubtedly equalled aspiration. The National Health Service, typifying as it does humanity fighting against natural ills, has become the true symbol of the welfare state. Based on need, largely free, and used by 95 percent of the population, it has become the most widely used and the most appreciated of all the social services. In a recent enquiry in Greater London into the impact of the services on the family as a whole, 92 percent of the families questioned, while stressing the fact that of all family difficulties illness was the chief source of worry, said that the National Health Scheme was "of great help" and 82 percent that it was of more help than any other service. [23] Doctors, too, after an initial period of hostility, have come to accept the Service with the same enthusiasm. For not only has it raised their standard of living to the point where they are now one of the highest paid professional groups in England, but in this age of science and specialization, it has given them more freedom to treat their patients according to their medical needs. By making available the costly new drugs and treatment essential to modern practice, the Service has made it possible for the general practitioner, as well as the specialist, to treat more serious illness among his patients and to do more preventive work. Of course, it could not ensure that doctors, now equipped with greater powers, would become "better" doctors than before, but it could and did provide, as Professor Titmuss has said, "that particular framework of social resources within which potentially 'better' medicine could be more easily chosen and practised." [24]

But quite apart from criticisms of individual features of the welfare state, there has been criticism of it on wider grounds. From the left wing have come voices proclaiming that the welfare state has not gone far enough, that it has merely damped down class antagonisms without resolving them, and that the social services, operating as they do within the interstices of a private ownership society, are limited by assumptions and regulations belonging not to the new society but to the old. At the same time, voices from the right wing, equally vociferous, have claimed that the welfare state has gone too far, that it has become a universal provider of such beneficence that the working population has become socially irresponsible and that what is needed now is an "Opportunity State" to match and sustain the welfare state. "The Welfare State as it exists today is the delayed reaction to Victorian poverty and interwar unemployment," writes Peter Goldman, Director of the Conservative Political Centre. "As standards of living continue to rise, many of the assumptions upon which it is based are seen to be falsified. . . . More and more people of working age are becoming capable of standing on their own feet; more and more can afford to make provision out of their earnings . . . for the necessities and against the hazards of ordinary life." Why, then, he goes on to ask, do we not make "a major shift" in the nature, direction, and emphasis of social spending—"away from the crude services which working people ought increasingly to be able to provide for themselves, and towards modern services crying out for community effort or finance." [25] Here, Goldman, without, it must be said, presenting any evidence that the English people *are* living in an affluent society, [26] has suggested an antithesis between the welfare state and an affluent society which has led one sociologist at least to ask whether these two are not irreconcilable rivals. The welfare state, T. H. Marshall claims, is a product of the "Austerity Society" of the 1940's with its rationing, its rent restrictions, its shortages, and its price controls. "It was not that these restrictions on the free market were regarded as good in themselves," he writes. ". . . But they provided as a background to the welfare legislation a society committed to 'fair shares' and to a distribution of real income which . . . was not the unpredictable result of supposedly blind forces of a competitive market, in which everybody was entitled to take as much as he could get." By the middle of the 1950's, however, the austerity society had passed away, and the affluent society, with its entirely different standard of values, was taking its place. In the ensuing clash between "the two opposed ideologies," the welfare state was at a disadvantage. "So it seems," Professor Marshall sums up, "that the Welfare State as we knew it in the 1940's . . . has been smothered by an Affluent Society." Obviously, he adds, there is need "for a new model." [27]

Here, then, is England's welfare state, meaning different things to different people and attacked by friend as well as by foe. No wonder, then, that Asa Briggs, for one, seeking the origins of the welfare state, was compelled to ask the question whether the end result, whatever it is, is still with us, or whether it was only flashed onto the screen of our consciousness in the 1940's and 1950's, and then disappeared altogether or changed into something else. [28] What is the verdict to be? Is the welfare state an image or reality? If a reality, why so many conflicting versions of it? If an image, has it no reality? And if the latter, what should be done about it? The matter is a little like a story Sir Lewis Namier is reputed to have told his students of the man who, during the horrors of a Lisbon earthquake in the eighteenth century when arraigned before a court for selling earthquake pills, silenced his accusers thus: "What," he asked, "would you put in their place?"

NOTES

1. *Hansard,* House of Lords (1953), vol. 182, 675 – 676.

2. Quoted in R. M. Titmuss, *Problems of Social Policy* (London: H.M.S.O., 1950), p. 508.

3. I.L.O. International Labour Conference, 34th Session, "Objectives and Minimum Standards of Social Security," 1950, pp. 3 – 4.

4. *Cf.* Asa Briggs' definition: "A 'Welfare State' is a state in which organised power is deliberately used (through politics and administration) in an effort to modify the play of market forces in at least three directions—first, by guaranteeing individuals and families a minimum income irrespective of the market value of their work or their property; second, by narrowing the extent of insecurity by enabling individuals and families to meet certain 'social contingencies' (for example, sickness, old age and unemployment) which lead otherwise to individual and family crises; and third, by ensuring that all citizens without distinction of status or class are offered the best standards available in relation to a certain agreed range of social services" ("The Welfare State in Historical Perspective," *Archives Européennes de Sociologie,* II, 2 [1961,] 228).

5. The two most comprehensive studies on this theme were published only in 1960 and 1961: David Roberts, *Victorian Origins of the British Welfare State* (New Haven: Yale University Press, 1960) and Maurice Bruce, *The Coming of the Welfare State* (London: Batsford, 1961). There were, however, earlier "pioneer" studies. See particularly Karl Polanyi, *The Great Transformation* (New York: Rhinehart and Co., 1944) and J. Bartlett Brebner, "Laissez Faire and State Intervention in Nineteenth Century Britain" in *Journal of Economic History*, Supplement VIII, *The Tasks of Economic History* (1948), pp. 59 – 73.

6. *Hansard,* House of Commons (1807), vol. IX, 798.

7. *Philosophy of Manufacturers* (London: A. G. Bohn, 1861), p. 404.

8. J. A. Froude, ed., *Reminiscences by Thomas Carlyle* (London: Longmans, Green and Co., 1881), II, 326 – 327.

9. Contemporary quotations taken from O. F. Christie, *The Transition from Aristocracy, 1832 – 1867* (London: Seeley, Service, 1927), p. 257.

10. J. Ralph, "The Best Governed City in the World," *Harper's Monthly Magazine* (June 1890). Quoted by Asa Briggs, *History of Birmingham* (London: Oxford University Press, 1952), II, 67.

11. "The Dwelling of the Poor" (1883), in Michael Goodwin, ed., *Nineteenth Century Opinion. An Anthology of Extracts from 'The Nineteenth Century,' 1877 – 1901* (Penguin Books, 1951), p. 75.

12. *Life and Labour of the People of London* (London: Macmillan, 1892), I, 165.

13. "A Victorian National Health Service: State Vaccination 1855 – 71," *Historical Journal,* V, 1 (1962), 1 – 8.

14. "The C.O.S. A Paper read at the meeting of the Fulham and Hammersmith Charity Organisation Society Committee, February 1, 1889, at Fulham Palace," *C.O.S. Occasional Paper,* 1st Series, No. 15, p. 25.

15. Sir Baldwyn Leighton, ed., *Letters and Other Writings of the Late Edward Denison M.P. for Newark* (London: Richard Bentley and Son, 1872), p. 103.

16. "Some Necessary Reforms in Charitable Work, Part I," *Charity Organisation Reporter,* XI, 434 (June 29, 1882), 196, and C.O.S. *Thirteenth Annual Report,* 1882, p. 20.

17. Oliver MacDonagh, *A Pattern of Government Growth 1880 – 1860* (London: MacGibbon and Kee, 1961), p. 17. See also "The Nineteenth Century Revolution in Government: A Reappraisal," *Historical Journal,* I, 1 (1958), 52 – 67.

18. G. Kitson Clark, " 'Statesmen in Disguise': Reflections on the History of the Neutrality of the Civil Service," *Historical Journal,* II, 1 (1959), 38.

19. *Report of the Royal Commission on the Poor Laws and the Relief of Distress.* Cmd. 4499, 1909. App. Vol. I. Minutes of Evidence. See answers to questions 2033 and 2036; also to questions 2027, 2229, 2230, 2375, 2366, 2318.

20. Speech at Bangor, January 19, 1906, in Philip Guedalla, ed., *Slings and Arrows—Sayings chosen from Speeches of the Rt. Hon. David Lloyd George* (London: Cassell and Co., 1929), p. 5.

21. "A Society for People" in Norman Mackenzie, ed., *Conviction* (London: MacGibbon and Kee, 1959), pp. 103 – 104. See also an article, "The Voiceless Millions" by Brian Abel-Smith in *New Statesman* (October 9, 1964), pp. 528 – 530.

22. "Whose Welfare State?" in Norman Mackenzie, ed., pp. 63, 62.

23. P.E.P., *Family Needs and the Social Services* (London: Allen and Unwin, 1961),

pp. 35, 36, 192. For an interesting discussion of the National Health Service, see W. A. J. Farndale, ed., *Trends in the National Health Service* (Oxford: Pergamon, 1964) and Richard M. Titmuss, *Essays on 'The Welfare State'* (London: Allen and Unwin, 1958), nos. 7 – 10.

24. Titmuss, p. 17.

25. In the Preface to *The Future of the Welfare State* (London: Conservative Political Centre, 1958), pp. 9, 10. For a further elaboration of his views, see Peter Goldman, *The Welfare State* (London: Michael Joseph Ltd., 1964); and for a pungent discussion of all conceptions of the welfare state, including his own, see David C. Marsh, *The Future of the Welfare State* (Penguin Books, 1964), especially Chapter IV.

26. And there would be many who would dispute this. See, e.g., Michael Shanks, *The Stagnant Society* (Pelican Books, 1961) and R. M. Titmuss, *The Irresponsible Society* (Fabian Society, 1960).

27. *Sociology at the Cross Roads and other Essays* (London: Heinemann, 1963), pp. 307, 285, 308. See also his later assessment of the welfare state in *Social Policy* (London: Hutchinson University Library, 1965), chapters 7 and 13.

28. Marshall, *Sociology at the Cross Roads,* pp. 221 – 258.

Most accounts of the development of the welfare state pay little attention to the contributions of the Labour party before 1945. They concern themselves particularly with nineteenth-century origins in various areas of legislation, with the programs of the New Liberalism after 1906, and with coalition planning for postwar security during World War II led by Sir William Beveridge, a long-time Liberal. Arthur Marwick, whose account of the domestic consequences of World War I appears earlier in this collection, dissents from this view. His article examines early Labour party policies on social welfare, arguing that Labour had thought hard about the issues involved over a long period of time. As a result, he concludes, its share in influencing the making of welfare policy was all the way through a substantial one. The article that follows appeared in The American Historical Review *(December 1967), pp. 380 – 403, and is reproduced by permission of the American Historical Association and the author.*

9

The Labour Party and the Welfare State in Britain, 1900—1948

ARTHUR MARWICK

In his detailed study of the establishment of the National Health Service Harry Eckstein insisted that, prior to the 1940's, the Labour party had contributed little to the concept of such a service: "The Labour Party was certainly not in the vanguard of the agitation. It joined the team, at best, in the middle of the game." [1] Alfred F. Havighurst endorsed this with the declaration that Labour issued no statement on a national health service until 1934. [2] A third American commentator on the British scene, Robert Brady, however, took an exactly contrary view, stating that "the programme which [Aneurin] Bevan inaugurated on the vesting day, July 5, 1948, was almost a verbatim copy of the one laid out by a Labour Conference thirty years earlier." [3] This opinion, expressed rather more cautiously, though extended to apply to the whole range of welfare state legislation between 1945 and 1948, was also voiced by G. D. H. Cole in one of his later essays. [4] Cole's earlier histories of the Labour party say little on Labour's attitude toward social policy. Henry Pelling similarly has largely confined himself to problems of power and organization, [5] and the latest narrative history of the Labour party, by yet another American historian, is equally reticent about pre-1945 Labour pronouncements on social welfare. [6] Maurice Bruce, in his admirable textbook on the British welfare state, is clearly not impressed by earlier Labour party contributions. [7] If, rightly or wrongly, the Labour party is now inextricably associated with the basic structure of the modern welfare state in Britain, [8] some examination of its previous policies on this topic would seem eminently worthwhile. In adjudicating between the two contrasting views quoted above, this paper attempts to answer two questions: what did the Labour party contribute to social legislation actually carried out prior to 1945, and what ideas and theories on social policy did the Labour party, essentially an opposition party during this period, put forward? The legislation of 1945 – 1948 will then be examined against this historical background. Out of all this something may be contributed to the wider and much-canvassed question of whether the welfare state should be seen as an inevitable facet of contemporary capitalist development or whether it contains explicit elements of political ideology. [9]

The welfare state can quickly be defined as one in which full community responsibility is assumed for four major sectors of social well-being: social security, which means provision against interruption of earnings through sickness, injury, old age, or unemployment; health; housing; and education. It may also be argued that it involves a responsibility to maintain reasonable standards of living and to look after the cultural health of society. In nineteenth-century Britain the sole public provision for social security was the poor law, which was administered in a spirit of harsh deterrence by local boards of guardians who were zealous stewards of ratepayers' money. Most of the wealthier trade-unions ran their own insurance schemes, and the city of Birmingham, under the influence of Joseph Chamberlain, had taken the lead in developing a municipal scheme for unemployment relief. Modest government encouragement for such schemes was provided in the 1905 Unemployed Workmen Act. The limited problem of industrial injury was dealt with in 1897 when employers were made liable for workmen's compensation. The weakness of the system in operation was that it might involve expensive litigation that would eventually provide the injured workman a lump sum rather than a weekly benefit. Free medical attention in the nineteenth century was provided through the charitable "voluntary" hospitals, a handful of local authority hospitals, and poor law infirmaries, though the wealthier trade-unions provided doctors who were contracted to provide medical attention in return for regular fixed payments. The housing acts of the nineteenth century were all permissive in character: public housing, being a charge on the rates, was provided only by the most progressive local authorities. When England's first major education act passed in 1870, it established a dual system in which locally elected school boards provided elementary education in areas where there were no efficient religious schools. Subsequent legislation rendered elementary education both compulsory and free.

When one looks back into the period of the origins of the Labour party—roughly the last two decades of the nineteenth century—one finds the dominant issues to be either the immediate ones of political organization or the fundamental ones of capitalism and socialism, yet it is possible to detect two welfare issues on which Labour sentiment was strongly and clearly expressed. The first was the demand, constantly repeated by Keir Hardie after his election to the House of Commons as an independent Labour candidate, that "remunerative and profitable" public work should be found for the unemployed. [10] The other was the question of old-age pensions, much discussed in high political circles in the 1890's but shelved as Joseph Chamberlain became more and more involved in imperial issues and the country in the South African war. On May 9, 1899, there was founded "The National Committee of Organized Labour (Trade Unions, Trade Councils, Federations of these Bodies, Friendly Societies, and Cooperative Societies) on Old Age Pensions, based on the principle that every old person on attaining a given age should be entitled to receive a free Pension from the State; and charged with the instruction to promote the legal enactment of this principle." [11] After the formation of the Labour Representation Committee (LRC) in 1900 as a federation of trade-unions and such socialist societies as the Independent Labour party (ILP) and the Fabian Society, old-age pensions became the one social issue dealt with in the propagandist literature issued by the new political organization in the first four years of its existence.[12]

The Trades Union Congress (TUC) in 1898 had, it is true, adopted a comprehensive and uncompromising resolution on educational reform that called for "Equality of Opportunity," raising the age of compulsory schooling to sixteen, and "such maintenance provided by the state as shall place secondary education within the reach of every worker's child"; [13] when the motion was formally readopted the following year, however, its seconder alleged, with apparent justice, "that Congress never properly interested itself in this question of education." [14] Thereafter, during the controversies over educational administration aroused by the 1902 Education Act, the fundamentals of educational policy disappeared. In drawing up the act, which made subsidized secondary education possible for at least some working-class children, abolished the school boards, and gave rate support to the religious schools, the Conservative ministry of A. J. Balfour was greatly influenced by the Fabian Society in one of the most striking triumphs for the society's avowed policy of "permeating" the major political parties.[15] It is significant that Ramsay MacDonald, secretary of the LRC, and the LRC conference as a whole, strongly opposed the Fabian minority and the act itself, because of the abolition of the separately elected school boards and the granting of their powers to the ordinary local authorities. [16] Labour opinion, as distinct from that of the intellectual Fabians, continued to support this idea of directly elective educational machinery and pointed approvingly to Scotland where the system of school boards lasted until 1929. The 1905 LRC Conference turned again to broader issues, calling for a system of free primary, secondary, and technological education, backed by maintenance scholarships. The beneficiaries of this proposed scheme were defined the following year as "all children whose usefulness could be enhanced by such extended education." [17] There is a similar ambiguity in the 1907 call for a scholarship system "within reach of every child." [18] The limited character of Labour attitudes on education is brought out by the conference debate of 1912 on a resolution proposing the raising of compulsory school age to sixteen (in theory the age was now fourteen, but there were so many exceptions and qualifications that many children in fact left school at twelve or thirteen). The motion passed, but the distinguished miners' leader, Robert Smillie, despite his own inclinations, had to voice the official hostility of his union; there was also strong opposition from the textile areas, home of the child "half-timers." [19]

In other spheres the metamorphosis after the 1906 general election of the LRC into a Labour party with a parliamentary strength of thirty did involve a more positive Labour contribution to welfare policies. It was now possible to apply direct pressure on old-age pensions, one of the first topics on which the new parliamentary Labour party initiated a debate. [20] Of the debate itself the Reverend T. H. Stead (admittedly a committed observer) wrote:

> . . . I was forcibly impressed by a new and revolutionary fact. That was the profound deference paid in all parts of the House to the Labour Members. . . . Too often it was the homage of conscious ignorance to expert knowledge. But there was more than that. There was a tremendous foreboding that these Labour men, so few in number, but so determined in purpose, had behind them unmeasured potencies of electoral strength. [21]

Two by-election victories during 1906 by Labour candidates who made old-age pensions a main issue seemed to emphasize this last point. Yet the speech from the throne delivered the following February made no mention of old-age pensions, as Hardie was quick to point out. [22] An amendment lamenting this omission was moved the following day by G. N. Barnes. [23] Extra-parliamentary activity culminated in January 1908 in a special Labour conference on old-age pensions. [24] Finally, in June 1908, the Liberal government put its proposals for maximum pensions of 5s. per week for a single person and 7s.6d. for a couple before the House. A Labour amendment, strongly supported by a Conservative opposition that was only too happy to embarrass the government, secured the raising of the married couple's pension to 10*s*. [25] Labour members played a part in another of the social reforms of the 1906 Liberal ministry: the provision of free school meals, long the special interest of Fred Jowett from Bradford (where there already was a municipal scheme in operation). [26]

With regard to social security generally, Labour advocated the abolition of the hated poor law; it recommended that most of the poor law services go to the local authorities, though it also favored the creation of a ministry of labour that would observe working-class problems. [27] On unemployment the parliamentary Labour party extended the original Hardie approach into a "work or maintenance" policy embodied in three "Right to Work" bills, sponsored between 1907 and 1909. [28] But more sophisticated, though not necessarily more enlightened, ideas were now in the air. Politicians' attention had for some time been focused on the German experiment with national insurance (for sickness, but not unemployment), while a young Liberal journalist, William Beveridge, argued the merits of the establishment of a system of labor exchanges. Since 1905 a royal commission had been examining the working of the poor laws. [29] Fabian influence on this commission was exerted through Mrs. Sidney Webb, while George Lansbury could put forth the more purely Labour case. In the end, as is well known, the Fabian ideas were embodied in a *Minority Report,* which actually was in many respects not widely different from the *Majority Report.* [30] The Liberal government, in any event, having taken up the idea of labor exchanges, proceeded to draft its famous national insurance scheme of 1911. Labour responses were mixed. Officially the parliamentary Labour party accepted the contributory insurance basis proposed for both unemployment and sickness. In the words of MacDonald, now chairman of the party: "We accept, and I believe that the great mass of the people of this country accept without questioning, the insurance method of dealing with this problem." [31] But a substantial section of the parliamentary party, led by Snowden, did not accept the proposal. MacDonald's parliamentary report to the 1912 Labour party conference attempted to arraign the rebels, [32] but it was clear that the conference supported them rather than the leadership. A resolution expressing reservations on many aspects of the government scheme was carried on a show of hands by 241 to 39, with MacDonald being attacked for what a delegate termed a "flippant speech." [33] The 1913 conference, rejecting by 976,000 to 569,000 an amendment generally favorable to the government moved by Mrs. Webb, called for the repeal of Part I (health insurance) of the

1911 act and its re-establishment on a noncontributory basis. [34] The parliamentary party was instructed to adopt the same approach in regard to Part II (unemployment insurance). [35]

Labour policy in face of the manifest ill-working of the existing system of workmen's compensation had clear overtones of class war. The 1911 conference agreed that "Workmen's Compensation should be organized and provided by the State, by charges upon the industries concerned, and free from any contribution from the worker." [36] The more farsighted proposal that compensation should be "a charge upon, and payable by, the Imperial Exchequer" was voted down. [37]

The winning of old-age pensions and of a free school meals service, marginally at least, owed something to the Labour party, though these two achievements cannot be compared to the passing of the Trades Disputes Act of 1906 as a triumph for the new party. In public health Labour had no direct influence in this period, unless one counts the efforts of Mrs. Webb and Lansbury on the Poor Law Commission. The Webbs' ideas on public health, as expressed in their *The State and the Doctor,* were, in fact, extremely narrow and certainly went no further than those of the most informed medical and lay experts of the day. [38] What the Webbs advocated was a "united State service" administered by a central public health department either separate from or within the existing Local Government Board. There would be a rigid test of the applicant's financial resources (Means Test) "persuading" all but the very poorest to make use of a private doctor. [39] The limits of the Webbs' vision are all too apparent in the following passage:

> Nor can anyone be warranted in giving support to the proposal that the whole of this outdoor medical service of the Poor Law should be superseded by a publicly subsidised system of letting the poor choose their own doctors. Any such system would lead, not only to a most serious inroad upon the work and emoluments of the private practitioner, but also to an extravagant expenditure of public funds on popular remedies and "medical extras." [40]

Labour attitudes, as expressed at party conferences, surpassed those of the Webbs. Following resolutions in 1909 and 1910 calling for the nationalization of all hospitals "in order that the best medical aid may be at the service of all classes of the community," [41] the 1911 conference approved a demand for a state medical service which "was a real medical service . . . that would be applied to everybody." [42] This insistence upon a comprehensive, classless (or "universalist") service, henceforth a central characteristic of all Labour thinking on the subject, contrasts sharply with the Webb idea of a service for the very poor only. In any event, the change embodied in the 1911 act from a mainly contractual medical service to a panel system administered by local insurance committees, combined with health insurance administered through private insurance companies (the "approved societies"), owed nothing to the Labour party, and only a little to the Webbs. Poor law hospitals, voluntary hospitals, and local authority hospitals continued their separate existence.

On housing, Labour had remarkably little to say, first raising a cry for state subsidies in 1914. [43] Housing, however, was included in the most significant of all the pre-1914 Labour contributions to the ideology of welfare policy, the concept of the "national minimum," involving

> a legal minimum wage in agriculture and all industries, the reduction of the hours of labour to 48 hours per week, complete provision against sickness, the guarantee of a national minimum of child nurture, the prevention of unemployment, the building of healthy homes for all, and the abolition of the Poor Law. [44]

In origins the concept sprang on one side from the insistence on "work or maintenance" and on the other from the more passive Fabian faith in "the constant elaboration of the collective provision for those unable to provide for themselves, of whatever may be regarded for the time being as the national minimum." [45] Presented to the 1913 party conference by the ILP, it is as fine an advance definition of the welfare state as can be found anywhere in Labour party literature prior to 1940. In its specific application to the size of welfare benefits, the "national minimum" was a notion that long remained with the party, until, in fact, the party was in a position to turn notion into fact.

Essentially a pressure group, limited and halting in most of its pronouncements, the Labour party of 1914 was changed by the upheavals of war into a major political party. Organizationally the change was reflected in the new party constitution of 1918; in terms of social policy it was reflected in the policy manifesto *Labour and the New Social Order* and in the conference resolution on health noted by Brady. *Labour and the New Social Order,* a curiously ill-constructed document, sprawls awkwardly over what are called the "Four Pillars of the House" (four is something of a magic numeral in British Labour iconology). [46] The first pillar was "Universal Enforcement of the National Minimum," which included health, housing, and education. There was much on unemployment, but the only precise suggestion was that the existing national insurance scheme be extended to occupations so far not included in it and that increased benefits be paid. [47] The second pillar was "Democratic Control of Industry," which included the nationalization of industrial insurance (that is, insurance to cover burial costs). Under the subheading "Local Government," education, housing, and health were again mentioned: there should be free educational provision up to whatever standard the child was capable of reaching; housing should be financed by interest-free loans or government grants, but should not be a charge on the local rates; and there should be a reorganization—the document is not very precise here—of local health services.[48] The third pillar was "Revolution in National Finance," and the fourth was "Surplus Wealth for the Common Good." This last section stated that the surplus should be used for extending health services, education, and cultural facilities. [49]

The health resolution of 1918 is important enough to deserve quotation in full, though it is too much a child of its times to bear the responsibilities Brady places on it. Moved by Dr. Marion Phillips of the Women's Labour League, and carried unanimously, the resolution ran:

> That this conference declares that the organization and development of a unified Health Service for the whole community are questions of urgent importance, and that steps should be taken without delay to establish a Ministry of Health based upon Public Health Services, and entirely disassociated from any Poor Law taints.
> (a) That to such a Ministry of Health should be transferred all the Health Services now coming under the Local Government Board, Board of Education, Home Office, Privy Council, National Health Insurance Commissions and Poor Law Acts.
> (b) That a Department for the care of Infancy, Maternity and Old-age, largely staffed by women, should be established, and increased powers be given to Central and Local Authorities for work of this kind.
> (c) That all duties relating to Housing should be transferred to the new Ministry, and that in this Department also the services of women should be fully utilised.
> (d) That there should be no representation of special interests, such as those of Insurance Societies in the formation of such a Ministry.
> (e) That the Public Health Committees of the Local Authorities, with such further provision as is necessary in view of their increased duties on the lines of the composition of the Education Committees, should be the centres of local administration.
> (f) That the Public Health Acts should be extended so as to include within their scope all those duties now so inadequately provided under the Poor Law, and all further services that are necessary to secure and maintain the health of the community. [50]

Plans for the establishment of a ministry of health were already well advanced, though it is possible that without the sort of outside pressure represented by this motion, they might, like so much of the government's reconstruction policy, have been shelved. The resolution is typical of Labour thinking at this time in the emphasis it places on control by local authorities (an amendment seeking to place health officers under the ministry rather than the local authorities was rejected): [51] ironically it was a major weakness of the Ministry of Health as it finally emerged that too much power was left in the hands of the local authorities. [52]

Much more significant than this resolution on national health is the flurry of special conferences and policy documents of the 1920's; it is curious that these have been completely ignored both by historians of the Labour party and of the welfare state, though their content is infinitely more interesting than that of the slender and noncommital *Dawson Report* to which historians have usually given far too much attention. First of all an Advisory Committee on Public Health, consisting of the following members, was appointed: the Right Honorable John Hodge, M. P. (chairman), G. P. Blizard (secretary), Mr. James Bacon, Dr. Ethel Bentham, Dr. E. J. Bygott, Mr. G. W. Canter, Mr. P. W. Cole, Dr. F. Lawson Dodd, Dr. David Forsythe, Dr. Arthur Greenwood, Dr. Somerville Hastings, Dr. Leonard Hill, Mr. G. A. Isaacs, Dr. James Kerr, Mr. William Leach, Dr. Benjamin Moore, Miss Enid Orange, Dr. C. A. Parker, Mr. W. C. Robinson, Dr. Alfred Salter, Mrs. E. W. Salmond, Dr. Lauriston Shaw, Dr. Jane Walker, Mrs. Sidney Webb, and Lieutenant Colonel Joseph Kynaston. [53] This committee agreed that "all the present voluntary hospitals should eventually be merged into the public hospital system," but it would not accept the recommendation of an influential minority, in which Hastings was a leading figure, that the doctor should become a salaried servant of the state. [54] A memorandum prepared by the committee formed the basis of the most complete blueprint for a future national health service yet put on paper, which the Labour party and Trades Union Congress published jointly in 1922. [55] "The Labour party," this document ran, "considers that the health of the community, being a matter of national concern, should be entrusted to the care of a complete Public Medical Service." [56] Although the blueprint saw this service as being administered by the local authorities, it stressed that they, in turn, would be under the supervision of the minister of health. [57] Still more important, the document imaginatively recognized that "the country should be divided into areas of sufficient size to allow of complete medical organisation," though in practice it equated these areas with the existing counties and county boroughs. [58] It was also precocious enough to recognize that "the several activities of this National Health Service should all pivot upon the local hospital as an Institute of Health." [59] In elaboration of this, it continued:

> the only possible method of coping with the urgent necessity for increased accommodation is for local authorities to establish their own hospitals. . . . Public hospitals when established should become *the health centre* or institute of each local health authority and should provide accommodation within their walls for all medical activities.[60]

The document here, it may be noted, stopped a little further from the brink of the controversial nationalization of hospitals, so confidently advocated in prewar days, than the Advisory Committee memorandum. It was unequivocal, however, in stating that the service should be "free and open to all," and this principle, it argued, would render obsolete the insurance element in existing public health provision. [61] The authors, well aware of the revolutionary nature of their proposals, suggested a transitional stage in which medical benefits would be made a charge on public funds and payable by the local authorities instead of insurance committees, and an immediate program of hospital building, appointment of specialists, and so on would be launched. [62]

The seriousness of the Labour party's interest in the problems of a national health service is borne out by the conference held at Caxton Hall, London, April 28 – 29, 1924, with representatives of the British Medical Association, the Medical Practitioners' Union, the Medical Women's Federation, the Federation of Medical and Allied Services, the British Dental Association, the nurses organizations, the approved societies, insurance committees, and big hospitals. [63] Hastings presented the Labour view, Lord Knutsford that of the voluntary hospitals, and Mr. Bishop Harman that of the doctors. [64] It was not possible to secure more than a vague resolution of agreement on general principles, disagreement being sharpest over the continued desire of the Labour representatives for the integration of the voluntary hospitals into a public system. [65] In January 1927 there was a further conference, this time with representatives of the nursing profession. [66] None of this important work had any direct effect immediately, and it indeed figured in only the briefest form at party conferences and in propagandist literature. Labour could, certainly, assert some direct influence (this was true of all aspects of social policy) through its representatives on the local authorities. It made large gains in the local government elections of 1919, which gave it control of Bradford and of twelve London boroughs, and majorities in the counties of Durham, Glamorgan, and Monmouthshire. Labour could also attempt to assert influence through the elective boards of guardians, though the judiciary frowned on any sharp deviation from the normal pattern of behavior, [67] and, in Scotland through the elective school boards until 1929. It became avowed Labour policy in local government not so much to create new social policies but to get local authorities to carry out the existing legislative legacy of the war period. [68]

Labour was in office briefly in 1924 and again for eighteen months between 1929 and 1931. Unemployment, housing, and, to a lesser degree, education were the social problems that received most ministerial attention. The 1924 Labour government was no more successful than any other in dealing with the basic economic problems underlying unemployment, and it attempted no fundamental change in the structure of unemployment insurance. Benefits for the adult male were raised from 15s. to 18s., scarcely a perceptible nod in the direction of the national minimum. The government also shortened the "waiting period" imposed upon the unemployed man after the benefits to which his insurance contribution entitled him were exhausted, and before he moved on to what was first called "uncovenanted benefit" and later "extended benefit" (or, in the nasty phrase of the Right-wing press, "the dole"). When again in opposition, the party proved more adventurous, and the evidence put forward jointly by the Labour party and the TUC to the Blanesburgh Committee on Unemployment Insurance (appointed by the Conservatives) makes interesting reading. Strong hostility, which was to mark Labour thoughts on the subject in the 1940's, was aroused by the dole [69] —that is to say to the distinction between benefit to which a man was entitled and "extended benefit" to which he had no claim as of right. At the same time the contributory principle was attacked on the grounds that flat-rate contributions were not commensurate with the ability to pay nor with risk of unemployment, [70] the latter being a strangely unsocialistic argument. The Labour party and TUC put forward two sets of recommendations, one "ideal," one immediate. The first "ideal" recommendation embodied the national minimum principle: the unemployed should be paid full maintenance. The other recommendation was that the full cost should fall upon the state, with the poor law at the same time being abolished. [71] As an immediate program, the representatives recommended a rise in benefits to one pound per week, a further extension of the classes in the community covered by unemployment insurance (there does not, however, seem to be any question of the middle classes being included; though accepting the universalist principle for the medical service, Labour had not yet arrived at it for social insurance), the ending of the concept of "extended benefit," a reduction in the employee's contributions, and an increase in those of the Exchequer (if the contributory principle had to be maintained, the delegation would have liked contributions to be linked to earnings, but this, for some reason, they felt impracticable); as a final immediate task, the delegation recommended the setting up of training centers for the unemployed. [72]

The uneasy eighteen months of Labour government between 1929 and 1931 again revealed Labour in office as unwilling or unable to carry through any fundamental change in the structure of unemployment insurance. The government's failure to improve the lot of the unemployed raised to crisis point tensions that had long been building up on the back benches of the parliamentary Labour party. The party leadership had refused, prior to the 1929 election, to commit itself unequivocally to raising unemployment benefits to one pound per week for an adult male, but a small group of candidates, mainly concentrated in the ILP, had pledged themselves to that figure. Only when they were joined by the trade-union group of M.P.'s were the ILP dissidents able to secure any concessions from the government: the gratuitous and humiliating proviso that an applicant for unemployment benefit must prove that he was "genuinely seeking work" was abolished, and the conditions governing the granting of "transitional benefit" (the new name for extended benefit) were made less harsh. At the same time the Labour government, in face of the bitter hostility of the small ILP group, enacted its Anomalies Bill, which was supposed to deal with those who, without genuine need or qualification, were receiving unemployment benefit.

By 1930 the ILP—the most active component in the original LRC—had little influence on the labor movement, but in the middle 1920's, when it was still of considerable importance, its leading intellectuals had produced a vigorous policy document with clear overtones of the national minimum entitled *The Living Wage*. Among other things, *The Living Wage* called for the institution of family allowances. [73] At the 1926 Labour party conference P. J. Dollan of the ILP moved to establish family allowances, but encountered so much opposition from trade-unionists, who feared that their introduction would undermine trade-union bargaining and make an excuse for lowering wages, that the matter was referred to the Labour party executive, [74] and from there to a joint Labour party-TUC committee. [75] A majority of the committee, in 1930, favored family allowances and recommended, another controversial point, that they should be paid directly to the mother. [76] But there was still a strong body of opposition to the whole idea, and so, for the time being, the matter rested there.

The one conspicuous domestic achievement of either of the first two Labour governments was the 1924 Housing Act, conceived and executed by the most brilliant of the Clydeside ILP figures, John Wheatley. The basic principle behind the act was the same as that embodied in the Addison Act, passed by David Lloyd George's government in 1919: that of a state subsidy for housebuilding by local authorities, a somewhat clumsy system since the local authorities must in the first place borrow the money needed to launch their housebuilding program. Wheatley was, in fact, acting contrary to a decision of the 1920 party conference that favored the granting by the central government of low interest loans to the local authorities. [77] There could be no doubt, however, as to the practical success of the Wheatley Act until it was suspended by the succeeding Conservative ministry. Arthur Greenwood's Housing Act of 1930 was a more limited measure, concentrating state subsidies on the specific problem of slum clearance, thus setting the tone for Conservative as well as Labour policy in the 1930's.

Labour's policy on education in the 1920's, though far in advance of that of the other political parties, was so burdened by an awareness of the dreadful inadequacies of the existing system as to seem positively pedestrian. It was dominated by the too facile slogan "Secondary Education for All," the title of a study published in 1922, which was mainly the work of R. H. Tawney. Labour's objective was

> both the improvement of primary education and the development of public secondary education to such a point that all normal children, irrespective of the income, class, or occupation of their parents, may be transferred at the age of 11+ from the primary or preparatory school to one type or another of secondary school, and remain in the latter till sixteen. [78]

Tawney was aware of the dangers, which, half a century later, had become an unfortunate feature of the post-1944 educational system: "All educationists are agreed that classifications of children made at eleven and twelve should be, at most, provisional, because the younger the children the more likely they are to be mistaken." [79] What was lacking in *Secondary Education for All* was any real conception of education as an essential ingredient in the regeneration of society. To find this one has to turn to the ILP publications of the midtwenties. [80] Most staggering was the omission of any proposals for dealing with the fee-paying Public Schools (the equivalent of the exclusive and expensive American private schools). It is not altogether surprising that the party conference of 1926, admittedly the peak of Left-wing sentiment in the 1920's, passed a resolution strongly criticizing recent educational publications of the Labour party and TUC, and calling for more "Workers' Control" in education. [81] In office Labour's education policies were entrusted to C. P. Trevelyan, a former Liberal who had moved into the Labour party by means of the ILP; he was able in 1924 considerably to relax the economies that had recently been imposed upon the public education system, but in 1930 he resigned from the government, partly because of the frustration of his proposals by the Conservative House of Lords, but mainly because of his conviction that the Labour government was insufficiently socialistic in its responses to the world capitalist crisis.

The 1931 crisis and its aftermath had the clearly marked effect of turning Labour's social thinkers away from planning for the future to the immediate task of safeguarding the existing social services. [82] Labour's concern here brings out the more permanent ambivalence in a party committed to attacking existing social provision as inadequate, but at the same time governed by the ILP tradition of local government service and the Fabian heritage of belief in the "inevitability of gradualness" and pride in "the constant elaboration of the collective provision . . . of . . . the national minimum." Thus the educational economies of the National government were attacked as reversing "the policy followed by all its predecessors since 1902." [83] The severely limited nature of Labour social planning in the 1930's has perhaps been responsible for the general neglect by historians of the real advances in social thinking made by Labour in the 1920's. It is typified by the concentration in housing policy on the necessary, but essentially negative, topic of slum clearance [84] and in education on the need for maintenance grants for secondary-school children rather than on any further expansion of the educational system. [85] The unproductiveness of Labour's social thought in the 1930's contrasts curiously with the detailed work done by such organizations as Political and Economic Planning and the Next Five Years Group. [86]

The one exception to this picture is the appearance in 1931 of the Socialist Medical Association (SMA), a body within the Labour party that advocated the sort of state medical service whose shape had already been worked out in the early 1920's. At the 1932 party conference, Hastings, now representing this new association, called for a "State Medical Service" "free and open to all." "It seems to me," he said, "it would be as sensible to make the salaries of the clergy dependent upon the amount of crime in their congregations as our present system of making the remuneration of the doctor depend upon the amount of disease he fails to prevent." [87] Enunciating once again the universalist principle, Hastings declared that his service would not be for the working class alone; he wanted no trace of the stigma of the poor law attached to it. "I want a service that the millionaire may take advantage of, and I want it to be so efficient that he will be glad to do so." [88] In the discussion that followed, a delegate received no reply when he inquired whether the proposals involved the nationalization of all hospitals. The party's post-1931 state of mind is indicated by the conference chairman's cautious remark that the implications of the SMA resolution were "very far-reaching." [89] The matter accordingly was referred to the executive, where it became so bogged down that Hastings had to ask the following year what had happened to it. Even he seemed to share the general diffidence about ambitious social planning, remarking that he realized the introduction of such a medical service might not be the first duty of a Labour government, but that it was necessary to have a "mental picture of the service we want to develop." [90] After another year the executive presented what it called a Preliminary Report, which was duly approved by the conference. [91] It is this document of 1934 that Eckstein and Havighurst erroneously regard as Labour's first venture into a discussion of the problems of national health. What is striking about the report [92] is the extreme caution with which it is phrased. It began by remarking that a state medical service could be built either upon the existing national health insurance scheme or upon the existing local authority services; the report favored the second alternative, so that health insurance would be confined to the payment of benefits (as distinct from the provision of free medical attention through the panel system). The approved societies would remain, and the income limit for participation in the scheme would be raised to about five hundred pounds per annum (a complete retreat here from the universalist principle). Reflecting the grim aftermath of 1931, the report also regretted that "for financial reasons" it would not be possible to forgo contributions. As to the medical service itself, the aim here was that it should be free and universal, but this could only be achieved in stages.

The report cited three prerequisites: there must be a consolidation but not under poor law control of existing local authority services; "efforts" must be made to take over the voluntary hospitals whose "valuable services" were recognized, a form of words even more noncommittal than the formulas of the 1920's; the public medical service must be equal to or, "rather, very much better than" the insurance system—no starry-eyed objective.

> Bearing these requirements in mind, it is suggested that the first main stage of a developing Public Health Service might be the provision of free domiciliary and institutional medical care to all insured persons, all insured persons of similar income, and all dependants of either category. Uninsured persons over the insurance income limit and their dependants might continue to make their own arrangements for non-institutional treatment on payment of reasonable charges according to means. In certain cases where free treatment is now available irrespective of means, the practice might be continued. [93]

Hastings was remarkably kind to this hesitant and etiolated document, describing it as an "embryo" of the sort of service he and the SMA visualized. [94] The report was published as an appendix to the 1934 party conference report, but unlike many other policy statements of the time was not accorded the status of separate publication in the form of a pamphlet, though it was mentioned in the propaganda leaflet *For Socialism and Peace*. [95] Until the outbreak of war no further hint was given of Labour thinking on public health.

The advent of the Second World War, Labour's participation in the Churchill coalition, and the wide interest everywhere aroused in the problems of social reform—an interest less novel, but more practical, than that during the First World War—restored Labour's confidence in its social mission; a clear eye and a ringing tread mark the series of vital policy statements turned out during the war. Labour was enjoying the uniquely happy role of being at one and the same time a government party, with all the prestige and experience that role conferred, and an opposition party, with complete freedom to work out policies of its own and, at party conferences, to criticize government policy (the implication on these occasions being that government policy was really Conservative policy). At a time when there was an overriding need to maximize national productivity, the trade-union leadership, too, enjoyed a strong bargaining position. Starting from the anomalies and inadequacies of the existing national health insurance scheme, the general council of the TUC "came to the conclusion that what was necessary was the complete overhauling of the whole scheme and the related Social Services." [96] A deputation in February 1941 to Minister of Health Ernest Brown stressed "the necessity for the linking up of all the Social Service Schemes into an adequate and properly coordinated scheme" and for drawing up a "comprehensive plan" in readiness "for implementation immediately after the war." [97] In May it was announced that a comprehensive survey of the social services would be undertaken under the auspices of Arthur Greenwood, a Labour representative in the government and the minister responsible for reconstruction problems. It was intended that the survey would be carried out by an interdepartmental committee of civil servants under the chairmanship of Beveridge, who had been involved in the problems of social policy since before 1914. Because of what might be termed the "sacred egoism" of Beveridge, the report associated with his name [98] had a far greater impact than might have been predicted from its original terms of reference. The 1942 Labour party conference welcomed the appointment of the interdepartmental committee; the resolution, moved by James Griffiths, stated the Labour view that there should be:

(a) One comprehensive scheme of social security.

(b) Adequate cash payments to provide security whatever the contingency.

(c) The provision of cash payments from national funds for all children through a scheme of Family Allowances.

(d) The right to all forms of medical attention and treatment through a National Health Service. [99]

From the floor of the conference there was again strong opposition to the idea of family allowances, and another amendment expressed hostility to putting the new social security system on a contributory basis. Both, however, were defeated. [100]

The *Beveridge Report* was published at the end of 1942 and was the subject of a parliamentary debate early in 1943. [101] Officially the government accepted in principle the Beveridge recommendation that there be one comprehensive system of social security, but their first two major spokesmen (both Conservatives) were so Laodicean in their advocacy that the parliamentary Labour party, despite the fact that its own leaders were in the government, felt bound to table an amendment expressing their disappointment with the government attitude. [102] When it came to a division, ninety-seven Labour members, together with twenty-two Conservatives and Liberals, voted against the government. Labour's formal attitude to the *Beveridge Report* was that, although amendments and improvements might be necessary, a scheme based on it should be ready to put into practice at the end of the war. [103] In 1944 the government announced its policy on social insurance, following in general the lines of the Beveridge recommendations. [104] Labour's critique of the government White Paper concentrated on the inadequacy of the proposed benefits and on the proviso that, in order to preserve the sanctity of the insurance basis, benefits would be paid only for a limited number of weeks. [105] In connection with the former point the following statement was given priority in practically every Labour pronouncement on social policy: "The Labour party is pledged to work towards the realisation of a national minimum standard below which no citizen should be allowed to fall." [106] A third significant feature of Labour thinking on social security was the emphasis on the nationalization of all insurance; during the 1945 election campaign, however, pledges were given that a place would be found in the new dispensation for bona fide friendly societies. [107]

The Labour policy document *National Service for Health* picks up and, on one point, extends the policies of the 1920's. *National Service for Health* was the first policy statement to appreciate fully the dependence of social policy upon efficient local government, and instead of basing its proposed health service on existing local authorities, as all previous Labour schemes had suggested, it postulated a scheme based on regional authorities. [108] The region was a new larger local authority unit described in the sister document *The Future of Local Government,* [109] to which all readers of *National Service for Health* were referred. After this courageous pronouncement, which if implemented would have given the health service a single coordinated and elective system of administration, the regional authorities having control over all branches of the service, with the Minister of Health assuming "powers of default," [110] the remarks on the future of the voluntary hospitals were again less than crystal clear. "Surely," said the document, in a manner suggesting that the authors were not quite sure, "the conclusion must be that public and voluntary hospitals alike must be brought within a National Health Service on equitable terms." [111] But there was no avoidance of the Labour party objective of a "fully salaried medical service." [112] The government White Paper, *A National Health Service,* [113] was vaguer than, but not radically different from, the Labour proposals and was given a qualified welcome by the 1944 conference. [114] During the succeeding year, however, Henry Willink, Conservative Minister of Health in the Churchill government, entered into negotiations with the British Medical Association. The final result of the negotiations was a weakening of the original proposals; this the 1945 Labour party conference repudiated. [115]

Labour's housing policy was enunciated in *Housing and Planning after the War.* Here there was an implicit rejection of the Wheatley and Greenwood policy of state subsidies in favor of a return to the 1920 idea of state loans of low interest.[116] Housing was the issue on which, according to a public opinion poll, the electorate felt strongest, [117] and in its election manifesto Labour promised that it would set up a separate ministry of housing. [118] Education was the one major sector of the welfare state of the 1940's for which legislation was passed before the war ended. The Butler Education Act of 1944 followed closely the "Labour Secondary Education for All" policy of 1922, and Labour was closely implicated in it through R. A. Butler's second-in-command, Chuter Ede. The attempt of Labour backbenchers to strike a mortal blow at the class basis of the British educational system by an amendment to make all schools free was resisted. [119]

The 1945 general election put Labour into office with a commanding majority. All political parties, it is true, were committed to bringing in some form of welfare state. In that sense the emergence of the welfare state in Britain can be seen as the product of a specific phase in capitalist development, precipitated by the experience of the Second World War. But Labour had said enough in the previous few years to reveal the distinctive image that it wished to give the postwar welfare state: it had, before the appearance of the *Beveridge Report,* stated its own "four essentials":

> We have to provide full employment; we have to rebuild Britain to standards worthy of the men and women who have preserved it; we have to organise social services at a level which secures adequate health, nutrition, and care in old age, for all citizens; and we have to provide educational opportunities for all which ensure that our cultural heritage is denied to none. [120]

It fell down in its failure to realize the extent of the changes necessary to realize this image, and, curiously, in its continued failure to appreciate the central importance of education. In a sense it was a prisoner of the twin Fabian and ILP-local government traditions of taking the existing structure of welfare provisions as given and from there working out the desirable improvements. It also put too much faith in the naturally enduring quality of the social harmony and community spirit engendered by the war. The ideal image existed; a series of policies on the different aspects of welfare legislation existed—some dating from the forties, some with a much longer ancestry—but all this did not add up to one integrated policy, despite constant lip service to the principle of "unification" and an addiction, after 1945, to talking about the "mosaic" of social services that Labour would fit together. [121] The mosaic quickly became a crazy pavement.

In passing the major acts that established the contemporary welfare state, Labour was governed not only by its own recent pronouncements but also by attitudes formed over a much longer period. It was guided by the best contemporary expert thinking as embodied in the *Beveridge Report,* and it was restricted by the lines of action that the coalition government had already laid down. It was hemmed in by the grim facts of the postwar economic situation and was affected by all the pressures, whether of official civil service opinion of outside vested interests, that are brought to bear on any democratic government, however strong its majority.

In its social security legislation the Labour government accepted completely, as MacDonald had done in 1911, the inevitability of insurance. As against an earlier hostility to the contributory principle, there was an even deeper hostility to any sort of "dole" to which prior entitlement had not been secured. Along with the insurance principle went a whole wilderness of qualification and requalification conditions and limits upon the length of time for which benefits would be paid. Heavily attacked by Left-wing Labour backbenchers, [122] this respectable core to the act remained substantially intact, preserving the fiction of insurance and providing employment for an army of administrators. In the end the friendly societies were not given a place inside the new system, but, despite earlier Labour sentiment on the subject, private insurance outside the state system was left untrammeled—perhaps one of the largest single reasons why the classless welfare state failed to materialize. In introducing the national insurance bill, James Griffiths claimed that it marked the beginning of the establishment of the "principle of a National Minimum Standard," which is interesting as illustrating the continuity of Labour thought, though scarcely of Labour action since Griffiths declared at the same time that it was administratively impossible to tie benefits to the cost of living, [123] and the government's expressed intention of holding the cost of living steady proved only a pious wish. The inclusion within the national insurance framework of provision for industrial injuries meant the final abandonment of the idea of making such provision a charge on industry itself, an abandonment of an earlier class-war stand that is paralleled in the party's acceptance of family allowances (enacted by Churchill's government before it left office). The preservation of the concept of national insurance demanded the continuance of some form of public assistance; hence the passage of the National Assistance Act of 1948, which, in the wide scope of its provisions did have something of the breadth of the wartime Labour vision. It formally repealed the poor law, [124] though there was still a breath of the nineteenth century about the continuance of the personal Means Test.

The National Health Service Act of 1946 was the only major piece of welfare state legislation whose passage the Conservatives contested. [125] This in itself was a measure of how far the responsible minister, Aneurin Bevan, was in advance of the political "consensus" on welfare issues. By plunging directly into the nationalization of the hospitals, Bevan, too, showed himself to be in advance of the previous vague Labour utterances on the subject. But he was unable, after long negotiations with the medical profession, to persuade it to accept the official Labour policy of a fully salaried service. His big failure, and it was a critical failure on the part of the whole government, was to carry through the local government reforms that *National Service for Health* had declared to be basic to the entire program. The new national health service, therefore, began with a clumsy tripartite administrative structure which the strict control vested in the Minister of Health could not really mitigate. The only vestiges of the regional ideal appeared in the system for hospital administration: local executive councils, with strong professional representation, looked after the General Practitioner services, and a place was reserved for the old local authorities, to whom was entrusted the task of building health centers, which the Labour planners of the 1920's had recognized as being of vital importance to any efficient public medical service. Few health centers were built.

Labour's housing legislation, again Bevan's responsibility, provides a good example of the universalist principle: public housing, it was made clear in the debates on the 1946 act and repeated explicitly in the 1949 act, was to be available to the whole community, not to the working classes alone. [126] But this good intention, whose success in the first place depended on a class unity that did not survive the war, foundered completely on the sheer failure of the government to build desperately needed houses. Bevan, who is alleged to have made the outrageous remark, "I never spent more than an hour a week on housing. Housing runs itself," [127] was clearly too preoccupied with the problems of launching the national health service. The government was rightly criticized by the Labour rank and file for its failure to keep the election promise to set up a separate ministry of housing. [128] Nor did the government follow its avowed policy of financing housing by loans at low interest; instead it adhered to the stereotype of annual government subsidies, in face of Left-wing opposition. [129] In education, the government was content, mainly by administrative action, to implement, as far as possible, the terms of the 1944 act. The more imaginative side of its vision of the welfare state is better seen in the town and country planning legislation, in its modest support for the arts, and, of course, in the direction of its economic policies toward the maintenance of full employment.

When Labour fell from office in 1951 it left behind several imposing chunks of masonry instead of the complete welfare edifice it had hoped to build; the cement of social harmony and community spirit that it had believed would bind the whole together was already crumbling. Its endeavors had, nonetheless, permanently changed the social face of Britain. And these endeavors were not simply the inevitable response that any government would have made to the particular historical circumstances of 1945. They were the endeavors of a political party that, over a long period of time, had thought hard, if unevenly, about the issues of welfare policy. This paper began with a number of quotations. Enough has been said, it is submitted, to show that the Cole and Brady versions, even if a trifle facile, come closer to the truth than the interpretations of those historians who have followed an established fashion in neglecting earlier Labour pronouncements on welfare policy.

NOTES

1. Harry Eckstein, *The English Health Service: Its Origins, Structure and Achievements* (Cambridge, Mass., 1958), 108, n. 4.

2. Alfred F. Havighurst, *Twentieth Century Britain* (New York, 1962), 375.

3. Robert Brady, *Crisis in Britain: Plans and Achievements of the Labour Government* (Berkeley, Calif., 1950), 356.

4. G. D. H. Cole, "The Growth of Socialism," in *Law and Opinion in England in the Twentieth Century,* ed. Morris Ginsberg (London, 1959), 86.

5. G. D. H. Cole, *British Working-Class Politics 1832 – 1914* (London, 1941) and *A History of the Labour Party from 1914* (London, 1948); Henry Pelling, *A Short History of the Labour Party* (London, 1961); Frank Bealey and Henry Pelling, *Labour and Politics 1900 – 1906: A History of the Labour Representation Committee* (London, 1958).

6. Carl F. Brand, *The British Labour Party: A Short History* (Stanford, Calif., 1965). An impressive attempt to redress the balance, however, is Richard W. Lyman, "The British Labour Party: The Conflict between Socialist Ideals and Practical Politics between the Wars," *Journal of British Studies,* V (No. 1, 1965), 140 – 52.

7. Maurice Bruce, *The Coming of the Welfare State* (London, 1961), 12 – 13, 16, 140 – 41.

8. Asa Briggs, "The Welfare State in Historical Perspective," *Archives Européennes de Sociologie,* II (No. 2, 1961), 211.

9. See esp. Leonard Krieger, "The Idea of the Welfare State in Europe and the United States," *Journal of the History of Ideas*, XXIV (No. 4, 1963), 553 – 68; C. L. Mowat, "The Approach to the Welfare State in Great Britain," *American Historical Review*, LVIII (No. 1, 1953), 55 – 63; and Dorothy Wedderburn, "Facts and Theories of the Welfare State," in *The Socialist Register 1965* (London, 1965), 127 – 46.

10. *Official Report, House of Common Debates*, 4th Ser., XIX (Dec. 19, 1893), col. 1769.

11. F. H. Stead, *How Old Age Pensions Began to Be* (London, 1909), 64 – 65.

12. Labour Representation Leaflet, No. 6, *The Labour View of Pensions for the Aged* (London, 1904). Sixteen Labour Representation Leaflets were issued between 1900 and 1904.

13. *Official Report of 31st Annual Trades Union Congress, 1898* (Manchester, Eng., 1898), 70 – 71.

14. *Official Report of 32nd Annual Trades Union Congress, 1809* (Manchester, Eng., 1899), 75 – 76. Olive Banks, *Parity and Prestige in English Secondary Education: A Study in Educational Sociology* (London, 1955), 116, gives a stronger, and, I believe, incorrect emphasis to early trade-union interest in education. For a full account of working-class attitudes toward education, see Brian Simon, *Education and the Labour Movement, 1870 – 1920: Studies in the History of Education* (London, 1965), esp. 126 – 62.

15. M. I. Cole, *The Story of Fabian Socialism* (London, 1961), 332; Fabian Society, *The Education Muddle and the Way Out* (London, 1901).

16. LRC, *Annual Conference Report, 1902* (London, 1902), 25 – 26. The ILP was divided on the issue: Philip Snowden opposed the local boards and "favoured the expense of education being met by the Imperial Exchequer." (*Ibid.*, 26.)

17. *Ibid., 1905* (London, 1905), 55; Labour Party, *Annual Conference Report, 1906* (London, 1906), 68.

18. *Ibid., 1907* (London, 1907), 62.

19. *Ibid., 1912* (London, 1912), 105.

20. *Official Report, House of Commons Debates*, 4th Ser., CLIII (Mar. 14, 1906), cols. 1330 ff.

21. Stead, *Old Age Pensions*, 205.

22. *Official Report, House of Commons Debates*, 4th Ser., CLXIX (Feb. 12, 1907), cols. 106 – 107.

23. *Ibid.* (Feb. 13, 1907), col. 222.

24. Labour Party, *Annual Conference Report, 1908* (London, 1908), 68.

25. *Official Report, House of Commons Debates*, 4th Ser., CXC (June 24, 1908), cols. 1775 – 94. For an excellent analysis of the issue, see Doreen Collins, "The Introduction of Old Age Pensions in Britain," *Historical Journal*, VIII (No. 2, 1965), 246 – 59. Collins does not mention the part played by the Labour party. See also Bentley B. Gilbert, "The Decay of Nineteenth-Century Provident Institutions and the Coming of Old Age Pensions in Great Britain," *Economic History Review*, 2d Ser., XVII (No. 3, 1965), 240 – 52.

26. A. F. Brockway, *Socialism over Sixty Years: The Life of Jowett of Bradford* (London, 1946), 78 ff.; Simon, *Education and the Labour Movement*, 248 – 89.

27. LRC, *Annual Conference Report, 1905*, 68; *Official Report, House of Commons Debates*, 4th Ser., CLXXXIII (Feb. 6, 1908), cols. 1122 – 23.

28. *Ibid.*, CLXXVII (July 10, 1907), cols. 1447 – 48; *ibid.*, CLXXXVI (Mar. 13, 1908), cols.10 – 99; *ibid.*, 5th Ser., IV (Apr. 30, 1909), col. 633; see J. Ramsay MacDonald, *The New Unemployed Bill of the Labour Party* (London, 1908).

29. *Sessional Papers*, 1909, XXXVII, cd. 4499.

30. For some perceptive comments, see Karl de Schweinitz, *England's Road to Social Security* (London, 1943), 184 – 98; see also Bentley B. Gilbert, *The Evolution of National Insurance in Great Britain: The Origins of the Welfare State* (London, 1966).

31. *Official Report, House of Commons Debates*, 5th Ser., XXVI (May 29, 1911), cols. 725 – 26.

32. Labour Party, *Annual Conference Report, 1912*, 29.

33. *Ibid.*, 96 – 98.

34. *Ibid., 1913* (London, 1913), 104 – 106.

35. *Ibid.*, 106.

36. *Ibid., 1911* (London, 1911), 105 – 106.

37. *Ibid.*

38. R. M. Titmuss, "Health," in *Law and Opinion*, ed. Ginsberg, 308 ff.

39. Beatrice and Sidney Webb, *The State and the Doctor* (London, 1910), 219, 225, 256 – 58.

40. *Ibid.*, 230 – 31.

41. Labour Party, *Annual Conference Report, 1909* (London, 1909), 88; *ibid., 1910* (London, 1910), 96.

42. *Ibid., 1911*, 106.

43. *Ibid., 1914* (London, 1914), 150.

44. *Ibid., 1913*, 107.

45. Sidney Webb, *Towards Social Democracy? A Study of Social Evolution during the Past Three-Quarters of a Century* (London, 1916), 39.

46. Labour Party, *Labour and the New Social Order* (London, 1918). The 1942 policy document *The Old World and the New Society* also set the Labour party four aims. Clause four of the party constitution is well known.

47. *Labour and the New Social Order*, 5 – 6, 8 – 11.

48. *Ibid.*, 14 – 17.

49. *Ibid.*, 21.

50. Labour Party, *Annual Conference Report, 1918* (London, 1918), 124 – 25.

51. *Ibid.*

52. See the interesting article by Philip Abrams, "The Failure of Social Reform: 1918 – 1920," *Past and Present*, No. 24 (Apr. 1963), 43 – 64.

53. Labour Party, *Memoranda Prepared by Advisory Committee on Public Health* (London, n. d.), I.

54. *Ibid.*, 5, 11.

55. Trades Union Congress and Labour Party, *The Labour Party and the Preventive and Curative Medical Services* (London, n.d.).

56. *Ibid.*, 3.

57. *Ibid.*

58. *Ibid.*, 3, 12.

59. *Ibid.*, 4.

60. *Ibid.*, 6 [italics mine].

61. *Ibid.*, 3, 7.

62. *Ibid.*, 10.

63. Report of Conference, printed as Labour Party, *The Hospital Problem* (London, 1924).

64. *Ibid.*, 3 – 6.

65. *Ibid.*, 12.

66. Labour Party, *The Labour Party and the Nursing Profession* (London, 1927).

67. See, e.g., the case of *Roberts* v. *Hopwood*, 1924.

68. See, e.g., Labour Party, *Continued Education under the New Education Act* (London, 1919).

69. Trades Union Congress and Labour Party, *Unemployment Insurance: Principles of Labour Policy* (London, n.d.), 4.

70. *Ibid.*, 5.

71. *Ibid.*, 6 – 7.

72. *Ibid.*, 10 – 15.

73. H. N. Brailsford *et al.*, *The Living Wage* (Manchester, Eng., 1926), 20 – 26.

74. Labour Party, *Annual Conference Report, 1926* (London, 1926), 274 – 75.

75. *Ibid.*, *1930* (London, 1930), 303 – 307.

76. *Ibid.*

77. Labour Party, *Annual Conference Report, 1930* (London, 1920), 181.

78. Labour Party, *Secondary Education for All* (London, n.d.), 7. Condensed versions of this were published jointly by the TUC and Labour party as *Education of Children over Eleven* (London, n.d.) and *From Nursery School to University* (London, n.d.).

79. *Secondary Education for All*, III.

80. See, e.g., *New Leader*, Oct. 12, 1923.

81. Labour Party, *Annual Conference Report, 1926*, 264 – 65.

82. See, e.g., *ibid.*, *1931* (London, 1931), 217 – 22.

83. *Ibid.*, *1932* (London, 1932), 250.

84. See, e.g., *ibid.*, *1933* (London, 1933), 196 – 98.

85. See, e.g., *Official Report, House of Commons Debates*, 5th Ser., CCLI (Feb. 12, 1936), col. 583.

86. Arthur Marwick, "Middle Opinion in the Thirties: Planning, Progress and Political Agreement,'" *English Historical Review*, LXXIX (No. 2, 1964), 285 – 98.

87. Labour Party, *Annual Conference Report, 1932*, 269.

88. *Ibid.*

89. *Ibid.*, 270.

90. *Ibid.*, *1933*, 141.

91. *Ibid.*, *1934* (London, 1934), 215.

92. Printed *ibid.*, 256 – 58.

93. *Ibid.*, 258.

94. *Ibid.*, 215.

95. Labour Party, *For Socialism and Peace* (London, 1934).

96. *Report of 73rd Annual Trades Union Congress, 1941* (London, 1941), 114.

97. *Ibid.;* see also Trades Union Congress, *The T.U.C. in Wartime* (London, 1942), and William (Lord) Beveridge, *Power and Influence* (London, 1953), 282 ff.

98. *Sessional Papers*, 1942 – 43, VI, cmd. 6404.

99. Labour Party, *Annual Conference Report, 1942* (London, 1942), 132.

100. *Ibid.,* 132 – 37.

101. *Official Report, House of Commons Debates,* 5th Ser., CCCLXXXVI (Feb. 23, 1943), cols. 1615 – 2054.

102. Labour Party, *Annual Conference Report, 1943* (London, 1943), 80.

103. *Ibid.,* 5 – 6, 20 – 26, 136 – 42.

104. *Sessional Papers,* 1943 – 44, VIII, cmd. 6550.

105. Labour Party, *Preliminary Observations on the Government White Paper on Social Insurance, Workmen's Compensation and a National Health Service* (London, 1944).

106. *Ibid.,* 5.

107. Brady, *Crisis in Britain,* 329.

108. Labour Party, *National Service for Health* (London, 1943), 15, 21.

109. Labour Party, *The Future of Local Government* (London, 1943), 8.

110. *National Service for Health,* 21.

111. *Ibid.,* 13.

112. *Ibid.,* 18.

113. *Sessional Papers,* 1943 – 44, VIII, cmd. 6502.

114. Labour Party, *Annual Conference Report, 1944* (London, 1944), 151 ff.

115. *Ibid., 1945* (London, 1945), 138 – 40.

116. Labour Party, *Housing and Planning after the War* (London, n.d.), 8.

117. R.B. McCallum and Alison Readman, *The British General Election of 1945* (London, 1947), 237.

118. Labour Party, *Let Us Face the Future* (London, 1945).

119. *Official Report, House of Commons Debates,* 5th Ser., CCCXCVII (Mar. 28, 1944), col. 1287.

120. Labour Party, *The Old World and the New Society* (London, 1942), II.

121. See, e.g., Labour Party, *The Welfare State* (London, 1946); Douglas Houghton, *The Family Circle* (London, 1946); Andrew Gordon, *A Guide to the National Insurance Act of 1946* (London, 1946).

122. *Official Report, House of Commons Debates,* 5th Ser., CCCCXXIII (May 22, 1946), cols. 369 ff.

123. *Ibid.,* CCCCXVIII (Feb. 6, 1946), col. 1740.

124. 11 & 12 Geo. VI, Chap. xxix, cl. 1.

125. *Official Report, House of Commons Debates,* 5th Ser., CCCCXXII (Apr. 30, 1946), cols. 43 ff.

126. *Ibid.,* CCCCXXI (Mar. 20, 1946), col. 236; 12 & 13 Geo. VI, Chap. LX, cl. 1.

127. Hugh Dalton, *High Tide and After: Memoirs 1945 – 1960* (London, 1962), 358.

128. Labour Party, *Annual Conference Report, 1949* (London, 1949), 211.

129. *Official Report, House of Commons Debates,* 5th Ser., CCCCXXI (Mar. 26, 1946), cols. 266 ff.

David C. Marsh is a sociologist who at present is Head of the Applied Social Science Department at the University of Nottingham. Author of National Insurance and Assistance in Great Britain *(London, 1950) and* The Future of the Welfare State *(Harmondsworth, 1964), from which the following chapter is taken, he is one of the most perceptive students of the social services in Britain. This latter book examines the ways in which the British have attempted to attain the social justice and equality postulated in the nineteen-forties. It reveals the author's scepticism about the concept of the "welfare state." The excerpt reprinted here is a concluding chapter which summarizes various judgments, including his own, on the handling of basic social issues. It ends, as Professor Marsh puts it, by raising questions about British "aims, principles, and practices in social, economic, and political affairs." Permission to reprint has been granted by Professor Marsh.*

10

The Future of the Welfare State: Whither or Wither?

DAVID C. MARSH

'Would you tell me please which way I ought to walk from here?' said Alice. 'That depends a good deal on where you want to get to' said the Cat.
Lewis Carroll, Alice's Adventures in Wonderland.

(i) What is the appropriate label for our society?

Where one wants to get to and how to get there depend in part on where one is starting from, and if, like Alice, one does not much care where one gets to as long as it is somewhere then as the Cheshire Cat so wisely observed 'it doesn't matter which way you walk' as you are sure to get somewhere 'if you only walk long enough'. In many ways the development of the welfare state in Britain is the result of walking long enough without any clear indication of where we wanted to get to or of following any well-defined paths. By a series of historical accidents we have arrived at what many people now believe to be the affluent society carefully engineered and controlled by the paternalistic welfare state. The future therefore, assuming the absence of a major war of annihilation, is reasonably foreseeable; we shall maintain and improve our welfare policies so as to make our society even more affluent than it is today. But is ours an affluent society in the sense in which these words were first used by Professor Galbraith in his analysis of American society? Or have we merely borrowed the phrase in order to use it as a vote-catching label designed to make us believe that we have attained the kind of society which the word affluent conjures up in our imagination?

Undoubtedly there is more affluence for more people than ever before in our history, but two astute observers of economic and social affairs have argued strongly that far from being an economically affluent or even a welfare society ours is in fact stagnant and irresponsible. [1] Michael Shanks shows that our rate of economic growth has fallen behind that of every other developed country in the world, and that if we are 'to improve our economy to the point where we can achieve the same rates of growth as other Western countries . . . and match the even faster growth rates of the Communist countries' we shall have to reform drastically many of our long-cherished ideas about and attitudes towards economic activity and industrial relations. He believes that 'industrial democracy can go a long way to reducing inequalities of power and some way to reducing inequalities of status. It cannot, however, go very far towards securing greater equality of opportunity. But this inequality is, to my mind, the most damaging of all from the point of view of national welfare and efficiency.'

Professor Titmuss is concerned about the 'changing concentrations of economic and financial power' in our economic and political systems and shows that 'as the power of the insurance interests (in combination with other financial and commercial interests) continues to grow they will, whether they consciously welcome it or no, increasingly become the arbiters of welfare and amenity for larger sections of the community'. He believes that the concept of the 'Welfare State for the working classes' is largely a myth, and that there is little 'to suggest that much progress has been made, during the last nine years in which great fortunes have been accumulated, to concentrate help through the public services on those whose need is greatest . . . . Those who have benefited most are those who have needed it least.' Inequality, far from being reduced, has been increased, and the concentrations of economic power he sees as 'accelerators of inequality; inequalities in the distribution of income and wealth, educational opportunity, vocational choice, pension expectations, and in the right to change one's job, to work in old age and in other spheres of individual and family need.' [2]

For both writers the term affluent society is no more than a label, and perhaps even a dangerously misleading label because it creates an impression of material and social well-being all round which they, and many others, would regard as quite false. And they see very little hope of improvement in social and economic conditions in the future if the fundamental problem of greater equality of opportunity for all remains unsolved: a problem which has been at the centre of controversy about the nature and aims of the welfare state in this country ever since the phrase was first used.

(ii) Equality, individual freedom, and the limits of State action

Those who see the welfare state as being designed primarily to reduce inequalities between individuals and groups are quite explicit about the kinds of inequality they wish to be reduced and, preferably, abolished, but they are by no means as explicit about the degree of equality they wish to be achieved. Presumably reducing inequalities results in more equality and that in an imperfect world of imperfect human beings the only practicable goal to aim at is that of eliminating unnecessary and palpably unjustifiable differences in the opportunities afforded to individuals to live their lives. To suggest that all things could ever be equal for all men at all times, or that all men would take equal advantage of equal opportunities and conditions at all times, is utopian. There are few protagonists of the welfare state who would make such claims, yet many critics of what they assume to be the welfare state as it exists in this country imply that the sole aim of the protagonists is to ensure absolute equality.

The two major political parties who have held office since 1945 are often assumed to be opposed to each other primarily because of fundamental differences in their attitudes towards the kinds and degrees of equality which the State ought to aim at achieving. The Conservative accuses the Labour Party of being interested only in equality. Thus Mr Iain Macleod in an article entitled 'The Political Divide', in a booklet published in 1958 by the Conservative Political Centre, *The Future of the Welfare State,* argues that 'there is another conflict peculiar to our times, which can also be reduced to a phrase or slogan: Opportunity versus Equality. These may well be the battle cries of the next election. If so, we should welcome it. Socialism, so Professor Lewis tells us, is about equality. It is a drab slogan, but then socialism is a sad creed. On our banners we will put "Opportunity", an equal opportunity for men to make themselves unequal'. Is the Labour Party concerned only with equality, and has the Conservative Party deliberately used the power of the State, during the years in which it has been in office, to provide an equal opportunity for men to make themselves unequal? Never having been a member of either party or for that matter any party, and therefore never having taken part in discussions about policy at the seats of power, I am obviously not in a position to answer categorically these questions, but from reading pamphlets and books and the interminable speeches of politicians, purporting to represent the aims and policies of both sides, and having observed systematically the kinds of policies preached and practised, I would not have thought that 'the political divide' was as clear-cut as Mr Macleod suggests.

An examination of recent political publications reveals that there are occasions when it would be difficult to identify the political allegiance of the writers or to recognize the real political divide. For example, what is the fundamental difference between these two statments?

(a) 'It is no part of my argument to say that we should spend less on social provision. My argument, on the contrary, is that we should aspire to spend more, much more, and establish conditions in which our resources will expand to meet these aspirations. It does, however, seem to me that there is both a need and an opportunity now and in the years ahead for a major shift in the nature, direction, and emphasis of social spending . . . towards modern services crying out for community effort or finance: namely the vigorous creation and maintenance by public authority of the finest environmental conditions for our people, and the generous application of public money to the subtler problems of personality, social adjustment, and education in its widest sense.'

(b) 'Looking to the future, there can be little doubt that what is needed is the direction of an increasing flow of savings into the British domestic areas of public squalor . . . . To raise the quality of environment for all our people should be at the very centre of social policy.'

The first of these two statements is from the preface to the Conservative Political Centre booklet *The Future of the Welfare State,* and was written by Mr Peter Goldman, Director of the Centre, and Conservative candidate at the celebrated Orpington by-election; the second is from the Fabian pamphlet *The Irresponsible Society* written by Professor R. M. Titmuss. Both are agreed on the need to raise the quality of the environment for all our people by social spending, presumably to make a better society for all, which is surely a fundamental aim of a welfare state, and there are many other aims which are held in common by apparently strongly opposed political writers. Where, however, there is a real political divide is in the means of achieving aims and in the interpretation of the ultimate effects on our society of using different means.

From the spate of articles, pamphlets, and books, and the torrents of words uttered by politicians and the avowed supporters of the major parties, there would seem to be at least two areas of fundamental difference in the means of achieving the well-being of individuals in society. The one concerns the role of the State, and the other (not of course unrelated) is concerned with the extent to which the availability and the provision of services conducive to individual well-being should be determined by the operation of market forces.

Much of what the State now does and ought to do is, apparently, not in dispute. A member of the Bow Group (founded in 1951 by ex-members of university Conservative associations) has argued that 'rigorous *laisser faire* is neither possible nor desirable, and it is one of the essential functions of the State to see that valid social interests are not neglected', but 'perhaps the most urgent and valuable task which Tories interested in the theories as well as the practice of politics can argue is this question of where we should draw the limits of state action. Not many can be said to have attempted it.' [3] Nor indeed, one suspects, have many Socialists or Liberals. In a democracy there are functional limits beyond which the State cannot go if it is to remain democratic, and in a welfare state there are presumably limits to which it must go if its welfare aims are to be achieved. All too often, however, discussions of the role of the state and the limits of its actions are bedevilled by the assumption that any extension of the functions of the State inevitably leads to a diminution in the freedom of the individual. Thus Mr Timothy Raison (op. cit.) argues that we have to make a choice 'between freedom or liberty for the individual on the one hand, and, on the other, paternalism by a government which claims that it knows best or feels that the rights of the individual can only be secured by a government prepared to intervene extensively.'

Is the choice quite so simple? Is it not possible that the liberty and freedom of the individual will in fact be increased rather than diminished by the actions of a government prepared to intervene extensively? Surely there are obvious examples in this country of where State intervention has substantially increased the individual liberty and freedom of the majority of citizens, and of where the rights of the individual could be secured only by extensive intervention on the part of the State. And there is of course always the possibility that too little intervention by the State will allow the many to be dominated by the few who may curtail the individual liberties of the many to an extent inconceivable in a democracy. There are some people who believe that the Government has intervened too little in recent years in this country, and that as a result we are already in danger of losing some of the individual liberties we now possess. Thus Professor Titmuss (in *The Irresponsible Society*) suggests that 'the growth of a "Pressure Group State" generated by more massive concentrations of interlocking economic, managerial and self-regarding professional power, points in the other direction: towards more inequality, towards the restriction of social rights and liberties and the muffling of social protest among a large section of the population.'

The assumption that every extension of State intervention in economic and social affairs leads inevitably to restrictions on individual liberty and freedom is, surely, as yet unproven. We need far more systematic studies of the consequences of State action than have as yet been carried out before we can reach positive conclusions about their beneficence or harmfulness, and then we would be in a position to follow the excellent precept laid down by Mr Timothy Raison (op. cit.) that 'one of the essential political principles of today ought to be that you should never act in ignorance if it is possible to act with knowledge'. And nowhere does this need to be applied more urgently than in that vast area of State activity, the provision of social services.

(iii) The attitudes of the political parties towards the social services

The differences in the attitudes of the main political parties towards the social services appear to be quite substantial. The views of some leading Conservative Members of Parliament and of influential Conservative study groups have been explicitly stated in, for example, a pamphlet *The Social Services, Needs and Means* written by Iain Macleod and Enoch Powell; an article with the curious title of 'A Policy of Sewage' by Enoch Powell, in *The Future of the Welfare State;* and an article in the Bow Group essays for the 1960s, by Geoffrey Howe on 'The Reform of the Social Services'. The predominant theme of these Conservative thinkers is that 'even in a prosperous society necessary claims on public expenditure can only be met if the social services, as we have come to know them, are drastically refashioned, so that their claims are diminished. Over the whole field of social policy our firm aim should therefore be a reduction of the role of the State,' but 'few Conservatives would doubt that the social services for the most part are here to stay. But we should hesitate to agree with Sir Keith Joseph [4] who, while seeking "scope for sensible men to provide additional protection or amenity for their families and themselves *on top of* the State provision", plainly expects the State to go on making the basic provision for all of us for ever' (Geoffrey Howe, op. cit.).

The Labour Party and its supporters have been far less explicit in their published attitudes towards the social services, but Professor R. M. Titmuss has replied to the main Conservative views in Chapter 2 of his *Essays on the Welfare State,* and it would seem that the Labour Party sees the social services as an essential means of correcting social inequalities and that what is needed is more and not less social provision. The Liberal Party, in recent years, has also produced a series of policy statements indicating that they favour an admixture of private and social provision.

No political party has publicly declared that it is against the provision by the State of social services of any kind, though there are some individual writers like Colin Clark who would obviously like to 'denationalize' the statutory services, [5] and the main area of dispute seems to centre around the extent to which individuals ought to provide themselves for their own welfare. The Labour Party clearly is in favour of communal provision, and social services should be provided as a right of citizenship and paid for by the community as a whole. The Conservatives on the other hand appear to believe that 'it is in keeping with the Conservative tradition to ask people to contribute to their own welfare and advancement', and therefore, for example, 'now that there is a demand for the grammar-school people may be expected to pay something for it. [6] The essence of Conservative policy ought to be that 'a deliberate move must therefore be made towards the creation of a "self-help" State in which the individual is more and more encouraged to provide for himself and his family. [7]

The Labour Party view is presumably based on the assumption that in an industrialized, capitalist, competitive economy the only possibility of ensuring a reasonable degree of equality of opportunity is through communal provision, and there is a far amount of evidence which at the very least suggests that without communal provision of a variety of services our society would be very different today from what it is. Underlying the Conservative (and to some extent the Liberal) views there are a number of assumptions, for example, that services provided by the State are not paid for by individuals; that where an individual pays individually and directly for a service he necessarily has a different attitude towards and sense of responsibility for the service from what he would have if he paid indirectly for it through taxation; and that services paid for communally make us utterly dependent on the State and less responsible as individual citizens.

How valid are assumptions of these kind? Obviously to assume that the State obtains its income other than from individual citizens or groups through taxation and other forms of statutory charges is untenable. The assumption that where an individual pays a share of the cost of communal services through taxation he has a very different attitude towards them from that which he would have if he paid the market price directly out of his own pocket is still unproven, and raises a number of important and, as yet, unanswered questions. The theory is that if, for example, I am made to pay fees weekly, monthly, or every term for my son's education then I will have a different attitude towards and a greater sense of responsibility for education than I would have if the costs of education are met out of rates and taxes to which I make a contribution. Would I, and would most people? And does this theory imply that the whole costs of education must be met only by those who make use of education services? I cannot speak for everyone else in Britain (though it would be a relatively simple matter to find out the facts), but my own feelings and attitudes are quite positive. Education is an essential service in a modern industrialized society, it should be a charge on the community as a whole, I have no objection whatsoever to paying taxes to meet the costs of education even though neither I nor my family may be using the services directly, the price of education ought not to be determined by the operation of market forces, and my attitude towards and sense of responsiblity for education would most certainly not be improved by having to pay individual bills rather than making my contribution through taxation. And, furthermore, under a 'get-as-you-pay' scheme, what would the State do about parents who refused to pay for the education of their children?

Do communal services make us less self-reliant and utterly dependent on the State? What proof does Godfrey Hodgson possess for his assertion (in the Bow Group essays, op. cit.) that 'one of the overall results of the individually attractive programmes of our political opponents has been to make the people of this country ever more and more dependent on the universal provider (i.e. the State), and ever further from a sense of responsibility for its actions'? If this is true the electorate would be uninterested in what the Government does and would presumably not bother to record its opinions at, for example, general elections. The fact is that despite the ways in which Governments since the war have created the impression of being more interested in retaining political power than in serving the needs of the nation, and the growing disillusionment of many citizens at the ineffectiveness of the House of Commons to provide a genuine forum for political debate, most of us do record our votes at general elections, and it may well be that if politicians treated us as reasonably sensible adults and not as morons more of us would show an even greater sense of responsibility for the actions of the State. Surely before making dogmatic assertions about the supposed effects on us as individuals of the actions of the State it would be preferable to find out what the citizens think and feel about, for example, the choice between communal and private provision, which would after all be in line with the excellent principle laid down by Mr. Raison in the same series of essays of never acting in ignorance if it is possible to act with knowledge.

The belief that all 'public' spending is harmful whereas all 'private' spending is beneficial seems to be most widely held by those who assume that the amounts they pay in taxation are in inverse ratio to the benefits they receive from the State; those who believe that if Joe Bloggs, through no fault of his, received more by way of 'benefits' from the State than he contributes in taxation then he is doomed to an attitude of dependence on the State and loses all sense of personal responsibility for everything; and those who believe that it is in the accumulation of private wealth as distinct from public wealth, and through the operation of market forces, that the best economic, political, and social interests of the nation are served. Thus Geoffrey Howe (in the Bow Group essays) argues that private wealth is 'an important equipoise to political power and a mainspring of economic expansion', a view obviously not held by Professor Titmuss who (in *The Irresponsible Society*) sees the growth in the economic power of 'the great insurance corporations' as constituting 'a major shift in economic power in our society. It is a power, a potential power, to affect many important aspects of our economic life and our social values in the 1960s. It is a power concentrated in relatively few hands, working at the apex of a handful of giant bureaucracies, technically supported by a group of professional experts, and accountable in practice to virtually no one.' For Titmuss the answers to the problems of achieving the best interests of the nation and reducing inequalities 'lie in many fields and forms of public ownership, public responsibility, and public accountability. . . . To substitute the professional protest for the social protest and the arbitrary power of the City for the accountable power of the Commons is no answer'; a view shared by the Economic Editor of that sober and respectable Sunday newspaper the *Observer*, who in an article on 'Tax Wealth, not gains' (8 April 1962) argued that 'excessive and growing concentration of money and power in very few hands is itself a threat to political and economic freedom'.

Serious study of the political and social history of this country over the past century provides little evidence to support the view that private wealth has been an important equipoise to political power. There are of course examples of individuals who have amassed great fortunes who seem to have had no interest in or effect on the distribution of political power, and have in fact used their wealth for the benefit of their fellow men. But in the complex society in which we live today can we, and do we want to rely on the accumulation of private wealth as the means of ensuring the highest standards of individual well-being for all? Whether we want to or not we obviously in practice cannot, because we have reached a stage of economic and social development where even the richest individual or group could not finance most of the major projects which are accepted as essential for the maintenance of living standards. Indeed even projects which have no direct bearing on basic living standards are looked upon and accepted as being entitled to communal support. For example, when the Cunard Shipping Company had to face the problem of replacing the liner *Queen Mary* the ultimate decision depended on the extent to which the State was prepared to subsidize the capital cost of replacement, and there are a host of economic projects, far more vital to the nation than a prestige liner, which would never have been started, and certainly could not continue in being, without the support of the taxpayer. Are we entitled to assume that because the State undertakes partial or full responsibility for financing an industrial project the directors, managers, and everyone else employed in the firm cease to exercise any initiative and abandon all their responsi-bilities? And that if, for example, a new *Queen Mary* was in fact built at the public expense then the passengers who sailed in her would behave differently from what they would have in a liner built by private enterprise? Surely not; yet there is an assumption that if, for example, education or health projects are communally financed then those who run them and those who use them imme-diately become irresponsible.

While we persist in assuming that the accumulation of private wealth and private spending are in all respects beneficial and conducive to the public good, despite some evidence to the contrary, and that the accumulation of public wealth and public spending are in most respects harmful, despite the evidence of numerous indices of social and individual progress, so will all our discussions about the kind of society we would like ours to be and the methods of achieving it be obscured by charges and counter-charges based not on facts, but on untested assumptions and unsubstantiated beliefs. Much of the criticism against and much of the fervour for the imagined or actual welfare measures in operation in this country are based on partial knowledge, and of-ten on sheer ignorance of what in fact they are achieving. To believe that they are only helping the feckless and shiftless and penalizing the worthy, or bring-ing incalculable benefits to everyone, is to ignore the facts. And what we need to do, far more than we have done, is to search for facts so that we can devise policies based on knowledge of how best to serve the interests of society as a whole. But what are the best interests of society?

(iv) What are the best interests of society as a whole?

Much has been said and written in recent years of the deterioration in moral standards and in the sense of social responsibility of the British people. Those who make accusations of these kinds seem to direct their attacks against par-ticular segments of society, especially those who are relatively defenceless, to have no sense of perspective or of the relationship of cause and effect, and themselves to acquiesce too readily in double standards of morality. One law for the rich and another for the poor may have been acceptable in the past, and could perhaps even have been justified, but it is not conducive to the de-velopment of 'one nation', which Mr Iain Macleod has assured us (in *The Fu-ture of the Welfare State*) it 'is the task of the Tory today to create'.

Our society today is riddled with differential privileges, powers, status, and standards of conduct, which are incomprehensible to the enlightened visitor from abroad, and rarely do we pause to consider whether these differences are really necessary and in the best interest of the nation. Even more rarely are we prepared to examine objectively how other societies organize themselves and whether we could learn from them, despite our membership of international organizations regularly providing comparative data of a most useful kind, not least in relation to the provision of social services and methods of financing them.

There are in our own country today people in high places and at the seats of power who believe that the burden of social service expenditure in Britain is heavier than it is in any other country, and yet numerous official reports from international governmental organizations, and even articles in reputable national newspapers, have shown conclusively that the financial burden is in fact far less here than it is in many other countries. Equally it has been shown that social service benefits are often provided at a higher level in other countries than they are here, and that employers abroad bear a heavier burden of the share in financing social security than they do in this country. Yet the Labour Party spokesman on social security could say publicly, in an interview on B.B.C. sound radio on 2 April 1963, when giving his views on Labour's 'New Frontiers for Social Security', that 'he had been surprised to find how much employers abroad contributed'.

Politicians cannot be expected to read all that is published, but surely they ought to be aware of what goes on elsewhere, and as the more reputable Sunday newspapers (to which politicians of all parties are frequent contributors of articles) have shown an increasing tendency in recent years to comment and publish informative articles on social affairs at home and abroad there is no justification for anyone being uninformed. Thus Conservative politicians who persist in their belief that the welfare state in Britain imposes intolerable burdens on the nation's economic effort and is responsible for our slow rate of economic growth would at least have been given food for thought in an article by Mr Andrew Shonfield in the *Observer* on Sunday, 22 January 1961. After having examined comparative data on labour costs Mr Shonfield stated categorically 'so much for the myth that it is the sheer volume of taxation in Britain required for the support of the namby-pamby welfare state which is responsible for our lack of competitive power and the slow growth of the nation's wealth. Germany, which has the record for growing fast, carries a bigger social burden—and does not seem to be slowed down, even to the extent of feeling the need to grumble endlessly about it. Nor does it prevent Sweden from staying the richest country in Western Europe'. Equally members of the Labour Party could have learned from this article the proportion of the burden of social security finance borne by employers in Western Europe, and they need not have waited until 1961 because *The Times* in a leader published on 30 September 1954 had already made this point clear, and the Conservative Political Centre in its pamphlet *The Future of the Welfare State,* published on 10 January 1958, had an interesting article on the same theme, 'Lessons from Abroad', written by Mr Richard Bailey, the director of the independent research organization Political and Economic Planning.

Far more attention should be paid by politicians and administrators to the lessons which can be learned from abroad, and far more publicity needs to be given to the fact that Britain does not now lead, and never has led, the world in its attempt to establish a welfare state. Nor indeed will it ever if political parties continue to delude themselves, as the Labour Party appears to do in its latest proposals for 'New Frontiers for Social Security' by claiming that 'Under a Labour Government—when Aneurin Bevan launched the first comprehensive free Health Service in the Western World, and James Griffiths laid the foundations of our modern National Insurance—Britain led the way in social security'. Political point scoring may be a justifiable part of the game of politics, and the interpretation of Western world can vary, but if New Zealand, Norway, Denmark, and Sweden are deemed to be part of it, then quite certainly, we did not lead the world in 1948. For too long we have assumed that other countries should always learn from us, but we could learn nothing from them; that the British way of life would always serve as a model for the rest of the world; and that the slogan which used to apply to our manufactured articles, 'British is Best,' applied equally to our economic, political, and social systems. We have been made to learn by bitter experience that 'British-made' is no longer a passport to world markets, and that Britain is no longer a great power in the realm of international politics. We have not yet learned the reasons for our fall from grace in the eyes of neighbouring states, and we never shall if we persist in ignoring their achievements and fail to submit ourselves to critical self-examination.

Even ordinary observation would reveal that there are many features of our society which are not to be found at all or at most to a lesser degree abroad: our highly stratified class structure; our class consciousness and assumptions about the rights, duties, and privileges of the different social classes; our worship of pomp, ceremony, and tradition; our archaic ideas about employer-employee relations; our fear of economic planning and inability to clarify the role of the State; the high status we accord 'the professions' without really knowing what a profession is, and the low esteem in which we hold manual work; our respect for the 'amateur', especially in politics and public administration; our outmoded system of local government and the false assumptions we make about local democracy; our respect for 'classical' education and relative neglect of scientific and technological education; and perhaps our greatest failing as compared with many other peoples is that we refuse to apply the principles of pragmatism.

A systematic and objective examination of other societies which have succeeded in recent years in achieving rates of economic growth and standards of welfare higher than ours would doubtless show that they have aims, policies, and methods which we could usefully import, imitate, and adapt to suit our needs. We have from time to time sent 'working parties' abroad to investigate particular methods of working in other countries, and during the long and abortive Common Market negotiations there were presumably searching examinations of the kinds of changes we would have to make in our social and economic policies to enable us to become partners in the European Community. All too often, however, there is an extraordinary reluctance to accept the need for change of any kind and even where evidence is produced of our obvious backwardness in particular fields (as it has been by some working parties) the usual reaction is for entrenched vested interests either to suppress the evidence or dismiss it irrationally as untrue. Facing facts and abandoning long-cherished principles and practices can be painful processes, but the pain must be borne, and if needs be an operation performed, if we are to move forward rather than remain static.

The natural inclinations of British politicians, administrators, businessmen, and trade-union leaders are to despise facts and mistrust theories, with the result that the actual as distinct from the assumed situation in governmental and industrial fields is rarely closely examined, and theoretical concepts of possible courses of action are hardly considered. If scientists had been equally reluctant to search for, examine, and re-examine facts, and had refused to give serious consideration to 'theories' which at first glance seemed to have no possibility of practical application, then the material world of today would be very different from what it is. Scientific attitudes and methods are just as practicable and essential in trying to understand the problems of government, industry, and human relations as they are in discovering the secrets of nature, and if our educational methods had concentrated more on making us use our critical faculties and less on rote learning, then far fewer of us would be prepared to accept unthinkingly so many of our existing social, economic, and political institutions. And, of course, the growing power of the advertiser, and, more menacingly, the 'hidden persuader', would presumably not have been as effective in influencing the directions of our economic effort and the patterns of our social behaviour.

Advertising is no longer an essentially economic function; it has become a powerful political weapon. Every major party employs advertisers euphemistically called public relations consultants—to exploit the party image, and to project a glorified image of the party leaders. National elections are fought not on the basis of the real differences between the programmes of the parties but on the most favourable image created by the advertisers, with the result that the voter has to make his choice from slogans and catchphrases rather than from systematic policy statements of aims and methods of achievement. If the 'brand image' type of political discussion was confined to electioneering, then we might suffer it as we do other kinds of advertising. But there is a dangerous tendency for all political discussion and publications of party statements to be couched in advertising terms. Rational debates on the merits of rival party programmes are extremely rare, and even the House of Commons has virtually ceased to be a debating chamber. Issues vital to the nation as a whole are often discussed perfunctorily, and the most assiduous reader of *Hansard* would be unlikely to find from the reports of debates in recent years any consistent themes of the aims and policies of the parties for the present and future well-being of the nation. Indeed there is among many members of Parliament a growing awareness of the ineffectiveness of the House of Commons to control public policy, and there is a demand for radical reforms in parliamentary procedure. If there is no clear lead from the 'Mother of Parliaments' on the future policies of the nation, how are we, the citizens, to know which way we 'ought to walk from here'?

If we continue along traditional lines we shall remain a static society in a dynamic world of change, and there is little point in setting up 'signposts for the sixties' (as the Labour Party have done) or in looking ahead to the seventies (as the Conservative Party is reported to be doing) when we shall continue in our muddled way just walking and getting nowhere. Ultimately we will not remain static; we will become a society in decline and, like some great Empires of the past, wither away. But is this what the majority of British people would hope for, or have we more positive ideas about the way our society should change and of the kind of society we would like it to be?

Do we want an 'acquisitive society' in which the material rewards go to the few who have the power to divert an undue share of the nation's resources for their own benefit, hence gaining more power and a status very different from the rest of us? Or would we prefer a society in which all had a reasonable share of the nation's resources, and differential rewards were based on responsibilities and contribution to the social good, and equality of opportunity a civic right? Apart from material rewards, on which even now we lay an undue emphasis, do we want the kind of society in which the few have rights and privileges denied to the many, or would we prefer to see privileges earned and accorded by society as a mark of distinction for outstanding contribution to the well-being of society? And so we could continue theorizing about the kind of society we want ours to be, giving it a distinctive label such as 'welfare', 'acquisitive', 'protective', 'consumptive', 'competitive', 'egalitarian', 'élitist', and the like, but all too often using words without precise meanings or even defined limits. What, for example, is 'the social good', what are 'privileges', and what is 'power'? Each of us will have our own interpretation of words of these kinds, and concepts of 'liberty', 'individual freedom', and 'justice' are equally open to a variety of interpretations. We need far more precision in the use of terms commonly accepted as describing social objectives if we are to gain agreement about the aims and methods of achieving the best kind of society, and this requries far more knowledge about the structure and mechanisms of society, and about human relationships and aspirations than we have now, or are likely to have if we pay as little attention to social research in the future as we have in the past.

(v) Will social policy in the future be based on facts or assumptions?

Framing social policy cannot always be delayed while exhaustive research is carried out to determine the facts on which to create policy; on the other hand policies should whenever possible and practicable be based on facts and not on assumptions and hunches. Politicians, administrators, and even hard-headed businessmen have a strange faith in the power of their own intuition, and they honestly believe that they know what other people think and desire even though the belief is based on very limited contact with very few other people. Only slowly have businessmen come to recognize the value of market research as a method of obtaining facts and opinions, and politicians and public administrators have still to become aware of the potentialities of social research as a tool for the creation of social policy. The reluctance of politicians and civil servants to recognize that facts can be found, and the foolish position in which they find themselves as a result of not encouraging systematic research into the consequences of social action, was admirably summarized by Mark Abrams in an article 'Pattern of Welfare', published in the *Observer* on Sunday, 16 April 1961. In that article Mr Abrams commented:

'When earlier this year the Commons prepared to debate the new health charges the Labour Party happily looked forward to great Parliamentary clashes which would restore the party's self-confidence and shatter that of the Conservatives. In fact, despite the noise, the attack would seem to have been completely ineffective. There were many reasons for this, but one of them was probably that moral indignation is no substitute for facts, and neither side was in a position to say quantitatively how many and which members of the public would be seriously affected by the new charges and how those hit might react. That the two parties should be in this state of ignorance is remarkable and deplorable. Currently the country is spending £ 3,000 million a year on the social services; a fair slice of this goes on providing each service with information officers and public relations units, but practically nothing is spent on finding out how consumers of these services use them and view them. Fortunately with a grant from the Nuffield Foundation, P.E.P. has now thrown some light on this neglected aspect of the workings of the Welfare State.' 8

This is not the only occasion in recent years for the parties to be in a state of ignorance. For example, the Government introduced the Rent Act without knowing what its impact would be, and the Labour Party opposed it in an equal state of ignorance; and the estimates of the number of contributors who would contract out of the Graduated Pensions scheme was hopelessly wrong. Why the Government should be in such a state of ignorance so often is difficult to understand when there is within the machinery of the central government an efficient and well-organized social survey unit capable of providing facts on most social questions. It can, however, undertake research only when it is requested or ordered to do so by other Government departments, and in spite of the well-deserved reputation that it has earned for itself among those who know something of the problems and techniques of social research, it is still all too rarely used, and is, in comparison with many other departments, pitifully small in the number of staff it is allowed and the budget on which it has to work. Can it be that the politician and the administrator is chary of asking for the facts to be found out because they prefer to act on assumptions, opinions, and beliefs which in the main are not capable of being rationally debated?

If our social policies henceforth are to continue to be based on what politicians, civil servants, businessmen, and trade-union leaders assume to be what the people of Britain desire, then it is unlikely that we shall see much change in what we have presumed to call the welfare state. We shall go on modifying a little here, patching up a little there, and be as much in the dark about the obvious weaknesses in our economic and social systems as we are now, and about the kind of society we want. Perhaps the younger generation, growing up in a world where social techniques are rapidly and continuously changing, where traditional attitudes, patterns of behaviour, and standards of value are constantly under attack, where the marvels of science and technology promise to bring the moon within the reach of man, and where the interest in education is more intense than ever before, will be less hidebound and more venturesome in their approach to and methods of social change. Despite obvious inequalities in educational opportunities, and the defects of our highly specialized and traditionalist education, young people today are more aware of the world around them than their fathers were, they are more eager to experiment and less conformist than previous generations, and of course there are far more of them continuing their full-time education beyond school-leaving age. It is unlikely that they will be content with a static society or that they will accept the dictum so commonly held by previous generations of parents—'what was good enough for my father is good enough for me and therefore good enough for my children'.

The jeremiads—many of them in high places—who castigate modern youths for their interest in materials things, the way they spend their money, their lax morals, cupidity, and selfishness, seem to forget that these failings are not peculiar to the present generation, or to a single age group or social class. And if modern youth is in fact guilty of charges of these kinds could it not be that they are following the example set by their elders and supposedly betters? If working-class teenagers spend their money on exotic clothes, pop records, tape-recorders, and juke boxes, is this kind of expenditure so much less socially worthwhile than the vast sums spent on coming-out parties for debutantes? Are the misdemeanours of followers of professional soccer teams, who are constantly accused of damage to railway carriages when following their team to an away match, so much more harmful than the antics of the 'younger set' on the London underground after a coming-out ball? The proportion of teenagers from the 'working classes' who engage in anti-social conduct is probably no higher than that from the 'upper classes' whose conduct leaves much to be desired, and to stigmatize all the younger generation as irresponsible because of the behaviour of the few is to ignore the fact that the majority of young people today are, rightly, questioning the kind of society and the world we live in, and have aspirations for the future very different from those of earlier generations.

The elders in the major political parties have already found that the younger members are not content simply to follow the lead given by their seniors, and when the younger no longer accepts blindly but questions and analyses the words, statements, policies, and practices of the older generation in power then the nature, pattern, and rates of social change are bound to be different from what they were in the past. Our natural tendency to proceed by reform rather than by revolution will no doubt continue, but let us hope that they will be reforms based on knowledge, facts, ascertained needs and desires, and assessments of results. As the principles of scientific investigation become more widely known and applied to fields other than the physical and natural sciences so will we recognize that many of the features of our economic, social, and political systems which we now accept as necessary, desirable, and inevitable are in fact unnecessary, undesirable, and certainly not inevitable.

There are still many people who question whether scientific methods can be applied to the problems of man in society, and there are others who make exaggerated claims on behalf of social science. Whatever views we may hold about the achievements of social science so far it can at least be said that social scientists are attempting to examine objectively the workings of society, and it is only through sustained and dispassionate examination of aims, purposes, functions, methods, and results that we can ever achieve a real understanding of the society in which we live, and enable decisions to be made as to the kind of society we hope to see developed in the future. In a democracy these decisions are made (or should be) by politicians within a system of representative government, and in a highly complex industrialized society the 'rulers' must have at their command facts on which to frame policy, and methods of measuring the results. Formidable tasks, but not impossible if the permanent officials, the paid servants of the State, are educated, recruited, and trained for the functions they must of necessity perform, and politicians recognize that they have a duty to society as a whole never to act in ignorance if they can act with knowledge.

Only when we rid ourselves of the vast load of mythology which now colours so much of our thinking about the kind of society in which we live and the sorts of people we are will we be able to attach an appropriate label to our society and our state.

The most commonly used label since the Second World War is that of the Welfare State. Is it entirely appropriate in view of the limited connotation of 'welfare' and the confusion in aims, principles, and practices in social, economic, and political affairs? And will it be appropriate in the 1980s, or will we by then have found that labels really mean what they say, and what will the State label then have written on it?

NOTES

1. Michael Shanks, *The Stagnant Society* (Pelican, 1961). R. M. Titmuss, *The Irresponsible Society* (Fabian Society, 1960).

2. Titmuss, ibid.

3. Timothy Raison, 'Principles in Practice, Conservative Thought Today' in the booklet

Principles in Practice, a Series of Bow Group Essays for the 1960s (Conservative Political Centre for the Bow Group, 1961).

4. The Conservative Minister of Housing and Local Government in 1963 who, long before he attained Ministerial rank, held some rather advanced views, from a Conservatives standpoint, on the need particularly to reorganize the complex and clumsy organization of the statutory services.

5. Colin Clark, *Welfare and Taxation.*

6. Godfrey Hodgson, 'Education on Demand', in the Bow Group Essays, op. cit.

7. Geoffrey Howe, op. cit.

8. P.E.P. report, *Family Needs and the Social Services.*

While the decline of Britain's world power was precipitated by the First World War, it was not until after 1945 that many British people began consciously to accept the fact that their country was a small European state with limited resources. In the nineteen-fifties and sixties fundamental questions were posed about the American connection, about the viability of the new Commonwealth, and above all (although many for a long time were unwilling to recognize how fundamental the question was) about Britain's relations with a western Europe fumbling its way toward some kind of federalist arrangement of its economic if not its political life. Both major parties had "pro-Europe" and "anti-Europe" wings; both looked for cooperation without real commitment for many years. Even when each took hesitating steps toward cooperation, that action was accompanied by conditions that made rejection almost inevitable. In his book Britain's Future *(New York, 1968), David Calleo surveys Britain's post-war international history in an effort to draw conclusions about the direction British foreign policy may follow. The present chapter outlines the alternatives available after 1945 and the road taken. It makes clear how reluctant the approach to Europe was and how slowly real attitudes changed from the late forties until the late sixties. David Calleo is currently a professor at the School of Advanced International Studies, Johns Hopkins University. This chapter is reprinted from* Britain's Future *by David Calleo, published by Horizon Press, copyright 1968 by David Calleo.*

11 | Britain in Transit: the Postwar Muddle

DAVID CALLEO

Future historians will very likely see the third quarter of the twentieth century as the period in which Britain haltingly took stock of her transformation from a world power of the first magnitude into a European power of limited resources. They will probably feel that Britain, compared with the rest of Europe, took rather a long time to come to terms with her problems. For since World War II every one of the great nations of Western Europe has faced the same painful discovery of reduced power and place in the world, and broadly speaking, the same kind of crisis in national identity. Germany and Italy emerged from the war physically shattered and carrying a heavy burden of guilt and self-reproach. France, too, was in ruins and, despite de Gaulle's heroic rescue of her honour, the shame and ugly disunity of 1940 left wounds that would take long to heal. Moreover, France's precarious self-respect was soon to be shaken by a series of military disasters that would inexorably deprive her of a great empire.

By comparison the prestige of Britain's wartime victory concealed the extent of her decline; the gracefulness of her departure nearly obscured the end of her Empire. As a result, the British postponed facing their basic problems for almost a generation. Whereas the continentals, in those cold postwar years, huddled together and sought a new identity and self-respect in the ideal of European unity, British Governments, from the war's end until the early 1960s, refused to participate in and sometimes actively resisted Europe's federalist evolution. Not until Macmillan's time did any British government seriously deviate from Churchill's original policy for the postwar era, the celebrated "three circles".[1] Britain was to continue to play three roles: a European power, the special ally of the United States, and the head of the Commonwealth. The chief rule of British diplomacy was to avoid ever being put in a situation where one role might have to be sacrificed for another. Naturally, therefore, Britain was not interested in a European union that would freeze her either in or out of the continent. Thus Britain's official contributions to the European enterprise were mostly rhetorical, and even then, generally from the statesmen out of office.

Churchill in opposition was especially well-equipped for these activities and indeed stirred all Europe with his eloquence. One of his most famous speeches was given at Zürich in 1946:

> We must build a kind of United States of Europe.
>
> If Europe were once united in the sharing of its common inheritance there would be no limit to the happiness, prosperity, and glory which its 300,000,000 or 400,000,000 people would enjoy.
>
> And why should there not be a European group which could give a sense of enlarged patriotism and common citizenship to the distracted peoples of this mighty continent? And why should it not take its rightful place with the other great groupings and help to shape the honourable destiny of Man?
>
> Therefore, I say to you, "Let Europe arise!" [2]

When Churchill in power showed no interest in Britain's joining Europe, the memory of these speeches caused considerable bitterness on the continent. But the disillusion came from not having listened carefully. The rest of the Zürich speech, for example, revealed clearly what Churchill felt subsequently called upon to state with more brutal clarity: "We are with them, not of them." [3] The union Churchill had in mind for Europe was to be built, not by Britain, but by a reconciled France and Germany. England, the Commonwealth, "mighty America", and, Churchill hoped, Russia, would be only the "friends and sponsors" of the new Europe. In short, even in rhetoric, Churchill's enthusiasm was carefully measured. Britain was to be a "sponsor", but not a participant.

One significant continental view of Churchill's policy can be found in de Gaulle's *Memoirs*. Throughout the war, the General had tried to win the British to his plan for a European combination, based on France, to balance the super-powers on their periphery. When Churchill paid a moving triumphal visit to liberated Paris in November, 1944, de Gaulle pressed his familiar theme:

> You English, of course, will emerge from this war covered with glory. Yet to what a degree—unfair though it may be—your relative situation risks being diminished, given,

your losses and expenditures, by the centrifugal forces at work within the Commonwealth, and particularly, the rise of America and Russia, not to mention China! Confronting a new world, then, our two old nations find themselves simultaneously weakened. If they remain divided as well, how much influence will either of them wield? [4]

De Gaulle was especially worried about the settlement Roosevelt and Stalin
would impose on Europe:

The equilibrium of Europe . . . the guarantee of peace along the Rhine, the independence of the Vistula, Danube and Balkan states, the creation of some form of association with the peoples all over the world to whom we have opened the doors of Western
civilization, an organization of nations which will be something more than an arena for
disputes between America and Russia, and lastly the primacy accorded in world politics to a certain conception of man despite the progressive mechanization of society—these, surely, are our great interests in tomorrow's world. Let us come to an
agreement in order to uphold these interests together. If you are willing to do so, I am
ready. Our two nations will follow us. America and Russia, hobbled by their rivalry, will
not be able to raise any objection. Moreover, we shall have the support of many states
and of world-wide public opinion, which instinctively shies away from giants. Thus
England and France will together create peace, as twice in thirty years they have together confronted war. [5]

Churchill's answer was a more thoughtful version of what he had shouted in
anger the preceding January at Marrakech: "How do you expect that the British should take a position separate from the United States? . . . each time we
must choose between Europe and the open sea, we shall always choose the
open sea. Each time I must choose between you and Roosevelt, I shall always
choose Roosevelt." [6] In Paris, a mellower Churchill defended his own and indeed postwar Britain's policy by observing that:

. . . in politics as in strategy, it is better to persuade the stronger than to pit yourself
against him. That is what I am trying to do. The Americans have immense resources.
They do not always use them to the best advantage. I am trying to enlighten them,
without forgetting, of course, to benefit my country. I have formed a close personal tie
with Roosevelt. With him I proceed by suggestion in order to influence matters in the
right direction. [7]

De Gaulle's disappointed view: "The peace we French hoped to build in accord with what we regarded as logic and justice, the British found it expedient
to approach with formulas of empiricism and compromise." [8] The British, as de
Gaulle had occasion to remind them several years later, were not Europeans. [9]

De Gaulle was an early but by no means solitary sceptic about Britain's interest in European unity. Paul-Henri Spaak, with less controversial credentials
as a good European than the General, once resigned as President of the Council of Europe's Consultative Assembly, with an angry attack on Britain's lack of

support for the European Defence Community. If Europe were to be built, he concluded, it would have to be without Britain.[10]

The most bitter denunciations of Britain's European policies came, in fact, from European enthusiasts among the British themselves.[11] These formed a significant group, claiming at various times the apparent, if ambiguous, support of some of the most distinguished figures in the country. But in the nineteen-fifties, these British Europeans had little effect on British policy.[12] Until 1961, every government was tepid and often hostile towards the whole idea of a close European union. Certainly no government was ever prepared to base Britain's future on such a union, or take the lead in creating it.

In the crucial postwar years that set the whole pattern of subsequent Western relations, it was not, of course, the Tories, but Labour's Foreign Secretary, Ernest Bevin, who directed Britain's foreign policy. Labour's policy went through roughly three stages, each corresponding to a different American phase. In the early days, while America was still flirting with the dream of a new "progressive" world order built around a Russian-American condominium, Bevin frequently found himself alone against Molotov in opposing Russia's ambitions, notably in Greece and Persia, with Byrnes looking on as a sort of benevolent and large-minded mediator. During this period, Bevin took the initiative in organizing a regional European defence arrangement, a policy leading in 1947 to the Treaty of Dunkirk between Britain and France.[13]

In 1947, with the Truman Doctrine committing the United States to the defence of Greece and Turkey, America began a policy of actively opposing Russian expansion. In 1948, there came the Marshall Plan and the Organization for European Economic Co-Operation, and in 1949, NATO. This fundamental switch in American policy constituted not only a triumph for imaginative American statesmanship, but also a victory for British policy. The United States, at last, was involved permanently on the European side of the Atlantic.

America's various European ties were organized in two quite distinct patterns—that of the Marshall Plan and OEEC on one hand, and that of NATO on the other. The OEEC reflected the ideal of an Atlantic Alliance built around two equal partners—America and a United Europe. NATO, on the contrary, was predicated on a direct relation between the United States and each of Europe's national states, without any intervening European Union. One was the relation often expressed metaphorically as an alliance with "two pillars". The other, the NATO relationship, seems to have been less inspiring to literary fancy. Perhaps a hen and her chicks would be the most appropriate metaphor. At any rate, both patterns continue to the present day.

From the beginning, British Governments clearly preferred the "Atlantic",

NATO pattern over the two pillars pattern of the OEEC. True, in the Atlantic pattern America would always predominate, but that, the British felt, was a price worth paying for an American commitment to Europe's survival. Furthermore, the ties in so vast an assemblage could never be very tight. Britain's Commonwealth and American connections, and eventually Britain's own nuclear capabilities, would still assure her a major role—a "special" relationship within the Alliance. Meanwhile the presence of so many others would allow Britain room for manoeuvre in her relations with the Americans.

On the other hand, the two-pillars pattern, a European federation to match the American, had every disadvantage for Britain. In the unlikely event that Europe actually succeeded in uniting, Britain would be confronted with the unpleasant choice either of being excluded from Europe or else impairing her independent world standing, Commonwealth connections and national economic independence. A federal European Union would end Britain's special position in the Alliance. With the continent united, Britain would either be absorbed or overshadowed. Thus while Brtiain was all for European co-operation, she was not interested in a European federation. Hence, she constantly stressed the necessary Atlantic dimension to European union. Bevin's own words in 1948 spelled out the basic British position:

> . . . the organization of all the Western European democracies, excellent and necessary as it is, can hardly be accomplished save within the framework of a larger entity. I am not content to confine either propaganda or speeches of action to the assumption that Western Europe alone can save itself. [14]

The British went so far in their enthusiasm for an Atlantic rather than a European grouping that they drew strong criticism from the American Congress itself: especially from the architects and enthusiasts of the Marshall Plan. The whole idea of that great venture was not only to save Europe from the communist flood, but also to provoke the Europeans to create, by their union, a self-sufficient economic and political unit capable of existing without indefinite American assistance. [15] The tension between these aims and Britain's policy was soon apparent. Thus, while the Americans in establishing the machinery of Marshall Aid were able to insist that Europe's economic problems be treated as a whole, British resistance killed off more radical proposals for integration along the lines of a European customs union. [16] In the same period, Britain so succeeded in watering down the institutions of the Council of Europe, the first of the actual attempts to build an organized European union, that even General de Gaulle found the Council a ludicrously inadequate instrument for forging the continent into a new nation. [17]

There were prominent Britons who criticized Labour's policy towards Europe at the time, but in retrospect the policy is easy enough to understand. The Government could hardly be blamed for being more interested in preserving the American commitment than in advancing visionary schemes for European unity. Furthermore, postwar leaders of both parties were suspicious of American enthusiasm for European federation. In the idea of the two pillars, the British were quick to see a more sophisticated version of the old American isolationism—as well as American naïveté in applying the lessons of their own federalist experience to divisions of vastly greater magnitude in Europe.[18] Britain's main interest was to ensure that the United States could not find an excuse, once again, to withdraw and leave Europe to its fate. Thus Britain continually resisted American efforts to encourage European federation—not only from a desire to maintain national independence, imperial connections, and great-power status—but from the fear that federalism for Europe and isolationism for America were reverse sides of the same coin.

Furthermore, the goal of European union, as an end in itself, quite naturally had less appeal for the British than for many other Europeans. Whereas every major continental power, with the ambiguous exception of France, emerged from the war with its old nationalist allegiances discredited, Britain had triumphantly confirmed the grandeur and durability of her own traditional loyalties and institutions. It was not surprising that there was lacking in England the same rather desperate eagerness to renounce national identity. In an odd sort of way, the German occupation had perhaps given the peoples of Western Europe a common experience, an intimacy among themselves, that made it easier for them to think of a new order in which they would work closely together and indeed become more like one another. Britain had been spared this painful education. The British could hardly be expected to embrace their disgraced friends and recent enemies quite so eagerly or expectantly.

If the British in general lacked any overriding enthusiasm for European union as an aim in itself, the Labour Party in particular found it not only irrelevant but often harmful to the actual goals in which Labour was interested.[19] Labour was more drawn to the internationalist idea of the United Nations than to the limited regionalist concept of a European union. Not only might a federal Europe provoke American isolationism, but, if Britain were bound up in it, the continentals might well constrain the Labour Party from pursuing its own cherished domestic and international goals. Internationally, Labour's imagination was fired by the vision of a new "multi-racial" Commonwealth bridging the gap between regions, races and stages of economic development. This goal seemingly had little to gain from Britain's close association with unregenerate Belgian, Dutch and French colonialists. Not a few in the Labour Party still hoped that a socialist Britain might eventually act as a bridge between communist Russia and the West. Britain's freedom of action was unlikely to be improved by close association with the Catholic anti-communists of Europe's ruling Christian Democratic parties. Above all, the Labour Party was bound up in its vast programme of domestic reform. Socialism had at last gained the opportunity to rebuild English society. What Labour Government could be expected to renounce the hard-won machinery of the national state at just the moment when it could at last be put to good use? What kind of new society, Socialists asked, could be built in a federation with the right-wing, capitalist governments of France and Germany? In short, European union was not, in itself, an overriding goal for most of the Labour Party and there were many other factors restraining Labour's enthusiasm for a federal Europe.

The continentals, finding no lead from Britain, went their own way. In 1950, the Schumann Plan to place the coal and steel industries of France and Germany under a common "High Authority" became the first of the continent's major supranational initiatives. The plan had a rather *dirigiste* flavour, but the Labour Government clearly rejected for England any federal scheme that might hinder purely national planning. [20] The continentals went ahead and established the Coal and Steel Community without Britain and thus first brought into existence the non-British "Europe of the Six."

When the Tories came back to power in 1952, they soon dashed any hope that they might prove more sympathetic to European union. They had already made it quite apparent that they were no more willing to accept the supranational discipline of the Coal and Steel Community than was Labour. [21] The new Government's first major confrontation with the European federalist movement occurred over the ill-starred European Defence Community. The episode provides a classic illustration of Britain's unwillingness to co-operate closely with the continent. EDC's sponsor, French Foreign Minister René Pleven, envisaged nothing less than a common European Army. The whole scheme represented an ingenious "European" solution to the agonizing problem of German rearmament. [22] The Korean War had made a large new land army urgently necessary for Europe's defence. France, especially with her colonial involvements in Indo-China and Africa, was hardly able to put up enough forces. Neither America nor Britain was willing to contemplate a lasting commitment of a mass army adequate to match Russia. Inescapably, Germany would have to be rearmed. The French Foreign Minister saw in his European Defence Community the means to rearm the Germans without rearming Germany. Individual national units would be kept small. The whole force would not be at the disposal of national governments as such, but under a common European command, directed, in turn, by a European political authority in which Germany was not likely to gain hegemony.

The political consequences of such an arrangement were immense. Once military power was organized on a non-national, "European" basis, a full range of European political and administrative institutions seemed inevitably necessary to provide the army with its goals, directives, funds, arms and provisions. Indeed, supporters of the scheme were busily drawing up and debating a constitution of the federal government of Europe. [23]

Ultimately, so great a loss of national independence proved too much for the French themselves to swallow. On one hand, General de Gaulle, reappearing from recent retirement, attacked the EDC as marking the end of French independence. With his notorious scepticism of the efficacy of an anational structure, he saw the likely result of the EDC, not as the building of a new European superpower, but as the permanent domination of Europe by the non-European allies. The EDC, he believed, would destroy the independent political will of France. The supranational institutions that were to replace her would be weak, based on no authority profoundly rooted in the loyalties of the peoples of Europe. The result would be a vacuum, soon filled by the powerful state across the Atlantic. Thus, the European army would be an organization of mercenaries, directed by a foreign power. Indeed, de Gaulle predicted, the commander of the EDC would probably not even be a European, but an American. [24] Other French groups feared that in a purely continental structure, whatever the arrangements, Germany would soon dominate. The EDC would trap France in a German embrace. Without Britain there were not enough elements to establish an internal balance.

Both these arguments were greatly assisted by the policy of the British Government. The British gradually made it clear that they would never submit their forces to the proposed arrangements. That was hardly surprising. A Britain that could not contemplate putting her coal and steel under supranational authority, was unlikely to do so with her army, least of all under a Tory Government. Britain's reluctance to make any commitment to the EDC encouraged French fears that Europe's army would be dominated by Germany. British reluctance also seemed to confirm de Gaulle's thesis that EDC was a clever Anglo-Saxon device to achieve German military rearmament at the minimum political price for the U.S. and Britain. France, on the other hand, was expected to sacrifice her independence in order to prevent Germany from regaining hers. Britain, de Gaulle noted, had no intention of making a similar sacrifice. Only France, caught in the grip of self-abnegation, "neurasthenia"

as he called it, could contemplate so servile a surrender of national independence. [25]

The French may not have accepted the EDC in any event and it might not
have worked if they had, but it seems fair to say that Britain's reluctance to
make any substantial commitments to an EDC force probably ensured that the
French Assembly would eventually defeat the proposal, whatever the chances
may have been for its passage otherwise. [26]

But Britain's motives are perfectly understandable. EDC was the most radical of all federalist proposals for linking together the nations of Europe. In the
early 1950s Britain could still reasonably see herself as a world power, nuclear
after 1952, whose concerns were hardly limited to Europe. The sacrifice of independence would certainly have been more real for her than for the France of
the Fourth Republic. For those committed to the idea of a federal Europe, Britain's action was deplorably short-sighted. But it is squared with the basic assumptions of bipartisan British foreign policy towards Europe—scepticism of
Europe's federalist initiatives and fear of American disengagement.

And while Britain took no interest in federal military and political union, she
was taking what appeared to be an effective role in encouraging more conventional forms of European co-operation. Indeed, it was Britain that rescued Europe from the impasse over German rearmament. Britain calmed continental
fears of Germany by promising to station substantial forces on the continent as
long as Britain was in NATO. At Anthony Eden's initiative, Bevin's old Brussels
Treaty Organization—Britain, France and Benelux—was expanded to take in
Germany and Italy, fitted out with some bureaucracy and an advisory parliamentary assembly, and re-christened the Western European Union.

Perhaps, as some bitterly argued, if Britain had made similar commitments
in the first place, the French Assembly would have accepted the EDC. [27] In
any event Britain would have joined it. There was all the difference in the world
between giving a military guarantee and joining a common army. Neither
Party, let alone the British public, was ready to advocate Britain's tying herself
irrevocably into a European military union.

Possibly the Tories were right to treat the European army as a pipe-dream,
but it is more difficult to defend their reaction to the continental initiative that
led ultimately to the Common Market. The British Government not only disapproved of these developments, but failed, it seems, to understand even what
they were about. While the continentals set about to build a great new regional
state in Europe, the British, with rather arrogant irrelevance, lectured them
about the dangers of trade distortion in a customs union. Against the political
ideals of regional federalism, the British preached the economic ideal of uni-

versal free trade—and seemed surprised that the Europeans felt the British ideal had little to offer, as if, indeed, the political goal of a United States of Europe could be measured by the economic standards of nineteenth-century free trade! It is this profound failure of the British political imagination in the 1950s that seems responsible for much of Britain's embarrassment in the following decade.

The Common Market was conceived after the defeat of the EDC in 1954, when the Good Europeans decided to "re-launch" the European movement along economic rather than political and military lines. Following a memorandum of the Benelux governments, the foreign ministers of the Six met at Messina in early June, 1955, and ultimately voted a resolution calling for a European Common Market. They charged a committee to study the means not only to eliminate all internal tariffs and quotas, but also to create, throughout the market, the fundamental economic conditions that would allow all parts to participate successfully in the benefits of open competition. Thus the committee studied a common external tariff, the harmonization of regulations and economic, monetary, and social policies, the free movement of workers, and the use of a development fund to develop backward parts of the proposed Community. [28] It was generally accepted that these aims would require strong Community institutions. In short, from the first, the Six were thinking not merely of the usual advantages of free trade, but of the integration of Europe into a single managed economy. This Committee, called the Spaak Committee after its Chairman, met throughout the rest of 1955 and, in April 1956, issued its notable report—the basis of a Treaty, negotiated throughout 1956, signed at Rome on March 25, 1957, and ratified by the national parliaments later in the same year. In January, 1958, the European Economic Community was born.

The significance of these developments seems to have been little appreciated in England. Britain sent a representative to the Spaak Committee who eventually withdrew. The Tory Government was preoccupied with other worthy goals, and especially with encouraging a new spirit of conciliation between Russia and the West. There was the general feeling that relations with Europe were proceeding satisfactorily. Arrangements for co-operation had been worked out with the Coal and Steel Community in early 1955, and with the birth of the WEU, British military relations with the continent had reached a new degree of intimacy. More fundamentally, however, the British Government, and indeed the public generally, never took seriously the political aspirations of the European Movement and of its artefact, the Common Market. Thus there seemed little sympathy or even comprehension of what the Europeans were after nor of how powerful were the forces sustaining them.

Britain's miscalculations led her into a disastrous effort to transform the Common Market into a free trade area, an initiative that resulted in the establishment of a rival European bloc, the European Free Trade Area (EFTA) and set the seal upon Britain's exclusion from Europe. [29]

Britain's motives were open enough. Once it was clear that the Common Market was to be established, the Government began to fear the dangers to British trade of being on the wrong side of the Market's common external tariff. The Government thus proposed a wider European "free trade area", envisioning an end to all tariffs and quotas on industrial goods within ten to fifteen years. [30] On November 26, 1956, Harold Macmillan, then Chancellor of the Exchequer, explained to the Commons that Britain wanted an agreement that would supplement but not sabotage the continent's customs union, while associating England with it in such a way that she did not have to sacrifice either her economic interests or her vital links throughout the Commonwealth and across the Atlantic. [31]

The British free trade proposals touched off a great debate in Europe and many now familiar arguments were then heard for the first time. The British solemnly warned of the dangers of an "inward-looking" Europe, split into two blocs and pointedly began discussing the possibility of free trade with Canada. The French and the federalists warned of the danger of Britain's watering down the coherence of the Six. Within the Common Market Countries, England's role became a focal point in the struggles between the federalists, protectionists, planners and free-traders.

Serious negotiations started in the fall of 1957, after the Rome Treaty was out of the way. The basic protagonists were the British and the French. The latter enjoyed powerful support from the Common Market Commission while Britain could count on the sympathy of such groups in the Community as Erhard's supporters in Germany, who were more inclined to favour free trade than political integration. Britain's essential interests were to ensure first that her exports were not put at a disadvantage in Western Europe, and second that the network of Commonwealth trading arrangements was not significantly disturbed. The British position developed a theoretical economic rationale, namely, that free trade was of benefit to all, while a narrow, "inward-looking" customs union was "trade-distorting". Such unions created artificial barriers against the outside world and the members' increased trade with each other was not justified by genuine economic advantages. The results would be harmful to outside countries and, indeed, harmful to the members of the Union itself. The most efficient international division of labour and pattern of trade would be distorted by the arbitrary barriers imposed by the Union. [32]

The French argument, like the British, ran on both the level of national interest and economic theory. The French realized that they had to modernize their overprotected industry and that the competition of an open European market would be salutary if painful. But feeling themselves weak in relation to the industrial exuberance of Germany, they were anxious that they should compete on equal terms unhampered by the institutional factors which, in addition to their inefficiency, might render the French incapable of competing with Germany. The French therefore insisted on arrangements to guarantee roughly uniform conditions for competition, wages, welfare costs and tariff duties. They were also interested in the development of backward regions. With their predilection for planning, the French believed that central "European" institutions would be needed to bring about these uniform conditions. The French wanted, in short, a larger market in which competition would be controlled intelligently to secure the progress of the weaker as well as the stronger members. Hence they opposed any serious dilution of the Common Market by a free trade area because they saw it as undermining the safeguards built into the Rome Treaty to ensure the even development of the Common Market as a whole. Furthermore, the French insisted that a fair deal for them would have to include agricultural as well as industrial goods. If they were to buy cheaper German industrial products, then Germany should buy cheaper French food.

As the French saw it, the British were seeking all the advantages of a European customs union without any of the obligations the others had accepted in the interests of the whole—weak and strong elements alike. The British, on the other hand, saw the French view as nothing but old-fashioned French mercantilist protectionism. The economics behind the demand for equal conditions of competition was faulty. Didn't the French know that free trade would soon result in equalization of conditions? [33] The desire of the French to foist their agriculture on the rest of Europe was deplorable. Surely Britain could not be expected to abandon her traditional Commonwealth supplies of cheap food.

The British reassured themselves by condemning the French for backward protectionism. But, in doing so, they ignored the sound political logic behind the French position. France, to be sure, sought particular advantages for herself in the EEC, as did everyone else who joined it. But the French position also accepted the rationale behind the Treaty, which was that a common European economy might be the foundation for an ultimate political union. Thus the Common Market was inspired not by free trade, but by a different sort of economics, strongly tinged with the political ideal of federation. The object of the Common Market was to create a new kind of regional economic unit that would enjoy many of the characteristics of a national economy. By joining the Common Market, the Six were taking the first steps not simply towards a more

effective international division of labour among independent states, but towards economic cohabitation in a single community. It was the political logic
of nation-building and not the logic of free trade that dictated that the Six
should favour each other over outsiders, that Germany should buy food from
France and France manufactures from Germany, and that they should both
contribute to the economic development of Southern Italy.

Against the political logic of federalism, the British continually countered
with the economic logic of free trade. Not surprisingly, they got nowhere. Both
sides had recognizable national interests intertwined with the competing ideals
they presented to the rest of Europe. But the interests of French protectionism
were combined with the regional ideal of European political union whereas the
defence of Britain's traditional trading patterns was justified by the universal
ideal of classical economics. For a Europe determined to unite, the French position was obviously more attractive. In opposing it, Britain struck at the very
heart of the political aspirations of Europeans. What is so surprising is that the
fundamental philosophical differences involved in the conflict were not seen
more clearly at the time. Indeed, ten years later, they are barely appreciated
now.

Britain's failure was really a failure of imagination. There were some, but
not many, who saw the issues clearly at the time. One of the most interesting
critiques of the British position comes from the distinguished Canadian economist, Professor Harry G. Johnson, himself a leading advocate of liberal free
trade. Looking back on the negotiations, Johnson was struck by the startling
"insularity of the reactions of British economists, and the grudgingness with
which they tend to recognize the continental viewpoint", an attitude mani-
fested in their unshakeable assumption that the "desire to create a unified
economy is not a reasonable policy objective, but a delusion whose possessor
should be treated with due gentleness." Johnson's further observations are
worth quoting at length:

> . . . the most striking characteristic of the reactions of British economists to the Com-
> mon Market and Free Trade Area schemes, viewed in the light of subsequent devel-
> opments, was the solid Britishness they displayed. With few exceptions, if any, the
> economists seem to have agreed with the Government's general line both that free-
> dom of trade, and not freedom of factor movements or the co-ordination of economic
> policies and institutions, is the substance of economic co-operation, and that what
> had to be decided was the terms on which Britain would be willing to join with the Six.
> None, so far as I can recall, showed any very profound appreciation of the possibility
> that the Six might have quite a different conception of economic co-operation than the
> British, let alone any sympathy with this conception or willingness to consider its mer-
> its as against trade-oriented British conceptions. It has since become clear enough

that the Six, or at least the French, do take their alternative conception of economic co-operation seriously. But recognition of this fact has tended to be more a matter of growing irritation with French perversity than of British self-questioning: while the fact that Britain has been trying to muscle in on a scheme whose earlier development she had formerly been steadily resisting, has been conveniently forgotten. The celebrated *Times* headline, "France the Wrecker", epitomizes this attitude; a headline more in accord with the historical evolution of events might well have been "Britain the Un-invited Guest".[34]

The free trade negotiations of 1957 constituted the first of the great diplomatic duels between Britain and France over the organization of Europe. It is interesting to speculate on the different reactions during the fifties of these two great European countries both faced with a cruel reduction in their world positions. The Suez Affair saw them acting together. Both were deserted by their American ally and forced to acknowledge their decline into dependent, second-class powers. The French, although distracted for some time by the agonies of their dying empire, turned resolutely to Europe. The British, on the contrary, sought busily to restore their torn Atlantic connections. Ironically, at the same time in America the Common Market was reviving all the old enthusiasm for European political union. Thus the United States increasingly urged Britain to join Europe at the very moment that the British were preoccupied with moving closer to America. [35]

But it was not so much American pressure as a remorseless logic of circumstances that was steadily forcing Britain towards Europe. The Suez debacle in 1956 shattered the illusion of independent world power. By 1958, it was clear that there would be a European Common Market without Britain, a community that might even develop into a European federal union. Britain was not only being pushed out of the European "circle", but might ultimately come to be displaced in her specail relationship with America as well. A united European group would surely be of more importance to the Americans than Britain.

The change of Presidents in Washington, from Eisenhower to Kennedy, removed from the White House the figure who, more than anyone else, symbolized that wartime camaraderie of soldiers and bureaucrats in arms that formed so much of the substance of the "special relationship". The Prime Minister and the new President soon formed close personal relations of their own, but it was apparent that, for the new generation of American leaders, official Anglo-American relations would be more practical and less sentimental. In hard terms, Britain had much less to offer than a unified continent. The unseemly collapse of the Paris Summit Meeting in 1959 had brought to a disastrous close one of Macmillan's favoured roles for Britain, the wise and honest broker at the summit with Russia and the United States. [36] The new freeze that followed suggested that British enthusiasm for peacemaking had possibly been premature. At any rate it was unlikely to be a particularly promising role for the future. The new administration in Washington was itself far more vigorous in approaching the Russians than its predecessor had been. Henceforth, Russia and America would play alone without their British nanny.

Meanwhile, on the domestic front, the early successes of the Tories began to turn sour. After a euphoric spurt in the mid-fifties, the economy had to be checked between 1955 and 1957 by severe Government measures to deal with a declining balance of payments. In 1957, bank rate reached 7% for the first time in decades. The reflation of 1958 and 1959 had to be checked in 1960 because domestic demand appeared to be outrunning the capacity of the economy. Imports rose faster than exports and, once more, there were difficulties with the balance of payments. Restrictions returned and, at the end of June 1960, bank rate went back up to 6%. By 1961, the economy, after a short improvement, was again in difficulty.

Looking back over the fifties, Englishmen began to entertain the disquieting thought that something fundamental was wrong with their economy. True, it had grown faster than in a long time. [37] By 1960, national output per capita was 12½% higher than in 1955. But, as we have seen, Britain's continental neighbours had been growing at twice that rate. The depressing British pattern of Stop-Go was already familiar, and many observers began to doubt if there were any cure short of some drastic recasting of the economy. [38]

Accompanying these diplomatic and economic discouragements, there was abroad in England during the early nineteen-sixties a widespread sense of cynicism and disillusion—especially among the clever and articulate young. Macmillan, far from insensitive to the need for imaginative idealism in politics, sought a new cause that could bring challenge, opportunity and fire to national politics. His solution was to lead Britain to the Common Market. In his announcement to the Commons on July 31, 1961, Macmillan reversed the whole postwar policy of Tory and Labour Governments alike. Britain suddenly appeared to take a major step towards Europe. [39]

But Macmillan's step was not as unequivocal as a Good European might have wished. Doubtless he had his own hesitations. From the beginning, moreover, he was met by a strong bipartisan diffidence and uneasiness—which he knew might easily turn into active hostility. Tactically his Government's situation was extremely complex. Any number of entrenched interests and loyalties might be aroused to oppose Britain's entry. Negotiations had to be conducted simultaneously on several shifting foreign and domestic fronts. The entire performance was an extraordinary balancing act, with Macmillan in the essential role. Everything depended on his courage and skill. Although he held his own in Parliament, his position among the general public was much weaker. Public support for joining was hesitant and volatile. Throughout the whole year and a half of negotiations, polls never revealed a stable majority for or against. By late 1962, the portents were suggesting a swing against the Conservatives. [40]

The study of British opinion during the negotiations reveals two interesting points: the indecision of the general public and the strong European enthusiasm of the Establishment. [41]

If leading Britain to the Common Market was a revolution, it was a revolution led from the top, from the ruling cliques of the Establishment itself. Nearly all the serious papers supported the Government. It was Lord Beaverbrook, the perennial leader of unfashionable causes, who led the journalistic opposition. The chief pro-Market public-relations organization, the Common Market Campaign, was compact, distinguished, efficient, non-partisan, well-financed and had easy access to the corridors of established power. Its leaders were Lord Gladwyn, a Liberal City banker who had just retired as Ambassador to France, and Roy Jenkins, a rising Labour moderate MP, later Home Secretary and Chancellor of the Exchequer. The arguments and techniques of the group seemed obviously aimed at informed rather than mass opinion and were a far cry from such great popular economic crusades of the past as Corn Law repeal or Imperial Preference. The chief opposition counterpart, on the other hand, the Anti-Common Market League, was obscure, amateurish and poor. [42] It appealed to the mass public, partly, no doubt, because it was not taken seriously by anyone else.

There are many plausible explanations both for this sharp distinction among the activists as well as for the apparent apathy among the masses. Why were the established classes so disproportionately in favour of joining? Federalism generally appeals most to a cosmopolitan upper class, rather than to the local masses. Some elite groups anticipated that a Europeanized Britain was the postwar solution that would be most favourable to their interests and tastes. The possibilities of Britain's running Europe presumably appealed more to those who already ran England. Furthermore, while many of the pro-Market arguments put off both the expert and the mass reader, they struck just the right tone of technicality and progressivism to appeal to a general educated audience.

The gulf between general and elite opinion does not, of course, prove anything about the quality of the arguments on either side. While one could deplore the presumed apathy and prejudice of the general public, one could also conclude that the views of the masses really were less fickle and more profound than those of the more educated public. [43] It may well be that the hesitancy of the general public to commit themselves to Macmillan's daring but dubious venture was the appropriate response for a great people who realized instinctively what their Government avoided telling them whenever possible: that England had reached a profound crisis in her search for a new identity and purpose. A moment of choice had come that could probably mean the end of the dreams and loyalties people had for a century been taught to cherish.

It would be wrong, in any event, to assume that the case against Britain's joining was as weak as it was unfashionable. The Anti-Common Market case was powerful and not without distinguished advocates. It reflected both political loyalties strongly held by most people in England and also genuine hazards and sacrifices involved in merging the British economy with the Common Market. What were the arguments for and against Britain's joining the EEC?

The arguments that are said to have influenced Macmillan in 1961 had long been familiar in Europeanist circles in England. [44] Only by leading the Europeans could Britain gain enough weight to be a major force in world affairs. Only by extending herself into a continental home market could Britain keep up her great positions in finance and technology. Only by a "cold shower-bath" of competition in a large competitive market would British industry be stimulated to efficient growth. On the other hand, should Europe be forged without her, Britain would be left isolated, weak and threadbare. Without Britain's political weight and skill, to be sure, the prospects for a stable democratic union in Europe were much reduced. But if the whole enterprise did fail and Europe reverted to chaos, Britain would suffer as twice before in this century.

The Anti-Market case was similarly both economic and political. The economic arguments were the most precise and were backed by the authority of some of the nation's leading economists. These professionals and their students tended to be sceptical of presumed advantages that were as numerically indeterminate as "economies of scale" or "cold shower-baths of competition", while they found it easier to measure the likely short-term loss to trade. [45] Their economic objections turned around the probable effects on the balance of payments and on the prospects for long-range economic growth. Rough calculation of the effects of joining indicated that, in the short run at least, changes in the balance of trade would be unfavourable. Britain would lose preferences averaging 10% on the third of her exports that went to EFTA and the Commonwealth. In return, tariffs averaging 10 − 15% would be dropped on the sixth of British exports that went to the EEC. Furthermore, imports from the Six, mostly competitive manufactures, would increase. The Common Market's protectionist agricultural policies would not only seriously hurt Britain's traditional Commonwealth suppliers, but raise English food prices. The resulting increase in the cost of living would push up wages and prices and squeeze profits. These immediate adverse effects would be reflected in the balance of payments and would soon require compensatory deflationary measures, made less effective, to be sure, by the Common Market's freedom of capital movements. In such an unfavourable atmosphere, the British economy would never get off the ground to meet strong new competition. The cold shower-bath would be followed by shock and paralysis. Britain would languish and become a mere offshore island of a European economy whose vital centres lay elsewhere. The attitude of many economists at the time, even many in favour of joining, was well summed up by Sir Donald MacDougall: "Looked at as a purely commercial deal, and ignoring the indirect consequences, it is thus by no means obvious that entry into the Common Market would be a good proposition for Britain. It might well tend to worsen the balance of trade." [46]

The political opposition was more diffuse, but no less powerful. [47] In Macmillan's view, Britain was going into Europe not to lose her independence, but to gain power. Like de Gaulle, he saw no reason to take federalist pretensions of the Brussels bureaucracy too seriously. In a Europe of States, Macmillan believed Britain's stable political traditions would lend strength to the shaky democratic governments of the continent. Britain's leadership would make Western Europe "outward-looking" that is, pro-American and sympathetic to the Commonwealth. Opponents attacked every one of these expectations. The federalist framework of the Community, and the general right-wing capitalist bias of the Six would, they believed, impose great limitations on the British Government's ability to plan its own economy. Britain would be swept up into a political system dominated by alien ideals and practices. Britain would not swing the continent; the continent would dominate Britain. British politicians and civil servants would be baffled and ineffective in the continent's entirely different legal and administrative traditions. The colonialist, right-wing, capitalist, anti-communist policies of the continent would become the policies of Britain—to the detriment of herself, her Commonwealth and the world in general. Opponents of joining naturally made much of Britain's ties with the old dominions, the new "multi-racial" Commonwealth, or the economic allies who had stood by her in EFTA. A most popular charge saw the Common Market as a "rich man's club" in a hungry world. Britain, it was felt, had sterner duties. [48]

Behind the more elaborate anti-Market arguments lay the fundamental unwillingness of many British to jettison so many of their old loyalties and prejudices to seek a common future with Europe—at least on any terms the Six were likely to accept. Some of these feelings were part of almost every Englishman and when they were added to the quite genuine economic pitfalls and thorny political problems, they formed an extremely formidable obstacle to the whole-hearted pursuit of a European policy. While Macmillan, with his customary dexterity, was able to keep his forces in order and dampen the immense potential opposition in the country, he ended up making so many concessions to the opposition at home that he had very little chance of succeeding with the Six on the continent. Thus in spite of all the official protestations to the country, it is doubtful that the Brussels negotiations ever were near success. [49] The agricultural concessions Britain asked for alone made it impossible for France to agree without a quite unreasonable sacrifice of her own economic interests—national interests, in truth, more in harmony with progress towards European union than England's.

It is highly unlikely, on the other hand, that Macmillan, even if he had accurately judged the situation, could have made Britain's entry any more appealing to the French. Conceivably, if Macmillan had offered to build with France a joint nuclear deterrent and weapons system, the French might have been tempted. But de Gaulle too had to measure his political ambitions against the underlying economic strength of his country. Without the agricultural policy, a vital French economic problem would have remained unresolved. With Britain in the Common Market, the French would probably never have achieved the agricultural agreements of 1965. As it was, they came only after the most prolonged and bitter struggle with the Germans who, for the same reasons as England, preferred to import cheap food from outside Europe. [50]

In any event, it is rather idle to speculate on what would have happened if Macmillan had offered nuclear co-operation or modified his economic demands. For it is highly unlikely that he would have been able to do so without losing the domestic battle upon which his whole position depended. Macmillan had probably pushed his Party and the country about as far towards Europe as it was possible to go. Furthermore, Labour by then was committed to opposing the whole venture and not unlikely to win the oncoming General Election. [51] By the time of de Gaulle's veto in January 1963, Britain's step towards Europe had become very shaky indeed. In short, de Gaulle was presented with a situation in which British public opinion was deeply divided, the Government's position precarious, Labour opposed, and the application to join loaded with qualifications fatal to France's economic plans. His veto was not surprising. What was surprising was the astonishment of the British. And whatever

France's particular motives, the official French view was widely appreciated, if not exactly shared, among many devoted to the creation of a European Union. It was quite unlikely that the rest of Europe would band together to bring irresistible pressure on the French, however sympathetic they appeared to Britain in private.

In short, while it may be true that a less qualified British bid to join Europe would have succeeded, Macmillan's Government, even if willing, was unable, because of deep domestic divisions, to make a more straightforward application. Thus the Government's domestic struggles cost it the foreign war. In this sense, it is probably true that the vital struggle in the campaign to get Britain into Europe goes on primarily in Britain.

In announcing his veto in 1963, de Gaulle went out of his way to suggest that Britain's internal evolution might well lead her some day to make an offer the Europeans would have to accept:

> Lastly, it is highly possible that Great Britain's own evolution and the evolution of the world would lead the British to the continent, whatever may be the delays before complete realization. For my part, that is what I am inclined to believe, and that is why, in my opinion, it will be in any case a great honour for the British Prime Minister, for my friend Harold Macmillan, and for his Government to have perceived this so early, to have had enough political courage to proclaim it and to have had their country take the first steps along the path that, one day perhaps, will bring it to make fast to the Continent. [52]

Has not that evolution taken place to a remarkable extent? Three and a half years later, not a Tory but a Labour Government took the lead in bringing Britain to Europe. In certain respects, the situation in 1966 was remarkably unchanged from 1961. The British economy was once again in serious difficulty after a much-heralded attempt to promote growth and productivity. The old economic arguments, pro and con, were roughly the same. British trade had continued to grow more rapidly with the EEC than with the Commonwealth.[53] The old problems of agriculture and sterling remained. The new Prime Minister did, to be sure, make more of the fear that Europe's industrial technology would soon be hopelessly surpassed by the United States. [54] Only enlightened Government co-operation within a common economy could, he often said, save Europe from eventually becoming a backward area. Meanwhile, many of the old political arguments against joining had been diminished, ironically, by General de Gaulle himself. The General had at least temporarily quashed the federalist pretensions of the Common Market Commission. Membership in the Communities did not seem to have restrained unduly the French government's domestic or international freedom of action. De Gaulle's foreign policy could scarcely be called right-wing, colonialist, or anti-Russian.

And three years after the 1963 veto, still no alternative to Europe had caught the imagination of the British public. Enthusiasm for the "multi-racial Commonwealth" had declined steadily. While there was undoubtedly strong sentiment for "Atlantic" ties with America, the notion of an institutionalized junior partnership with the United States enjoyed a limited appeal, further constrained by the agitation over technology. And many British suspected that their own lack of enthusiasm was more than reciprocated by the great majority of Americans. Many, to be sure, were coming to believe that Britain should shed her extraneous foreign commitments and rebuild her own economic and political future by some thorough-going internal reformation. But the final desertion of the Labour's Government's National Plan in July 1966, suggested that Britain could not resolve her economic problems by herself.

In any event, by 1967 Britain was once again seeking to enter the Common Market. The old problems remained. Could Britain bring herself to be sufficiently "European", whatever that might mean, to make herself irresistible to the continent? Could she avoid those inhibitions abroad that public opinion demanded at home? Were there any attractive alternatives to Europe?

The French reaction in 1967 suggested that the question of Britain's joining Europe might be unresolved for many years. De Gaulle's obdurate refusal to admit Britain on any terms other than his own and his relentless exposure of the ambiguities in Britain's position at least had the advantage of driving Britain to face up to the fundamental questions. These basic questions about the kind of future Britain wants for herself and for the world will remain long after the immediate problems of joining or creating this or that international arrangement have been resolved. If, for example, Britain gains Europe, what will she do with it? It is this fundamental indecision about her role and purpose that has been troubling Britain since the war and so often made her policies ambiguous and self-defeating. But how can the British resolve this problem? What, in fact, are the basic alternatives for Britain? What are the prospects and the commitments involved in each?

NOTES

1. See Chapter I, note 3.
2. Churchill's speech at Zürich, September 19, 1946.
3. Churchill made this statement on May 11, 1953, referring to the powers attempting to build a European Defence Community. See Northedge, p. 159.

4. Charles de Gaulle, *Salvation*, p. 58.

5. *Salvation*, p. 59.

6. Charles de Gaulle, *Unity*, p. 253.

7. *Salvation*, p. 59.

8. *Salvation*, p. 57. It was chiefly thanks to Churchill, however, that France was readmitted to the great powers in the occupation of Germany and the founding of the UN. See Northedge, p. 17; and Hansard, 403 HC. Deb 5s. Col. 495 (September 28, 1944). For Churchill's analysis of his policy towards de Gaulle near the end of the war, see W. S. Churchill, *The Second World War*, vol. 6, *Triumph and Tragedy*. London: Cassell & Co., 1954, Chapter 16 and also p. 353.

9. Seventh Press Conference held by de Gaulle in Paris at the Elysée Palace, January 14, 1963. See Major Addresses, p. 213.

10. The Assembly of the Council of Europe had, according to Spaak, only 60 members out of 135 who believed in the need to create Europe. See Brugmans, *L'Idée Européenne*, 1918–1965, Bruges, 1965, p. 123. Since the Council had been created to satisfy Britain, its lack of enthusiasm was taken to reflect Britain's lukewarm attitude to European unity.

11. See A. Nutting, *Europe Will Not Wait*, London, 1960, and J. H. Huizinga, *Confessions of a European in England*, London: Heinemann, 1958. There is also Lord Boothby's extraordinary speech in the House of Lords on June 30, 1960. Also, Sir David Maxwell-Fyfe, *Political Adventure: Memoirs of the Earl of Kilmuir*. London: Weidenfeld & Nicolson, 1964.

12. For more than twenty years before the Macmillan application to join the EEC there had been a substantial body of opinion favouring a federal solution to the problems of Europe. The 1947 formation of Churchill's United Europe was a crucial stage in the development of what was later to become pro-Common Market opinion. The members included Robert Boothby, L. S. Amery and Sir David Maxwell-Fyfe. The group soon became divided on the extent and nature of the federation to be advocated: Its importance during the fifties was not as great as the distinction of its sponsors suggests. The 1958 Britain in Europe group, formed under the chairmanship of Gladwyn Jebb, was explicitly in favour of British entry into the Common Market and, despite a reluctance to define its position too closely, appears to have been federalist in its declared opposition to de Gaulle's Europe of States. By 1961, therefore, there were in Britain a considerable number of eminent and well-informed men who had helped to move public opinion towards acceptance of the EEC, and were able to help maintain the impetus of the new initiative once negotiations had started.

13. Northedge, p. 46. Northedge provides an excellent account of this whole period.

14. Northedge, p. 140. See Hansard, 450 HC Deb 5s Col 111o, May 4, 1948.

15. For a knowledgeable discussion of the events and policies referred to, see Nicholas, especially, p. 50 ff.

16. For an American view see Moore, pp. 21–22. Britain, as the leading member of the OEEC, saw her interests in the revival of world, rather than solely intra-European trade.

17. See Calleo, *Europe's Future*, p. 84. At this early date, de Gaulle offered a counter-proposal for a confederation—an early version of the Fouchet Plan—including a referendum among the peoples of Europe.

18. Northedge, pp. 138 – 40. It should not be forgotten that Roosevelt, at Yalta, had announced that American troops would be out of Europe two years after VE Day. Northedge, p. 17.

19. Northedge, p. 135 ff. also Henry Pelling, *A Short History of the Labour Party,* London: Macmillan, 1961, p. 99 ff, and Eugene J. Meehan, *The British Left Wing and Foreign Policy,* Rutgers University Press, 1960, p. 152.

20. Northedge, p. 150 ff.

21. Harold Macmillan, Council of Europe, Consultative Assembly, second session, seventh sitting, August 14, 1950, pp. 436 – 8.

22. A European army united command had been proposed by Winston Churchill at Strasbourg in 1950. Northedge, p. 153.

23. Calleo, *Europe's Future,* pp. 49 – 51. See also Raymond Aron and Daniel Lerner, *France Defeats EDC,* New York: Praeger, 1957; Henri Brugmans, *L'Idée Européenne, 1918 – 1965,* Bruges, 1965.

24. Charles de Gaulle, speech at Sainte-Mandé, November 4, 1951. *Speeches, Statements and Press Conferences,* 1946 – 1958, R.P.F. files, on microfilm, Bibliothèque de Fondation Nationale des Sciences Politiques.

25. Calleo, *Europe's Future,* pp. 87 – 88. De Gaulle, Press Conference, November 14, 1949, and interview with M. Bradford as representative of the United States at Colembey-les-deux-Églises, July 10, 1950.

26. One of the crucial arguments put forward by French Socialist opponents of EDC in the National Assembly was that British participation, not merely promises to maintain forces on the Continent, would be necessary if France were not again to find herself faced in Europe by a German-Italian alliance. See Aron and Lerner, Chapter 1, in particular pp. 7 and 15; and Northedge, p. 152 ff.

27. Paul-Henri Spaak was President of the Consultative Assembly of Europe when Britain announced that she would not join the EDC. Spaak, who is a distinguished Belgian politician and lawyer, had by 1950 been several times Prime Minister and Foreign Minister of his own country and chairman of numerous international and European organizations. He resigned in frustration on hearing the news. He had told Nutting that the British federalists "had waited too long for Britain to get aboard the European bus . . . the Eden plan was a neat halfway house arrangement which might suit Great Britain, but halfway houses were not enough for Europe." Nutting, pp. 44 – 5. See also note 10.

28. Camps, p. 25 ff. Camps provides a thoroughly detailed and well-documented study.

29. For EFTA, its origins and achievements, see Chapter VII, note 36.

30. "A European Free Trade Area, UK Memorandum to the OEEC," Cmnd. 72, HMSO, February, 1957.

31. Hansard, House of Commons, November 26, 1956. See also Harold Wilson's reply. For a short account see Camps, p. 106 ff.

32. For a discussion of the relative virtues of customs unions and of free trade, see James E. Meade, *The Theory of Customs Unions,* Amsterdam: North-Holland Publishing Co., 1966, esp. Chapters V and VI.

33. An attack on the "stupidity" of harmonization was made by R. F. Kahn in his contribution to *The Free Trade Proposals,* ed. G. D. N. Worswick, Oxford: Basil Blackwell, 1960, p. 62. The whole book is an interesting collection of reactions from professional

British economists, mostly with a free trade background.

34. See p. 139 of "The Common Market: the Economists' Reactions," in *The Free Trade Proposals,* pp. 135 – 42. Johnson is speaking here specifically of the contributors to this symposium.

35. See Nicholas, *Britain and the United States,* Chapter 10.

36. For a brief discussion of the events leading up to the 1960 Summit Meeting and Macmillan's role, see Northedge, pp. 272 – 6. For a discussion of Macmillan's relations with Eisenhower and Kennedy, see Sampson, Chapters 9 and 15.

37. British postwar growth, although disappointing by comparison with other countries, has been excellent if a longer perspective is taken. Between 1913 and 1950, for example, the annual rate of growth was 1.7%; between 1950 and 1960, 2.6%. See Maddison, p. 28.

38. See Dow, *Management of the British Economy,* p. 111.

39. See Lord Windlesham, *Communication and Political Power,* London: Jonathan Cape, 1966, Chapter VI, "Public Opinion on the Common Market."

40. See David E. Butler and Anthony King, *The British General Election of 1964,* Macmillan, 1965, Chapter II, for a discussion of the prevailing social malaise at the time of the first British application.

41. Gallup Polls between July, 1960, and January, 1963, reveal that at no time was more than 80% of the public decided; in July, 1961, as many as 42% answered, "Don't know" to Gallup's curious question: "If the British Government were to decide that Britain's interest would best be served by joining the European Common Market, would you approve or disapprove?" To the more straightforward: "On the facts as you know them at present, are you for or against Britain joining the Common Market?" in December, 1962, 36% were for, 26% against, and 38% didn't know; see *Journal of Common Market Studies,* September, 1966, p. 49 ff.

It is, of course, obvious that all the top political élite were not for joining the Common Market, e.g., Hugh Gaitskell and Harold Wilson. Nor were all company directors, university teachers or lawyers, e.g., John Paul, Sir Roy Harrod and Sir Derek Walker-Smith. But it seems incontestably true that the great majority of those in the higher ranks of British business and professional life favoured entry. In August, 1966, Gallup polled 411 people selected from "Who's Who" and found 90% approving, and 6% disapproving, with 4% answering, "Don't know". *(Daily Telegraph,* October 24, 1966). It is also generally believed among students of public opinion that the Common Market has been much more popular among the young.

42. The Chairman and driving force of the Anti-Common Market League was Mr John Paul, then a company director in the oil business and once Chairman of the South Kensington Conservative Association. Eventually, the Earl of Sandwich, formerly Lord Hinchingbrooke, MP, and now Mr Victor Montagu, became President of the League. For a general study of the group, see Windlesham, *op. cit.* Typical views of various prominent anti-Marketeers can be found in the pamphlet, *Britain not Europe,* ed R. Hugh Corbett, London: The Anti-Common Market League, 1962.

43. For a defence of popular judgment in foreign policy, see R. H. S. Crossman, "Democracy and Foreign Policy", in *Planning for Freedom,* London: Hamish Hamilton, 1965. Mr Crossman, Lord President of the Council in the present Labour Government, has been an opponent of Britain's entering the Common Market.

44. For a discussion of Macmillan's views of the advantage of entry as well as those of Sir Frank Lee's committee of top civil servants that reinforced him, see Camps, Chapters 9 and 10. Also for an excellent summary of the pro-Market case at the time, see U. W. Kitzinger, *The Challenge of the Common Market.*

45. See A. Lamfalussy, "Europe's Progress: due to Common Market?" *Lloyd's Bank Review,* October, 1961.

46. Sir Donald MacDougall, *Britain and the Common Market,* p. 15. Those who have been opposed to entry, or who have voiced strong reservations on economic grounds, include Thomas Balogh, Sir Roy Harrod and Professor Nicholas Kaldor.

47. For a comprehensive and powerful summary of the political arguments against joining see Willian Pickles, *Not With Europe.*

48. Denis Healey, for example, said during the 1962 debate that he feared the Common Market was becoming a "rich man's club" and for this reason alone the Commonwealth was preferable.

49. See Camps, chapters 14 and 15 for a detailed account and analysis of the final stages of negotiations. For some important interpretations of the state of the negotiations at their breakdown, see Charles de Gaulle, Press Conference, January 14, 1963, in "Major Addresses", 211 – 16; Mr. Heath's speech at the break up of the negotiations in Agence Internationale d'Information pour la Press, Luxembourg, EUROPE, Documents No. 186/187, February 5, 1963; also European Economic Community, Commission, Report to the European Parliament on the State of Negotiations with the United Kingdom, Brussels, February 26, 1963.

50. For a discussion of the implications of the common agricultural policy, see Calleo, *Europe's Future,* pp. 62 – 3.

51. Hugh Gaitskell, the Leader of the Opposition, had put forward five conditions which would have to be fulfilled if the Labour Party were to support entry. They amounted to a refusal to join:

1. Safeguards for the Commonwealth.

2. Safeguards for EFTA.

3. Suitable arrangements for British agriculture.

4. Freedom to pursue an independent foreign policy.

5. Freedom to formulate and carry out national economic planning.

52. Charles de Gaulle, Press Conference, January 14, 1963, in *Major Addresses,* pp. 215 – 16.

53. Between 1961 and 1965 exports to the Commonwealth from the UK increased by 18%; to the EEC by 37%. Source: Annual Abstract of Statistics 1966, pp. 223.

54. Chapter IV. 4, note 3.

The implications of the previous chapter are clear. Whatever the peculiar conditions that concealed her weaknesses after 1919, Britain in the wake of the second world conflict no longer could be counted as a world power of the first order. Certainly she no longer had the resources to undertake unlimited commitments in foreign policy while at the same time providing a decent and secure standard of life at home. But illusions are hard to slough off. Most politicians continued to employ the rhetoric of the past and many British people persisted in their confidence that somehow Britain's position, perhaps as a mediator between the U.S.A. and the U.S.S.R., could be maintained. In the essay that follows, F. S. Northedge emphasizes the mental adjustments necessary to accept the role of a power of the second or third rank. A productive student of British foreign policy, whose article on the implications of World War I was used to begin this collection, he here somewhat more didactically explores what is needed if the British are to come to terms with their new status in the world of the superpowers. This article was first published in International Affairs, January 1970.

12 | Britain as a Second-Rank Power

F. S. NORTHEDGE

Ever since he established the point in his book *U.S. Foreign Policy,* published in 1943, most people have agreed with Walter Lippmann that 'a policy has been formed only when commitments and power have been brought into balance'. It could be called the Micawber rule of foreign affairs: 'income, nineteen shillings and sixpence; expenditure, twenty shillings: result—misery. Income, twenty shillings; expenditure, nineteen shillings and sixpence: result—happiness'. The failure of American policy in Vietnam to realise its original expectations has shown that the resources needed to fulfil commitments are not necessarily to be measured in physical terms; they comprise all the capabilities, psychological as well as military, skills as well as economic strength, necessary to influence the other parties to the international process.

But even if we confine the definition of a country's resources for the fulfilment of foreign policy commitments to the military and economic, it is clear that at no time are these a fixed sum. Much will depend on what proportion of the country's net annual product its people are willing to set aside for foreign policy purposes—for defence, foreign aid, the upkeep of diplomatic services, contributions to international organisations and so on. And this in its turn will depend on how urgent prevailing foreign policy commitments seem to governments and ultimately, in a democratic state, to public opinion. In wartime a nation will pare its personal spending to the bone in the collective interests of survival; in peacetime a competition is bound to ensue between the advocates of spending on foreign policy and defence, on one side, and those who want lower taxes or increased outlays on the social services, on the other.

It has been a characteristic of thought in Britain about foreign policy since the Second World War that, on the one hand, most people have unquestioningly accepted the premise that Britain should continue to rank as a world Power of the first order, and, on the other, that the same people have insisted that living standards should go on rising and spending on social services should be shielded to the utmost against inroads made by taxation on behalf of the financing of foreign policy commitments. The question may therefore be asked, not so much whether Britain, given the will, can continue to think and behave as a Power of the first rank; but whether, since the will is evidently not there, the necessary mental adjustments can be made to maintain successfully the position of a Power of the second or perhaps third rank.

In the catalogue of collective neuroses political nostalgia must occupy a primary position, the tendency, that is, 'to think backwards while living forwards', as Kierkegaard formulated it. The British, because of their ancient security from foreign invasion, their remoteness in mind if not in distance, from the complexities of European politics, their long-assured supremacy at the apex of the international pyramid of power, are peculiarly prone to assume that in all essentials the world is still much as it always was, and that Britain, despite all the evidence to the contrary, will still manage to come out on top, almost without effort. Professor Kenneth Waltz, of Brandeis University, has shown, in a recent scathing criticism of the British political system called *Foreign Policy and Democratic Politics,* how British politicians and publicists have coolly assumed that, whatever the state of the British armed forces, no matter how weak the national economy and despite the reduction of the Commonwealth to an almost meaningless consultative association, British 'influence' will somehow still continue to penetrate the Cabinets and Foreign Offices of the world. As a striking example of this bland style of thought, he cites the thanks which the British Prime Minister paid in 1963 to Presidents Eisenhower and Kennedy for co-operating with him to make the partial nuclear test ban agreement a reality.[1]

The historian in particular is impressed by the way in which the unquestioning British confidence in finally coming out on top once the difficulties of the present are overcome has affected British thinking about past international crises. The Munich Agreement of September 1938 is a good example. It has been axiomatic in post-1945 British ideas about the country's pre-war foreign policy that it was conducted by naïve and gullible men supported and sustained by a timid, comfort-loving public opinion. Naïve the Chamberlainites of the 1930s might have been, and timid public opinion certainly was. But few who take this stereotype for granted seem to have seriously considered how it would have been possible for Britain and France in 1938, with Soviet Russia's intentions uncertain, Italy and Japan sympathetic towards the Third Reich, and the United States if anything even more isolationist than in 1914, to take on Germany whom they were barely able to defeat in the First World War when all those four Powers were on their side. The assumption that Hitler's bluff could have been easily called by a stout refusal to do business with him stems from the uncritical premise that, when all is said, Britain is, or at least was then, still at the top of the league table of Powers.

Similarly, it has been widely assumed in Britain since ex-President de Gaulle's first refusal to accept Mr. Macmillan's bid to join the European Common Market in 1963 that this was due to Gallic obstinacy and jealousy of Britain, and that the other five Common Market partners were only too anxious to welcome Britain into the club. But it is hard to see why this should be so. Few British politicians or sectors of British public opinion have shown much real interest, until recently, in the ideals or the practical problems of European integration. British Ministers have repeatedly pointed out that, once admitted into the Common Market, they would certainly not be at the head of the march towards political unification which the EEC is in theory designed to promote. Such is British indifference towards, or positive abhorrence against, the whole idea of European union that in January 1963, when the General's first veto was announced, an almost audible sigh of relief ran around Britain, as though a distasteful task had been deferred.

The British have shown in the years since 1945 no great skill in managing their own economy, and such ignorance about the way in which the West European countries manage theirs that an almost universal image has developed in Britain of the EEC as an inward-looking provincialist grouping which Britain can serve by helping to liberalise. The truth is in fact almost exactly the reverse; the Common Market's external tariff policy is at least as liberal as Britain's, if not more so, and, as far as economic assistance to the rest of the world is concerned, France and even Federal Germany notoriously have a better record than Britain.[2] One can thus understand the irritation of convinced Europeanists on the Continent at the idea prevalent on this side of the Channel that only old-fashioned French pride keeps Britain out of Europe and that, once this is overcome, Britain will bring a breath of fresh air into the Communities.

The political nostalgia underlying these insular notions has for special reasons affected Britain more than any other of the old European Great Powers during these last twenty years. Clearly, Britain's retention of her sovereignty during the Second World War while most European states lost theirs, either in its course or immediately after its end, fostered the illusion that Britain was still free to shape the world closer to her heart's desire. The idea that power independently to mould world affairs still lies in Westminster despite the dependence of the pound, for example, on decisions made in Bonn, Paris, Washington and Zurich, dies hard. Moreover, the Germans and Italians lost their empires in one fell swoop, the former as far back as 1919, and no longer hanker after having their fingers in pies abroad. The Germans, too, have had since 1945 the all-embracing problem of reunification in their thoughts, and this has concentrated their attention on European affairs. As for France, the loss of empire was more recent, as it was also far more violent, but there was always an alternative road for France in foreign affairs, that which led to a united Europe under French leadership, a road which inspired French leaders as far back as Napoleon I, if not Henry IV of France and Navarre. For Britain, on the other hand, once the Empire was gone very little was left. Britain's policy in Europe for almost two centuries had been that of neutralising the European Powers one against another so as to leave Britain free to cultivate her imperial garden. The Anglo-American 'special relationship', too, has been seen in British eyes as a means of influencing Britain's successor as the leading democratic nation and directing it towards policies helpful to the maintenance of Britain's world position as a maritime and imperial Power. Minds long inured to these oceanic conceptions of British policy do not readily accept the need for a downward revision of expectations to what is required of a second-rank state with strictly regional interests.

One consequence of this psychological inertia has been a most characteristic behaviour pattern of Britain since the Second World War: the tendency to be driven towards decisions and policies not because they are the most desirable, or least undesirable, options currently available, but because other options have ceased to be available. The pattern somewhat resembles the movements of an amoeba, which acquires its food not by deliberately choosing it but by attempting to digest the rest of its environment and finding it inedible. Devaluation of the pound in November 1967 is a now classical example from financial policy. Only when other options had lost all their credibility was this reluctant decision made, and when it was made there was no disposition to place the responsibility for it on Britain's management of her economic affairs. The Prime Minister told the nation in a broadcast on November 19 that devaluation 'tackled the root of the problem' and, almost in the same breath, that the activities of speculators, which the decision to devalue in any case did not seem to affect, had been the cause of the crisis. The implication was that the British people could continue as before, at least until the next crisis came.

But it is in foreign affairs that the British habit of 'business as usual', until old policies become definitely unworkable and the remaining options have to be recklessly seized, is best illustrated. In the conditions of 1945 the old Churchillian conception of the three over-lapping circles of British foreign policy—the Commonwealth, the Atlantic world and Europe—seemed sensible enough. But the way in which the first two have been emptied by time of most of their content, leaving Britain with scarcely any option but the third, illustrates the persistent failure of British policy-makers to think out, as far as possible in advance, what would be a suitable course for this country to follow in world affairs.

Before 1939 the Commonwealth, the first of the famous circles, served an important function in keeping the old, white Dominions in touch with British foreign policy in order to act in its support if, for example, a war which threatened their interests as much as it did Britain's resulted from the failure of that policy. But once, in the late 1940s, Britain's survival began to depend on the Atlantic alliance and its nuclear deterrent, whether in American or British hands, this *raison d'être* of the Commonwealth lost its meaning. The idea, so common on the political Left after the Second World War, that the Commonwealth could somehow serve to reconcile world-wide racial antipathies as its multi-racial character grew was also shot to pieces when South Africa left the Commonwealth in 1961. All in all, it is hard to resist the impression that in so far as the Commonwealth has influenced British foreign policy at all since the war it has done so by keeping alive images of global power and influence in Labour and Conservative governments alike.

In much the same way the so-called Anglo-American 'special relationship' must bear some responsibility for sustaining in successive British Ministers unreal notions as to Britain's rightful place at the top table of world affairs. There could be said to be some role for a powerful British voice in Washington so long as the intense anti-Communist frenzy held sway in the United States during the 1950s. Sir Anthony Eden, as he was then, performed a useful function in those years in helping to restrain the crusading zeal of John Foster Dulles. But with the advent of Mr. Kennedy to the White House in January 1961, and his address to the American University in Washington in June 1963 on the need for peaceful co-existence with the Communist world, this function came to an end. During the Cuban missile crisis in October 1962 Mr. Kennedy demonstrated the same combination of iron determination and a conciliatory manner once the main point had been gained as has distinguished diplomacy at its best throughout the history of the international system. British Ministers might well have taken the hint and embarked upon wholesale revision of the idea of the special relationship when President Kennedy, almost as an act of condescension, agreed to visit London to report to the Prime Minister after his talks with Mr. Khrushchev in Vienna in June 1961. Instead there followed the Johnson era in which British Ministers sought without avail to modify America's Vietnam policy in return for their loyal support of that policy, often at much cost in terms of respect from the rest of the world.

It is true that British Ministers have gone a long way to cut the special relationship down to size. Lord Chalfont, the then Minister in charge of British negotiations with the Common Market, said in October 1967 that Britain made no further claims on the United States by virtue of the 'special relationship', and that Britain had henceforward to think, not so much of the United States and herself, as of the United States and Europe, of which Britain hoped to be a part. [3] But here again, as in the case of the Commonwealth, the time-lag between substantive changes in the whole environment of foreign policy and the appreciation of such changes by Ministers, the press and public opinion has had the effect of causing alternative policies, and now its European policies, to be imposed on Britain by events. And yet it is clear enough that West European states, when faced by a country like Britain, have the strongest temptation to raise their price for its entry into the Communities since they know that many of the viable options have faded.

It is here that we encounter one of the central disabilities from which Britain suffers in her present approach to the Common Market states. The extraordinary change from diplomatic strength to diplomatic weakness in Britain's position *vis-à-vis* Western Europe in the years since the war has paradoxically had the effect of diminishing such enthusiasm as there was in Britain for membership of the European Communities; it is felt in this country, not only that its present position as a suppliant is humiliating, but also that this weak bargaining situation places a strong leverage in the hands of any Common Market states which want to make difficulties about Britain's entry. But it cannot be repeated too often that this diplomatic weakness is a consequence of the unanticipated obsolescence of alternative policies, and especially of the three-circle concept of the immediate post-war years. It is equally clear that the clinging to such a concept when two of the circles, the Commonwealth and the Anglo-American special relationship, had long been deprived of practically all their meaning is characteristic of British reluctance to abandon the notion of reviving an imperial past in a new form and instead to adjust as rapidly as possible to the requirements of a role as a Power of the second rank.

But what in effect are such requirements? What must Britain do if she is to behave less like the United States and the Soviet Union, and more like other second-rank states like France or Federal Germany, or even Holland and Belgium?

First, there are certain British habits in foreign policy—one is obliged to speak of them as such rather than as reasoned positions—which governments must either set aside or indulge in only very rarely. One is the almost automatic tendency to submit to the temptation to act as the world's mediator, as though other countries must rise with enthusiasm at the prospect of a friendly British intervention in their disputes. It is now painful to recall the innumerable occasions on which British Prime Ministers and Foreign Secretaries have invoked the British Co-Chairmanship of the 1954 Geneva Conference on South-East Asia as justifying British efforts to act as a mediator in the Vietnam war. Yet it has always been plain to see that Britain, having elected to support United States policy in Vietnam, albeit without conviction and principally out of loyalty to a declining 'special relationship' with Washington, has robbed herself of the possibilities of playing any significant kind of mediatory role. Indeed, one suspects that Mr. Wilson exerted himself so much as a would-be mediator in Vietnam partly in order to placate critics in his own party of his support for United States policy; if so, this would be another illustration of the thesis of Professor Waltz in the book referred to, namely, that problems of party solidarity are often more to the forefront of a British Prime Minister's mind in foreign policy than the actualities of the situation. However that may be, the numerous British ministerial visits to Moscow in recent years, ostensibly to get negotiations going over Vietnam, have done little to enhance respect for British sagacity and realism in foreign affairs.

Another aspect of the same habit of taking first-rank status for granted is the condescending attitude towards other countries now equal in rank to Britain, which again does little to increase the world's respect for British realism. This has been apparent in the hectoring tone which British newspapers, and possibly British Ministers in private, too, have adopted towards the West Germans for their alleged failure to support British membership of the EEC as against General de Gaulle, and for their Government's refusal, before the Federal German elections on September 28, to revalue the Deutsche Mark. The story, widely reported in the European press at the time, that Chancellor Kiesinger, when he visited Britain in October 1967, was threatened that Britain might revise its European policy, withdraw its forces from Germany and recognise the East German republic unless the Germans used tough language with de Gaulle on Britain's behalf in the Common Market negotiations may be apocryphal, but it is not uncharacteristic of the British manner. Again, if the

West German press had urged devaluation on the British during their election campaign in 1966 as openly as the British press urged revaluation on the Germans in their election last autumn there would no doubt have been an outcry in this country. Putting aside all question of diplomatic propriety, Britain is no longer in a position to lecture other states of equivalent rank as Queen Victoria used to lecture her grandchildren who sat on the thrones of Europe.

Much the same applies to the British attitude to nuclear weapons. The question has been, and is still, debated whether the British nuclear deterrent can really be independent when it relies so heavily on American vehicles for its delivery, and whether circumstances can be conceived in which British nuclear weapons could be used or even their use threatened without American acquiescence. It may be answered, reasonably enough, by the argument that, so long as American spokesmen make clear that their own nuclear forces would be unleashed only when America's own continental security was at stake, Britain has a right, possibly even a duty, to maintain such nuclear independence as she has. But it is difficult to see how this is consistent with British support of the nuclear non-proliferation treaty (NPT), British horror at the whole idea of West German access to nuclear weapons and the scarcely concealed British disdain for France's nuclear armoury. All the arguments in favour of the British nuclear deterrent apply *mutatis mutandis* to every other country in the world, and although there may be some case for saying that Britain has an almost unparalleled stake in peace which would justify her in having responsibility in using or threatening to use nuclear weapons, this is not an argument which necessarily impresses other countries. Above all, it is hard to see how Britain can join the European Communities on the assumption, however slight, that one day they will lead to a full-scale political union, while defending the view that only Britain and, though grudgingly and because this is now a *fait accompli,* France can be trusted, among the West European states, with national nuclear forces. This strongly suggests what may in fact be the real British position in the matter of the EEC, namely that Britain neither wants it nor believes in it but has to contrive to join it in order to take economic advantage of its larger market and so to restore Britain's position as a first-rank Power.

Is it not also time for Britain to recognise that, in her present position, she can exercise little or no influence on the shaping of the world-wide balance of power, no more in fact than France or Federal Germany? In the developing three-cornered relationships of the United States, China and the Soviet Union it is impossible to forecast what the pattern of alignments will be in the 1970s and 1980s, but whatever it is it will affect us all. During the acute phases of the East-West cold war in the 1950s Britain had a useful role to play in moderating the cold war between the two protagonists, and in urging on the United States the need for tension-easing agreements with the Communist world. That phase ended in the late 1950s and early 1960s with the acquisition of an assured second-strike capability by both super-Powers; henceforward both states had an equal interest in the avoidance of a war *à outrance* between them, the United States began to depend less on NATO for her continental security, and the main lines of communication in the management of East-West relations now lay directly between Washington and Moscow. It is hard today to understand precisely what security interest the United States still has in the NATO alliance, except possibly as a means for holding any territorial ambitions of Federal Germany in check and thus keeping the Soviet Union well disposed towards the West, although the Federal German elections in September seemed to show the declining interest in territorial revision in West Germany, especially among young voters.

In the resulting Soviet-American *détente* a purely British voice can only have an inconsiderable part to play, except in two respects. First, it is a British and a European interest that the Soviet-American arms race should not move upwards to another, unpredictable, rung of its escalation ladder as a consequence of competitive building of anti-ballistic missile systems. No one can say how such a competition would affect the relative stability in East-West relations which has been reached, and it is but common prudence to prefer the known devil to the unknown devil. In other words, there can be no strong British interest in a failure of the projected Soviet-American strategic arms limitation talks (SALT) or any other arms control negotiations at that level.

The second British interest in the East-West *détente* is to try to ensure that the super-Powers do not manage the *détente* in such a way as to damage British or West European interests. It is hard to see at present how Soviet-American relations could operate to the detriment of British interests, but it is even more difficult to decide how far Britain should go in backing Federal Germany against Soviet-American collusion at Germany's expense, as for instance in the matter of the NPT. All Britain's emotional tendencies are at present on the Soviet-American side in this respect, but can we any longer afford to club ourselves with the super-Powers against the 'have-not' nations as far as nuclear weapons are concerned? However one answers these questions, the fact is that Britain cannot, from the basis of her present strength, greatly influence Soviet-American relations in order to serve the two purposes mentioned above, or any other purposes. And yet there is little evidence that the British and other West European governments are doing much to hammer out a common viewpoint on these, or any other, global questions.

As to the third element in the world balance of power of the next ten or twenty years, China, it is also clear that Britain will, on her own account, have even less of a say in shaping Chinese relations with the two super-Powers, especially after the decision to withdraw militarily from the Far East by the end of 1971. Britain, like other West European countries, is long past the time when she had any considerable influence in that part of the world; indeed it seems that even the United States has come to recognise the limits of her own capacity to shape events in East Asia and is now calling on friendly nations there to save themselves by their own efforts. Yet there can be no doubt that the manner in which China, when the present revolutionary turmoil subsides, re-enters the international system will govern the course of international affairs for the next twenty years. The central question is whether China will enter as an active participant in the world balance of power, as the Soviet Union did in the 1930s after an early period of messianic hopes of world revolution; and, if she does, whether she will mend her fences with the United States or with the Soviet Union. A Chinese *rapprochement* with one or the other seems almost inevitable since it is contrary to all the rules of foreign policy that such a vast country should remain with powerful enemies on its land and maritime frontiers at the same time. Whichever course China finds it most in accordance with her interest to choose will profoundly affect the course of world affairs, including the interests of Britain and her continental European partners, though evidently little thought is being given to this eventuality in any of the world's foreign offices outside those of America and Russia. Britain, again, could hardly influence this coming transformation of world politics to her own advantage from the basis of her present strength. Since this is so, it is vital that Britain should begin to exchange ideas on this subject with her West European partners, whether her negotiations to join the EEC are successful or not.

A final question is whether the professional side of British diplomacy today is as resourceful, flexible and far-sighted as it needs to be for a country of second rank which no longer has any considerable margin of strength which it could afford to lose through diplomatic errors. Looking back on the quarter-century since 1945 one can agree that British foreign policy has notable achievements to its credit by way of the seizure of vital issues and contributions to the Western alliance. In recognising the danger to Western Europe and the United States of Soviet policies in Eastern Europe in the middle and late 1940s, in pressing for a *détente* with the Communist world in the 1950s, and in defending, as against the United States, the legitimacy of non-alignment policies adopted by the new Afro-Asian states, British Ministers and diplomats exhibited professional skill equal, and in many instances superior, to that of their closest allies. But there have also been too many mistakes and miscalculations for anyone to feel complacent on this score. Setting aside the Suez fiasco of 1956, there has been the long failure to recognise the validity of West

European integration and its value for Britain, the extraordinary over-estimate of the power of economic sanctions to bring the Smith régime in Rhodesia to heel, and, most strange, the apparent failure to recognise General de Gaulle's second refusal to admit Britain into the EEC until he had to spell it out in so many words on November 27, 1967. How the makers of British policy could have continued to believe that de Gaulle might change his mind when he categorically stated that he would not do so at a press conference in Paris as early as May 16, 1967—and that was before devaluation of the pound and even before the second British application to join the EEC—is hard to understand.

The recent Duncan Report has made controversial proposals for rationalising and concentrating the British Foreign Service. But should the starting point of such an inquiry be, as in the Duncan Committee's terms of reference, the saving of a few million or hundred million pounds? What the country requires, in conformity with its reduced world status, is not a cheaper Foreign Service, but a more efficient one, even if it is somewhat more expensive. There are at least two ways in which its efficiency could be increased. One stems from the remarkable fact that in this country serious thinking about foreign policy is done on two levels among others, the official and the academic, with hardly any formal contact between them. Of all the great departments of state the Foreign Office is almost alone in holding to the view that advising on foreign policy is the monopoly of the career civil servant and that he needs no assistance from the expert outsider. In hardly any other major country today is this practice pursued. In the second place, though this is a comment on public services in general, it is impossible to believe that we are even yet making anything like full use of the potential intellectual resources of the community. The restriction of university education to the children of the better-off and the professional classes, while those of the great majority pass almost automatically from school to manual employment, must cramp the capabilities of a country which, with its empire and front-rank status gone, has only its native resources of talent to draw upon. Britain, when a front-rank Power, saved herself more than once by her own efforts. The same formula is essential when Britain at length comes to terms psychologically with what it means to be in the second rank of nations.

NOTES

1. (London: Longmans, 1968), p. 151.

2. See David Calleo, *Britain's Future* (London: Hodder and Stoughton, 1968), Chapter II.

3. *The Times*, October 10, 1967.

The euphoria of "affluence" in the late nineteen-fifties and early nineteen-sixties caused some Conservatives to question whether social security for all, rather than policies directly applied to those actually in need, should continue to be guaranteed. Very soon, however, the future prosperity of Great Britain became an even more urgent matter of concern than her place upon the international stage. Observers noted the slow growth of the economy, worried over the lack of dynamism in industry and the low productivity of Labour, and concluded that drastic measures were required if Britain were to keep pace with other Western countries. One of the most effective of such economic analysts was Michael Shanks, whose Penguin Book, The Stagnant Society, *was first published in 1961 and issued again in a revised edition eleven years later. In it he outlined the case for a program of centralized economic control and authority within the framework of an acute criticism of the failures of government, industry, and above all the trade unions. The argument was somewhat one-sided, but it illustrated the growing strain of pessimism that developed during the course of the sixties. To show that Shanks's attitudes are more than unique and that they include even a significant disillusionment with parliamentary democracy, I have included a brief recent comment by a journalist who wrote at the time of the October 1974 election. Michael Mosettig is an NBC news editor and former UPI correspondent in Europe. His article appeared in* The New Republic *of October 12, 1974. It is reprinted by permission of* The New Republic, *copyright 1974, The New Republic, Inc.*

13

Epilogue: British Elections

MICHAEL MOSETTIG

The autumn has begun with crisp mornings and sunny days after a dismal and rainy summer. The civility and charm that have for so long attracted beleaguered American urbanites to London still abound. Prices, of course, are shooting up and are almost unrecognizable to one who lived here only five years ago. After four years of inflation, now reaching a 20 percent annual rate, England is no longer a low-cost country. Yet shops and stores are busy; a buy-now-before-it's-too-late philosophy is at work. The theater is thriving commercially if not artistically. Business may be off in the fanciest West End restaurants, but neighborhood bistros and trattorias of increasingly good quality are jammed with late-night diners.

Yet there are signs of fraying at the edges. Terrorist bombings are a reminder that the "Irish Question" remains, 300 years after Cromwell, 100 years after Gladstone and almost 60 years after the Easter uprising. Hooliganism is on the increase at football matches and on public transport. Buses and subways run less efficiently. Old buildings are too often replaced by ugly new ones. The poor and lower-middle classes have been pinched tightly by the unremitting inflation. The upper-middle class and rich can usually stay ahead or even, but it is the future that worries them. The general election this week—the second in nine months—promises no end to political stalemate or economic stagflation.

On Fleet Street, where doom and trivia are dispensed in equal dollops by a dwindling number of newspapers, the air is heavy. "I have a bet on," says a

Fleet Street editor, "that parliamentary democracy will not survive another five years. With every passing day, I look more likely to pick it up." *The Economist* predicts "a period of serious deterioration in the fabric of British society." From editors, businessmen, politicians comes a constant warning: no nation has sustained for any time at all a 20 percent rate of inflation and still maintained its democratic institutions.

Paper fortunes have been lost in the drop on the London Exchange to a postwar low. Businesses are squeezed for cash, and more bankruptcies are forecast. The housing and property market that inflated drastically in the last two years has ground to a halt; every London block is dotted with "For Sale" signs, but there is no mortgage money for prospective buyers. A vacation package tour group recently collapsed leaving thousands minus their annual holidays and next to no chance of retrieving their vacation money. The last major European nation to recover economically from World War II and to taste the fruits of consumerism and affluence now sees them being plucked away.

In a nation where central heating has still not won total acceptance, it is the demand for such items as dishwashers, modern kitchens and washing machines—without a concurrent growth in real income or productivity—that helps spur inflation. Young couples complain the mortgage crunch is keeping them from buying a suburban house, when only in the last decade has homeowning been open to any but the rich. Cars jam the city and suburban streets; and the high cost of gasoline, $1.25 a gallon at the pump and from the Arab wellhead, is adding heavily to inflation and Britain's balance of payments bills.

It is no comfort that no parliamentary democracy in the West is coping successfully with inflation and affluence. But in Britain a case can be made that the political establishment is not even confronting them. Rather than discussing ways of expanding real wealth, much of the debate revolves around how to divide up a dwindling pie. When in doubt revert to class warfare.

It is the pronounced division of classes that has prompted the retired Col. Blimps to form their citizen armies, ready to man the power stations in case of a late autumn general strike. On the other side these divisions have prompted more strident calls for extensive nationalization of private business and new wealth taxes. The working man's family, squeezed to the point that even the traditional Sunday roast has become a luxury, does not respond to suggestions for wage restraint, and his unions do not bother making the suggestion. The middle-class commuter is angry at the unions, dismayed at the political stalemate and frightened by prospects of higher prices and new taxes.

The skill of the British political establishment since the war had been to develop and gradually expand the welfare state and mixed economy while papering over divisions and avoiding outright class confrontation. Edward Heath, the last Conservative Prime Minister, broke those unwritten rules by deciding to take on the unions. He paid a price in losing last winter's election, called during the coal miners' strike and the three-day work week. The Tories talk of replacing Heath, the two-time (1966 and 1974) loser and one-time (1970) winner, with a fresher face. Their talk has the same wistful tone as the talk in Republican congressional lobbies, before impeachment, that Richard Nixon would somehow just go away. And the Tories go into the election divided between those advocating a tight-money and possibly high unemployment policy to combat inflation and those pushing milder restraints.

Ironically Laborite Prime Minister Harold Wilson campaigns as the candidate of conciliation—at least he will not provoke the labor unions and he may hold together a party divided over the Common Market and becoming further stretched between its Marxist and non-Marxist wings.

But England is no longer a two-party country. Neither is it a three-party country. The most important outcome of this election could be to confirm it—even if temporarily—into a multiparty country. Because of the nonproportional, single-member district voting, third and fourth parties have never gained more than diversionary strength since the war. But their votes in this election may prove enough of a diversion to make some form of peacetime coalition government a live prospect for the first time since the Depression.

Even with a big jump in their popular vote last February, the Liberal third party still collected only 14 seats in the House of Commons compared with 301 for Labor and 297 for the Tories. With candidates in virtually all the constituencies this time, the standard question is how many more seats can the Liberals pick up and will there be enough to hold the balance of power and perhaps to enter a coalition? Analyses built around that proposition are chewed over in political columns. They tend, however, to ignore several prospects: that the Liberals may have peaked as a protest vehicle in February; that this election may show the real blossoming of the Welsh and Scottish nationalist parties; and that the importance of the Liberal vote may be in the number of marginal seats it tilts in the direction of the Tories or Socialists, producing in a fluke manner a strong parliamentary majority for one of the major parties. Labor has spurned a coalition with the Liberals, even though both parties are committed to income redistribution. But the Tories have been nibbling at the coalition bait.

The urge to power and the morality of coalitions do not trouble the nationalist parties. In Wales and Scotland they are the beneficiaries of the general political malaise plus the regional and linguistic nationalism that is stirring throughout Europe from Croatia to Brittany and Flanders and now to Britain. In Wales the nationalist movement is largely linguistic. In Scotland it is becoming economic and for that reason more serious. North Sea oil has given Scottish nationalism a reason for being. The oil is the balm that all Britain is counting on by the 1980s, with hopes of self-sufficiency that could reverse its economic fortunes. While it is obviously better to be an oil exporter than importer, the North Sea has become the latest illusion for the ever-optimistic British. They talk of oil now as they talked in the 1960s of joining the Common Market, which would give the country new outlets for its products and political talents. Economically and politically the Common Market has been a disillusioning experience for Britain, just as the failure of Britain, especially under Wilson, to play a strong role has disappointed its more European-minded market partners.

And then there is Ulster. In addition to all its other problems, it now has Enoch Powell. Having split with Heath and the Tories, Powell is running for a Northern Ireland seat to Westminster. If elected he will become the *de facto* leader of the rump Ulster Protestant nationalist faction. These are the old Unionists who used to vote with the Tories in the House of Commons. They go their own way now, feeling betrayed by the tolerant policies with which the last Tory government tried and almost succeeded in bringing some peace to that province. The chances of a strong one-party government with a healthy working majority are slim indeed.

In Britain and on the Continent there are cynics who say the British actually enjoy all this, that they feel best coping with adversity. There are certainly plenty of reminders that they have endured and survived worse than this. Despite the builders and bulldozers the place is redolent of history. In an early evening one can walk across the river and catch the towers of Westminster jutting into a blue-gray dusk. On the last night of the Proms hundreds of fresh-faced kids jam Albert Hall, wave their Union Jacks and sing "Land of Hope and Glory" as if Queen Victoria herself were leading the chorus. The question in 1974 is not whether there will always be an England, but what kind of Britain will emerge from this unhappy decade. The British will be lucky if they have any better answer to that question after the election than they do now.

Bibliographical Note

Almost every brief bibliography appears to start with a note about the vastness of the literature in the field. Not to be out of style, I will make the same comment about works on twentieth-century Britain and move on to call attention to a few titles that are important for further study. By now, two standard works have emerged, one in the well-known *Oxford History of England* series, edited by Sir George Clark, the other a volume in Longmans' *History of England in Ten Volumes*, the general editor of which is W. N. Medlicott. The Oxford volume, A. J. P. Taylor's *English History, 1914–1945* (New York, 1965), is a sprightly re-creation of an era, unorthodox in some of its judgments, provoking in its challenges to easy generalization, constantly opening up new ways of looking at the period. Totally different in style is W. N. Medlicott's *Contemporary England, 1914–1946* (London, 1967). Much more systematic, skeptical of the sweeping *obiter dicta* Taylor delights in, Medlicott's work is a temperate, balanced, eminently sound account of recent British history, informed by a dry sense of humor that reflective readers will relish.

Two older works still merit notice and two textbooks provide a valuable introduction to British history after 1900. *Imperialism and the Rise of Labour, 1895–1905* (New York, 1951) and *The Rule of Democracy, 1905–1914* (2 volumes; New York, 1952), the conclusion of Elie Halévy's masterful *A History of the English People in the 19th Century,* have not yet become obsolete, nor has R. C. K. Ensor's *England, 1870* – 1914 (Oxford, 1936), the volume that precedes Taylor's in the Oxford history. The best short single-volume text is by all odds Alfred F. Havighurst, *Twentieth-Century Britain* (Evanston, Illinois, 1962), while the latter sections of R. K. Webb, *Modern England from the 18th Century to the Present* (New York, 1968) also provide a most useful introduction to the entire period. Finally, special mention must be made of Charles L. Mowat, *Britain between the Wars, 1918 – 1940* (London, 1955), a general study that is at the same time a work of detailed and liberal-minded scholarship.

While I have noted in my preface that much of the broad-gauged work on twentieth-century Britain has appeared in books rather than in briefer form, numerous articles of major value, particularly on special and sharply focused issues, are to be found in the relevant periodicals. I have found the most useful to be *The Journal of Modern History, The American Historical Review, The Journal of British Studies, The Journal of Contemporary History, The Cambridge Journal, The Journal of Social History, The English Historical Review, The Bulletin of the Institute of Historical Research, The Journal of International Affairs, International Affairs, World Politics, The Journal of Politics, The Political Science Quarterly, The Political Quarterly, The Journal of Interdisciplinary History, The Journal of Commonwealth Political Studies, Past and Present,* and *The Economic History Review.*

The American Historical Review is particularly useful for its bibliographies—or rather lists—of articles and books newly published. All of the recent books noted in the first two paragraphs—Taylor, Medlicott, Havighurst, Webb, and Mowat—provide guidance in the footnotes, selected readings, or critical bibliographies to the significant literature that appeared up to about 1967 or 1966. I, myself, published a bibliographical essay entitled "Some Recent Writings on Twentieth-Century Britain" in *The Journal of Modern History,* XXXII (March 1960), 32 – 47 and in a revised form as *Great Britain in the Twentieth Century* (2nd ed., 1966), Publication No. 28, Service Center for Teachers of History, American Historical Association, Washington, D.C. The *Journal of Modern History* essay, slightly updated, has also appeared in Elizabeth C. Furber, ed., *Changing Views on British History. Essays on Historical Writing since 1939* (Cambridge, Mass., 1966). Alfred E. Havighurst is preparing a bibliography of work on twentieth-century Britain that may well be in print before this book of readings is published.

Because so much in the way of bibliographic help is available, I shall limit myself to listing a few of the books, some bearing on the major topics I have selected for this collection, some touching upon areas that might well make the material for several other such collections, that I have found useful in trying to keep up with the history of twentieth-century Britain: C. L. Mowat, *Great Britain since 1914* (The Sources of History: Studies in the Uses of Historical Evidence; London, 1971); G. R. Searle, *The Quest for National Efficiency. A Study in British Politics and Political Thought, 1899 – 1914* (Berkeley and Los Angeles, 1971); Peter Rowland, *The Last Liberal Governments* (2 vols.; London, 1968 and 1971); A. J. P. Taylor, *Lloyd George, A Diary by Frances Stevenson* (London, 1971); Trevor Wilson, *The Downfall of the Liberal Party, 1914 – 1935* (London, 1966); R. H. Ullman, *Britain and the Russian Civil War. Volume II. Anglo-Soviet Relations, 1917 – 1921* (Princeton, 1968); Maurice Cowling, *The Impact of Labour, 1920 – 1924. The Beginnings of Modern British Politics* (London, 1971); Marvin Swartz, *The Union of Democratic Control in British Politics during the First World War* (London, 1971); Arthur Marwick, *The Deluge: British Society and the First World War* (London, 1965); Zora B. Steiner, *The Foreign Office and Foreign Policy, 1898 – 1914* (New York, 1969); F. S. Northedge, *The Troubled Giant: Britain Among the Great Powers, 1916 – 1939* (New York, 1966); Max Beloff, *Imperial Sunset, Volume I: Britain's Liberal Empire, 1897 – 1921* (New York, 1970); Keith Middlemas, *The Strategy of Appeasement. The British Government and Germany, 1937 – 39* (Chicago, 1972); N. Thompson, *The Anti-Appeasers, Conservative Opposition to Appeasement in the 1930's* (Oxford, 1971); Ian Colvin, *The Chamberlain Cabinet* (London, 1971); J. E. Naylor, *Labour's International Policy. The Labour Party in the 1930's* (Boston, 1969); David Carlton, *MacDonald versus Henderson: The Foreign Policy of the Second Labour Government* (New York, 1970); Michael R. Gordon, *Conflict and Consensus in Labour's Foreign Policy, 1914 – 1965* (Stanford, Calif., 1969): Sir Llewelyn Woodward, *British Foreign Policy in the Second World War* (3 vols.; London, 1970); Michael Leifer, ed., *Constraints and Adjustments in British Foreign Policy* (London, 1972); D. MacLean, *British Foreign Policy since Suez* (London, 1970); Grant Hugo, *Britain in Tomorrow's World. Principles of Foreign Policy* (New York, 1969); Max Beloff, *The Future of British Foreign Policy* (London, 1969); H. Duncan Hall, *Commonwealth. A History of the British Commonwealth of Nations* (London, 1971); W. B. Hamilton, K. Robinson, and C. D. W. Goodwin, eds., *A Decade of the Commonwealth, 1955 – 1964* (Durham, N.C., 1966); N. Mansergh, *The Commonwealth Experience* (London, 1969); A. J. Youngson, *Britain's Economic Growth, 1920 – 1966* (London, 1967); H. W. Richardson, *Economic Recovery in Britain, 1932 – 39* (London, 1967); S. Blank, *Industry and Government in Great Britain. The Federation of British Industries in Politics, 1945 – 1965* (Lexington, Mass. 1973); J. and A.-M. Hackett, *The British*

Economy. Problems and Prospects (London, 1967); Thomas Jones, *Whitehall Diary*, ed. by Keith Middlemas (3 vols.; London, 1969); Robert Skidelsky, *Politicians and the Slump. The Labour Government of 1929 – 1931* (London, 1967); F. Bealey, ed., *The Social and Political Thought of the British Labour Party* (London, 1970); Angus Calder, *The People's War. Britain 1939 – 45* (London, 1969); S. Haseler, *The Gaitskellites. Revisionism in the British Labour Party, 1951 – 64* (London, 1969); D. E. Butler and A. King, *The British General Election of 1966* (London, 1966); D. E. Butler and M. Pinto-Suschinsky, *The British General Election of 1971* (London, 1971); D. McKie and C. Cook, *The Decade of Disillusion: British Politics in the Sixties* (London, 1972); Robert Rhodes James, *Ambitions and Realities. British Politics 1964 – 70* (London, 1972); Frank Parkin, *Middle Class Radicalism. The Social Bases of the Campaign for Nuclear Disarmament* (Manchester, 1968); J. Mills, *Growth and Welfare. A New Policy for Britain* (London, 1972); W. Beckerman, ed., *The Labour Government's Economic Record: 1964 – 1970* (London, 1972); Michael Shanks, *The Stagnant Society* (rev. ed.; Harmondsworth, England, 1972); G. Jones and M. Barnes, *Britain on Borrowed Time* (Harmondsworth, England, 1967); D. Butler and D. Stokes, *Political Change in Britain* (London, 1969); R. J. Scally, *The Origins of the Lloyd George Coalition* (Princeton, 1975); R. McKibbin, *The Evolution of the Labour Party 1910 – 1924* (London, 1974).

Aside from the important diaries of Thomas Jones and Frances Stevenson cited above, I have not listed any of the almost unending memoirs, diaries, and apologia that fill the bookshelves. Similarly, I make no attempt to illustrate the scope of the numerous assessments of twentieth-century figures that have appeared in the last decade beyond noting the following handful of biographies that make useful contributions in varying ways to our further understanding of their subjects: Stephen E. Koss, *Lord Haldane. Scapegoat for Liberalism* (London, 1969); Sydney Zebel, *Baldwin. A Political Biography* (London, 1973); K. Middlemas and J. Barnes, *Baldwin. A Biography* (London, 1969); A. J. P. Taylor, *Beaverbrook* (London, 1972); Michael Foot, *Aneurin Bevan. A Biography. Vol. Two: 1945 – 1960* (London, 1973); Robert Rhodes James, *Churchill. A Study in Failure 1900 – 1939* (London, 1970). Finally, mention should be made of the multivolume biography of Winston Churchill in narrative sections with parallel companion volumes of documents, begun in 1966 by the late Randolph Churchill and now being continued by Martin Gilbert.

INDEX

F5